i

The Unbroken Chain

Determinism, Free Will, and the Nature of Choice

Thomas Winston Smith

To my son, Louis. May you always question.

Table of Contents

Chapter 1

What Is Determinism? – Defining the Unbroken Chain

Science, Religion, and the Question of Free Will

As human knowledge has advanced, traditional religious explanations of the world have gradually lost some of their authority. For many people, the detailed biblical creation story and the elaborate theological doctrines of the past no longer carry the same weight they once did. Biblical scholarship and scientific discoveries have shown, for example, that the Book of Genesis contains multiple conflicting creation accounts. Such revelations have led modern believers to view many scriptural details as non-essential. However, there remain a few core tenets of religious belief—the existence of God, the immortality of the soul, and human free will—that are considered vitally important. These three ideas, often termed "natural religion" doctrines, were thought (by thinkers like Thomas Aquinas and many others) to be provable by reason alone, without needing divine revelation. It becomes important, then, to ask what modern science has to say about these doctrines. Can science prove or disprove God's existence, an afterlife, or the freedom of the human will? My own view is that science at present can neither conclusively confirm nor refute any of these grand claims—indeed, no method outside of scientific inquiry can definitively do so either. Science can, however, provide evidence and arguments that affect how plausible we find these ideas. This is especially true of the question of human freedom versus determinism, which we will examine in this chapter.

Historically, the concept of determinism found its strongest support in the success of classical physics. By the late 19th century, physics had discovered precise laws (like Newton's laws of motion and gravitation) that seemed to govern all material movement, making events in principle predictable in advance. Nature appeared to operate like clockwork, following an unbroken chain of cause and effect. Oddly enough, in the 20th century the most potent challenge to determinism also arose from physics—specifically from the new physics of the atom. Before we delve into that modern challenge, however, we need to clearly define what we mean by *determinism*. What does it mean to say the world is deterministic? We must clarify the issue as much as possible before getting lost in endless debates. After all, if we don't define our terms clearly, we risk ending up like the devils in Milton's *Paradise Lost* who argued endlessly about "Providence, Foreknowledge, Will, and Fate" and *found no end, in wandering mazes lost*[1]. To avoid such fruitless confusion, let us begin by spelling out exactly what determinism entails.

Two Aspects of Determinism

---

[1] **John Milton**, *Paradise Lost*, Book II, lines 558–561 (London: 1667).

Determinism actually has a twofold character, which we should distinguish for clarity. On the one hand, it functions as a practical guiding principle for scientific research. On the other hand, it stands as a sweeping doctrine about the nature of the universe as a whole. These two aspects are related but not identical. The first can be useful even if the second turns out to be false or unproven. Let us examine each aspect in turn: first the practical scientific principle, then the broader universal doctrine.

1. Determinism as a Scientific Maxim (Cause and Effect in Research). In practice, determinism serves as a working maxim for scientists: it advises that we should *always look for causal laws* underlying the phenomena we observe. In simpler terms, scientists operate under the assumption that events do not just happen randomly or without cause; there are rules or laws that connect what happens now to what happened earlier. In our everyday life we already rely on casual cause-and-effect rules to get by, but these everyday rules are often imprecise and admit exceptions. For example, we might say: *"If I flip this light switch, the lamp will turn on"*—with the unspoken caveat *"unless the bulb is burnt out or the power is off."* Or *"If I strike a match, it will produce a flame"*—*"unless the matchhead is faulty and falls off."* Or *"If I dial this phone number, I will reach my friend"*—*"unless I misdial or there's a network error."* These are useful rules of thumb, but they are not ironclad laws; they trade some accuracy for simplicity.

Science, however, strives for invariant, exceptionless laws. The ideal model of a scientific law was provided by Newtonian astronomy: using Newton's law of gravitation, one could compute the past or future positions of planets with remarkable accuracy over vast periods of time. This was a triumph of determinism in science—given the state of the solar system at one time, the laws of physics could in principle determine its state at any other time. Encouraged by this success, scientists have sought similar laws in other domains. Outside of planetary orbits, finding perfect laws is harder because other systems (chemical reactions, weather, living organisms, economies, etc.) involve great complexity and many interacting factors. Even so, scientists have managed to discover dependable causal laws in chemistry, in electromagnetism, in biology, and even to some extent in fields like psychology and economics. The search for causal laws is the essence of the scientific method, and few doubt that it's a sensible strategy. If there truly were some realm of phenomena that had no causal regularities whatsoever, that realm would be essentially off-limits to science, because science advances by finding patterns and regularities. Thus, the maxim *"look for a cause"* is as fundamental to a scientist as *"look for mushrooms"* is to a mushroom hunter: it's almost definitional to the activity. In this practical sense, determinism—as the belief that phenomena follow laws—is a guiding light for scientific inquiry. Scientists assume determinism as a working hypothesis: whenever something happens, they seek to understand *why* it happened, confident that there is some explanation governed by consistent principles.

2. Determinism as a Universal Doctrine (The World as an Unbroken Chain). Beyond its role as a research strategy, determinism also embodies a general philosophical doctrine about reality. This doctrine asserts that *the state of the entire universe at any given moment is a consequence of its state at a prior moment, according to causal laws*—in other words, the complete future is theoretically fixed by the complete past. If we knew all the facts about the world at one time and knew all the laws governing change, we could (again, in theory) predict everything that would happen thereafter. According to this

4

view, the chain of cause and effect is unbroken and all-encompassing. Every event that occurs is the inevitable result of prior conditions plus the laws of nature. Whenever we observe something happen, a thorough enough investigation should uncover earlier circumstances and relevant laws that made that event unavoidable. Likewise, if we truly understand the laws, then whenever we see the same circumstances arise again, we should be able to predict that the same outcome will occur.

This broad doctrine of determinism paints a picture of a universe that is, at least in principle, completely predictable from moment to moment, given sufficient knowledge. It's an awe-inspiring idea, but also one that is difficult to state with precision. The trouble is that phrases like "in theory everything is predictable" can be slippery. What exactly do we mean by "in theory" here? If we say "everything is determined by laws," it rings hollow unless we also believe that those laws are actually knowable or discoverable in practice. We must be careful not to make determinism a vacuous claim. Obviously, whatever happens in the future will be what it will be — in that trivial sense, one could say it is already determined *simply because it will eventually happen.* For example, an all-knowing God (such as the God of traditional Christian belief) would, by definition, already know every detail of the future. If such an omniscient being exists, then indeed the future is in some sense "already written," because God's current knowledge would perfectly reflect every future event. But this kind of absolute foreknowledge is *outside* the realm of what science can verify or use; it doesn't help us as human investigators of nature. It serves little purpose, scientifically, to claim "the future is determined" if that determination is in practice completely hidden from us.

To make determinism meaningful as a doctrine that we can discuss scientifically, we need to frame it in terms of what is testable or knowable by humans, not by hypothetical omniscient beings. Otherwise, we run the risk of drifting off into metaphysical speculation that can never be resolved— again, *"wandering mazes lost"* in the words of Milton. So how can we define determinism in a way that is concrete and potentially testable, at least in principle? The key is to limit the scope to something an experimenter might conceivably deal with, rather than the entire universe at once.

Defining the "Unbroken Chain" of Causation

Let us attempt a more precise, workable definition of determinism—one that captures the idea of an unbroken causal chain but stays within the bounds of the observable and testable. We might frame it as a hypothesis about predicting events within a finite region of space over a finite duration of time, using finite resources. Consider the following thought experiment:

Imagine a sphere in space, with us (the observers) at the centre. Suppose that at the very beginning of a certain year— let's say the start of the year 1936—we somehow know every detail about everything happening inside that sphere at that exact moment. We choose the sphere's size such that it has a specific relation to the speed of causation in the universe. For definiteness, assume our sphere is so large that it takes light (and thus any signals or causal influences, since nothing can travel faster than light) one year to travel from the sphere's boundary to its centre. In other words, the radius of our sphere is such that light emitted at the perimeter at midnight on January 1, 1936, would reach the centre by midnight on December 31, 1936.

6

Now, if determinism is true, then everything that happens at the centre of that sphere during the year 1936 should depend *only* on the conditions inside the sphere at the start of the year. Any events outside the sphere cannot affect the centre within that year, because they are too far away for their influence to arrive in time (it would take longer than a year for any effect from beyond the sphere to get to the centre). Therefore, if we had complete knowledge of the initial state inside the sphere (as we supposed) and if we have the correct laws of nature, we ought to be able to calculate or predict all the happenings at the centre of the sphere for the entire year.

In reality, of course, we cannot gather all that data in advance—we would have to wait until the year is over to actually collect all the information from the sphere, because even information from the sphere's edge takes the full year to reach us at the centre. But in principle, after the year has passed, we could examine whether the information we gathered (about the state of the sphere at the year's start) together with our known causal laws is sufficient to explain everything that occurred within the sphere (and especially at its centre) throughout that year. If it is sufficient—if every event inside followed from the prior state according to our laws—then determinism holds for that sphere and that time period. If not—if things happened at the centre that had no traceable cause within the sphere's initial conditions—then determinism would fail in that instance.

Using this kind of reasoning, we can formulate the hypothesis of determinism more rigorously. It would go something like this:

Determinism Hypothesis: *There exist discoverable causal laws such that, given enough calculating power, an observer who knows the complete state of a closed system (for example, everything happening* *inside a sufficiently large sphere) at a given initial moment can predict all events that will occur within that system (for example, at the centre of the sphere) for a specified duration (such as the time it takes light to travel from the system's boundary to its centre).*

In plainer terms, determinism means that if we have enough information about the present state of a system and the laws of nature, we can foresee the system's future state with arbitrary accuracy (at least until influences from outside the system have time to enter). This definition tries to capture the intuitive idea of an unbroken chain of causation—every event is caused by prior events *in its vicinity*, such that nothing truly unpredictable or "from nowhere" ever occurs.

It's important to note what this hypothesis does and does not claim. We are not asserting here that determinism is definitely true in reality; we're describing what it *would* mean for determinism to be true in a scientifically relevant way. Whether this hypothesis holds is something that evidence would have to confirm or refute. In fact, no one currently knows for sure whether the universe really obeys such strict deterministic principles. Determinism, as defined above, is an ideal or model that science has often striven toward. We can't declare with certainty that it's either correct or incorrect in an absolute sense. As we shall see, when people argue for or against determinism, they often have a vaguer notion in mind than the precise formulation we've given. But at least we now have a concrete framework to test the idea: Does knowledge of the present and the laws truly allow us to predict the future? With this clarified definition of determinism in hand, we can proceed to examine how well it stands up, especially in light of modern scientific developments.

The Challenge from Modern Physics

For a long time, the deterministic outlook seemed highly successful. By the early 20th century, many scientists and philosophers were convinced that the universe was fundamentally deterministic—every effect following a cause—thanks to the tremendous predictive power of known physical laws. For the first time in history, however, determinism then came under direct challenge from scientists themselves, on scientific grounds. This challenge emerged with the advent of quantum mechanics, the new physics of the subatomic world.

The leading voice of this challenge was the astronomer and physicist Sir Arthur Eddington, who publicly argued that recent discoveries in atomic physics undermined the deterministic worldview. (It should be noted that not all prominent physicists agreed with Eddington—Albert Einstein, for instance, famously resisted these indeterministic implications of quantum theory. Still, Eddington's argument was influential and needs to be considered.) We will examine this challenge in as non-technical a way as possible, focusing on its philosophical implications.

Quantum mechanics, in a nutshell, suggests that at a fundamental level we cannot predict exactly what an atom will do, even if we know its current state perfectly. Instead, the theory provides a list of possible outcomes and their probabilities. In a given situation, an atom (or a subatomic particle) might have several different possible behaviours or paths it could take. Sometimes it does one thing, sometimes another, even if the starting conditions appear identical. We can often calculate the odds of each outcome with great precision, but not which specific outcome will occur in any single instance.

This is a radically different scenario from classical physics. To use a simple analogy: imagine a railway ticket clerk at a busy train station (say, London's Paddington Station). Over time, the clerk might observe that, on average, a certain percentage of travellers go to Birmingham, another percentage go to Exeter, and so on for various destinations. If the clerk tallies enough tickets, reliable statistics emerge: perhaps 30% of travellers head north to Birmingham, 10% southwest to Exeter, 5% to Cardiff, etc. However, the clerk cannot know the individual reasons or causes for each traveller's choice on a given day—only the overall proportions in the long run. Now, classical physics envisioned a universe where, given enough information, even the individual "reasons" for each event *could* be known: nothing would be left to chance. Quantum physics, by contrast, puts us in a position somewhat like that booking clerk. We can measure the statistical distribution of outcomes for countless atomic events, but when it comes to predicting a single event—like what one specific atom will do at a specific moment—quantum theory says we simply *cannot know* for sure. There is an irreducible element of unpredictability or randomness in each individual occurrence.

It's important to note that this unpredictability is not due to a lack of effort or technology on our part (at least according to the standard interpretation of quantum theory). It's not just that we're "missing some hidden detail." Rather, the theory itself states that nature, at the micro level, doesn't decide outcomes in a strictly deterministic way. We can know that outcome A will happen, say, 60% of the time and outcome B 40% of the time, but we cannot say which outcome will occur in the next trial. In the analogy, the physicist is like a clerk who can find out the overall travel patterns but is "asleep except during working hours" and never gets to learn the personal motivations of single travellers. Even when observing as closely as possible (in the laboratory), atoms don't reveal any further clues as to *why* one outcome occurred in one instance and a different outcome in another, seemingly identical, instance.

At first glance, one might think that this situation doesn't truly refute determinism—it might just reflect our ignorance of some underlying details. Perhaps there are deeper causes for each atomic event that we simply haven't discovered yet. After all, history offers many examples where events appeared random until science uncovered the mechanisms behind them. Isn't it possible that tomorrow we'll find a new law that determines what an atom will do, restoring order to the subatomic realm? Up to a point, this line of thinking is quite reasonable. Our detailed knowledge of atomic behaviour is relatively recent (quantum theory arose in the early 20th century), and it's certainly conceivable that further research could identify hidden variables or laws that remove the element of chance. No one can prove that such laws won't be found in the future. If we were otherwise strongly convinced that determinism *must* be true, we could assume that today's randomness is just a temporary placeholder for tomorrow's scientific discovery. In the past, phenomena that initially seemed capricious (like weather patterns or the spread of diseases) often turned out to follow laws when studied more carefully. So, a determinist might argue, why should atomic events be any different? Given more knowledge, we might find the causes that determine each supposedly "random" quantum jump.

However, the challenge of quantum physics goes further than just saying "we don't currently know all the causes." It suggests that even many of the classical laws we took for granted might not be ironclad deterministic rules, but instead *statistical outcomes of underlying randomness.* In other words, what if Newton's laws and other classical principles are not absolute dictates but averages that emerge when you have huge numbers of particles? This is a profound shift in perspective: it means determinism at the large scale might be an illusion, a by-product of probabilities smoothing out the chaos at the tiny scale.

To illustrate this idea, consider a fanciful thought experiment: imagine a giant who is so large that he cannot see individual human beings, but only large crowds. This giant observes the city of London from a great height. He notices that every morning, a huge amount of "matter" (which in reality is people, though he can't see individuals) moves into the city, and every evening a large quantity moves out. Day after day this happens, with great regularity. The giant might naturally conclude that there is some law of nature causing this daily inflow and outflow—perhaps he theorizes that the sun, when it rises, somehow draws masses of matter into London, and when it sets, the matter flows out again. Indeed, he might even note that on days when the morning is very foggy (and the sun's rays are obscured), the inflow is delayed or reduced, confirming his hypothesis that the sun's influence is the driving cause of the movement. From the giant's limited perspective, this hypothesis fits the observable facts well: more "stuff" enters the city by day than by night, and the pattern correlates with the sun.

Of course, we (with normal human perspective) know the real explanation: individual people commute into the city for work and leave in the evening. We also know that each person might have personal reasons for occasionally deviating from the pattern—someone might stay home sick, or leave early one day, etc. These individual decisions introduce small irregularities, but given the sheer number of people, the overall flow still looks smooth and law-like to a giant who can't see the individual cases. In our story, if the giant later acquires a better instrument (akin to a microscope for us) that allows him to discern individual humans, he would find that the perfect regularity he assumed was an illusion. The flows in and out of London are not driven by a strict natural law of the sun; rather, they are the net effect of countless individual choices (each of which might be considered somewhat unpredictable or "capricious"). The apparent law was really a statistical regularity resulting from averaging over large numbers.

According to Eddington and others, something analogous could be happening in physics. For centuries, we assumed physical bodies (like gases, planets, or projectiles) followed exact deterministic laws. But now it appears that the atoms themselves may only be following statistical tendencies. The atoms have certain probabilities of doing this or that, and because there are so many atoms in an object (trillions upon trillions), the random deviations average out and the overall behaviour *seems* perfectly regular to us. Just as the irregularities of individual commuters were invisible to the giant, the tiny quantum randomness is mostly invisible in everyday phenomena—hence classical physics found seemingly exact laws. If this is true, then the traditional case for determinism collapses. The success of classical physics in predicting, say, planetary motion or gas pressure doesn't prove the universe is strictly determined; it only shows that with large numbers of particles, the random wiggles cancel out and give a reliable average outcome. Underneath, at the atomic level, events might be happening without any deterministic rule at all in each instance.

By the early 1930s, physics indeed had evidence that many laws might be "merely statistical." For example, a chunk of radioactive material will emit particles in a very regular way when considered in bulk: perhaps a thousand decays per second on average, which can be predicted by probabilistic formulas. But no one can predict *which particular atom* will decay at which moment—each atom's decay seems to be spontaneous. Similarly, when studying the motion of molecules in a gas, scientists had long used statistical methods (since the 19th century) to explain things like temperature and pressure. A gas is composed of an enormous number of molecules moving randomly. From moment to moment, individual molecules speed up or slow down unpredictably by colliding with each other. Yet, collectively, their average energy can be measured as temperature, and laws of thermodynamics describe how heat flows—but these are laws of averages and probabilities. In fact, even before quantum mechanics, physicists recognized that many processes are *in principle* statistical. For instance, if you have a room with air evenly distributed and separated by a partition, when you remove the partition the air will mix evenly. It's *overwhelmingly probable* the air will remain roughly uniform in density and temperature. However, it's not *absolutely impossible* (just fantastically unlikely) that by sheer chance all the fast-moving molecules could end up on one side of the room and the slow ones on the other, making one side hot and the other cold without any external cause. That would be a fluke beyond any practical expectation, but it doesn't violate the fundamental laws—those laws just say it's so improbable we can ignore it.

What quantum mechanics introduced that was truly new was the suggestion that this probabilistic character is not just due to our lack of knowledge or the impracticality of tracking zillions of particles. Instead, it might be an irreducible feature of nature. The theory posits that there is no deeper deterministic story for each particle; the probabilities are the final story. This is a very difficult concept to accept—even many scientists (including Einstein) were uncomfortable with the idea that randomness is truly fundamental and not just apparent. If a single atom's behaviour is completely undetermined (except by probabilities), why do large collections of atoms display such consistent regularities? It feels as though there *must* be something enforcing the statistics. To return to our earlier analogy of travellers and diving boards: imagine a swimming pool with a high diving platform and several lower diving boards. You observe that, over the course of a summer, a certain percentage of dives occur from each height—say 5% of people dive from the highest platform, 15% from the next, and so on. If you saw these stable percentages year after year, you would suspect there is some reason behind individuals' choices—perhaps only the very skilled divers attempt the highest jump, which keeps that number relatively small but consistent. If, instead, each diver's choice of platform were completely whimsical, it would be quite mysterious that the overall statistics come out so uniform every season. It would almost seem as if some hidden hand is ensuring that exactly the right proportion choose each level to maintain the pattern. Pure caprice in each case doesn't obviously lead to neat regularities in aggregate, unless the number of cases is so astronomically large that even wild caprice averages out (and even then, the exact stability of the ratio might be puzzling without underlying causes).

15

In quantum physics we have exactly this puzzle: each atomic event might be a law unto itself with no cause, yet when you have billions of them, they collectively behave as if there were strict laws (even if those laws are now interpreted as laws of probability). Some physicists and philosophers argue that there must be some underlying factors or conditions that enforce those probabilities—that the regular ratios of outcomes we observe cry out for an explanation. Others accept the idea that probability itself is an "ultimate" law, with nothing further underneath it. This is an ongoing debate in the foundations of physics and the philosophy of science.

As a personal stance, I (the author) find it hard to believe that sheer randomness on the individual level can by itself produce the kind of consistent order we see on the large scale. The theory of probability itself, while mathematically well-defined, sits on somewhat shaky logical foundations when we try to interpret it in the real world. It almost feels like alchemy to say that by adding up millions of completely capricious events you get a perfectly exact law. If each coin toss were truly free of any cause (just pure chance deciding heads or tails), do we really have a solid reason to expect 50% heads and 50% tails in the long run? We observe it tends toward 50/50, but is that just another law we have to accept without explanation? Might not absolute caprice just as well lead to 100% heads all the time for no reason at all? Of course, probability theory tells us that the odds of extreme imbalances are incredibly low with large numbers, but that theory itself is a kind of secondary law we're invoking. My point is that if we suspect fundamental randomness, it's intellectually tempting to suspect hidden variables or causes that ensure the randomness conforms to those nice statistical patterns. This is not a proof of anything—this subject is far too subtle for dogmatism—but it suggests that we shouldn't too quickly assume that quantum indeterminacy spells the final death of determinism. It could be that the apparent spontaneity of atomic events will eventually be explained by deeper laws we haven't discovered yet. In any case, the debate is open: quantum physics has weakened the classical determinist view, but whether it has killed determinism outright is still unclear. Many scientists are content to work with the probabilistic models and not ask "why," whereas others, like Einstein, expressed the sentiment that *"God does not play dice with the universe,"* indicating their belief that a deterministic explanation must exist even if we haven't found it.

Can Determinism Be Saved? (Responses to the Quantum Challenge)

Faced with the quantum mechanical challenge to a law-bound universe, defenders of determinism have suggested a couple of possible counter-arguments to reconcile the new findings with the old principle of causality. Let's consider two major lines of response a determinist might offer:

First, one might argue that historical precedent favours determinism. In the past, whenever we encountered phenomena that appeared random or "uncaused," we often later discovered causes or rules that had been obscured by complexity. For example, the weather once seemed like the whims of gods; now we understand it as a complex but rule-governed physical system (even if we can't predict it perfectly, we know there are causes like pressure systems, temperature gradients, etc.). The same pattern holds in many fields: we initially think something is purely chance or fortune, but with study we find underlying mechanisms. So,

17

the determinist might say, *yes, atoms seem to behave unpredictably now, but give it time.* The atomic world is enormously complicated and only recently explored; it's premature to conclude that no strict laws exist there just because we haven't found them yet. If one has philosophical or a priori reasons to believe in an orderly universe, this argument can be reassuring: it suggests we simply haven't grasped the full picture. However, if one doesn't have a strong philosophical commitment to determinism, this argument by itself is not definitive. The sceptic can reply that quantum theory already provides an explanation for why large-scale phenomena appear regular (the laws of probability) *without* requiring that each micro-event be determined. In other words, the determinist's appeal here meets a strong rebuttal: "We don't *need* hidden individual causes to get regular large-scale behaviour; probability theory shows that large numbers will almost certainly exhibit stable averages even if individuals are random." The fact that big objects behave predictably (like planets orbiting or gas pressures being stable) doesn't prove each atom has a predictable trajectory; it might only demonstrate that with zillions of atoms the uncertainties even out. Thus, unless one has an independent reason to insist "there must be a precise law for everything," the mere success of past science in finding laws doesn't guarantee success in this new domain.

Second, a determinist might offer a more nuanced argument: *"All right,"* he says, *"you admit that even in quantum physics, when we look at large numbers of events, clear statistical ratios emerge (e.g. 60% outcome A, 40% outcome B). Now, isn't it reasonable to believe that those statistical ratios themselves are generated by underlying causes in each case? After all, whenever we see reliable statistics in nature, we usually suspect there's some reason behind each event that yields that overall ratio."* A classic example often cited is the ratio of male to female births. In most human populations, the sex ratio at birth is remarkably consistent—about 105 boys born for every 100 girls (often noted as roughly 51.5% male, 48.5% female). This is a statistical regularity across large numbers of births. Yet no one believes that each baby's sex is simply a matter of pure chance with no cause; on the contrary, biologists think there are specific genetic and physiological causes determining sex in each individual case (even if we don't fully understand all the influencing factors, we assume they exist). The aggregate ratio (around 105:100) would then be a consequence of those underlying mechanisms. In an analogous way, the determinist argues, if atoms show statistical regularities—say, an atom has a 20% probability to do X and 80% to do Y under certain conditions—there must be particular causes at work in each instance to produce that distribution in the long run. If there were absolutely no cause steering each atomic decision, why would the outcomes tally up so neatly over time? If individual events were truly lawless, we might expect chaos in the totals as well, which we do not see.

This second argument raises a deep philosophical question: Do consistent statistics imply underlying causes for individual events? Or can probability just "exist" without deeper reasons? To tackle this question, we can momentarily set aside the complexities of quantum physics and use a simpler scenario: coin tossing. We believe (based on physics) that if you flip a fair coin, the outcome of any given toss—heads or tails—is determined by the precise mechanics of that toss (the force of the flip, the air resistance, how it tumbles, etc.). In practice, we can't measure all those factors well enough, so each toss seems unpredictable. However, we *expect* that if you toss the coin a great many times, it will land heads roughly half the time and tails half the time. In fact, probability theory tells us that as the number of tosses grows large, the percentage of heads should get closer and closer to 50%. We also know it's possible (just very unlikely) to get runs of many heads in a row by chance. For example, tossing a coin 10 times, it's not too surprising to get maybe 10 heads in a row once in a while (the odds of 10 heads in a row are 1 in 1024, so if you did thousands of trials of 10 tosses, you'd expect it occasionally). But if you tossed a coin a million billion billion times, it's exceedingly unlikely you'd ever see 100 heads in a row within that vast sequence; the fluctuations tend to average out. So even without knowing the cause of each toss's outcome, probability theory predicts a stable overall ratio of heads to tails.

Now, in the coin's case, we actually trust that determinism *does* hold at the individual level—the coin's motion follows Newton's laws—so this analogy isn't perfect for the quantum question. However, imagine if someone insisted that each coin flip was governed by pure chance (like a little "gremlin" deciding heads or tails on a whim for each toss). Would we find it acceptable that this pure whimsy nonetheless yields an almost perfectly even split of heads and tails over millions of throws? We might start to suspect that if the outcomes balance that well, perhaps the coin (or the gremlin) isn't entirely whimsical after all but has some bias that ensures overall fairness. In reality, with huge numbers, even random events do even out, but the determinist in our discussion is essentially saying: It's hard to swallow that statistical laws are fundamental. If we see a stable pattern (like the sex ratio or coin flip frequencies), our intuition (shaped by experience) is that *something* is controlling things behind the scenes to maintain that pattern.

However, it's crucial to realize that this intuition is not ironclad proof. Probability theory, as a branch of mathematics, does allow that random independent events can produce stable frequencies given large numbers—this is the Law of Large Numbers. And quantum mechanics might be telling us that, at bottom, the universe operates on something akin to pure chance (within certain constraints), and yet because of large numbers, we get the orderly world we see. This point of view is conceptually unsettling for some (myself included, as noted earlier) because it leaves a gap in explanation: *why* those particular probabilities and not others? The debate here becomes almost philosophical or even metaphysical: determinists feel that a real explanation requires causes for individual events, whereas the new quantum perspective suggests that might be asking for something nature doesn't provide.

At present, there is no definitive resolution to this debate. Many physicists adopt an instrumental stance: quantum mechanics works extremely well as a predictive tool, so whether each event is truly uncaused or just caused by something we haven't found is seen as an almost metaphysical question rather than a practical one. Some interpretations of quantum mechanics (such as the "hidden variables" theories) attempt to restore determinism at the cost of other assumptions, but they remain minority views. The mainstream view accepts that on the micro level, events are fundamentally stochastic (random within a probability distribution).

To summarize this section: The successes of quantum physics have undeniably weakened the idea of an absolutely determined universe. They show that, at least in terms of what we can currently observe, the universe contains an element of unpredictability. Determinists can respond by arguing that this unpredictability may be only apparent or partial, maintaining hope that deeper laws or future discoveries will re-establish determinism. They also point out logical difficulties in accepting pure chance as an ultimate explanation. This back-and-forth indicates that determinism as a cosmic doctrine is no longer taken for granted; it's an open question in light of modern science. And ironically, where once physics was the staunchest ally of determinism, it has now become the main field in which determinism is questioned.

Quantum Physics and Human Free Will

The debate over quantum indeterminacy has implications beyond physics. Some thinkers saw in the new physics a glimmer of hope for the age-old problem of human free will. If nature at its fundamental level isn't strictly determined, perhaps that opens a door for human decisions not to be preordained either. Sir Arthur Eddington, in particular, not only challenged determinism on the level of atoms but also speculated on what it could mean for our freedom of will.

The basic idea proposed by Eddington was this: if certain events at the atomic scale are not determined but could go one way or another, then maybe the brain (being a physical system made of atoms) could exploit this indeterminism to allow for free choices. After all, if every particle in our brain followed rigid laws, then in principle our thoughts and decisions would be predetermined by prior states of those particles—leaving little room for a traditional notion of free will. But if there is a little bit of genuine randomness or freedom in how an atom behaves, then maybe an act of will could "tip" an atomic event one way versus another, triggering a cascade that leads to a larger effect (like raising an arm or speaking a word).

Eddington imagined that living matter, and the brain in particular, might be a kind of special environment where these tiny uncertainties are magnified into significant actions. The term sometimes used is "amplifier": some systems might amplify microscopic indeterminacies into macroscopic changes. For example, think of a delicate balance—like a very sensitive bomb trigger that could be set off by a single atom's decay. If the atom decays, the bomb explodes; if it doesn't, the bomb stays inert. Such a mechanism effectively turns a random atomic event into a life-size outcome. Eddington speculated that the brain could have something analogous: maybe there are neurons or molecular switches in our neurons that are so finely poised that a single quantum event could influence whether they fire or not. Then an *uncaused* volition (or perhaps a volition at the quantum level) could disturb one atom's behaviour, which would upset a delicate neural balance and initiate a large-scale neural event—resulting in a conscious action that is not traceable solely to prior physical causes.

This is a fascinating idea because it attempts to link the notion of free will with the new scientific understanding, granting a possible mechanism for how "mind" might influence "matter" in a way not ruled out by physics. According to Eddington, quantum physics doesn't change any of the established laws for large-scale phenomena (a rock or a planet still obeys the same gross behaviour as before), but it replaces certainty with *overwhelming probability*. So, normally, the random atomic deviations average out. But what if in the brain there is a special kind of instability where a very small push can produce a large outcome? (In chaos theory this is sometimes called the "butterfly effect," where a tiny perturbation grows over time into a major effect.) Eddington's suggestion is that the brain's biology might

23

allow a single atom's "choice" to be that butterfly that causes a storm, so to speak, in the neural circuitry, thereby affecting behaviour.

Now, even Eddington admitted this was mostly speculative—a "bare hypothesis," as he put it. It's important to recognize that even if quantum indeterminacy exists, using it to rescue a meaningful form of free will faces serious challenges. For one, randomness alone is not the same as *control.* If my decisions were random at root, that hardly sounds like free will in the sense people usually desire (which is about being the author of your actions, not having them happen by chance). Eddington's hope was that the mind or will could selectively influence those random events toward desired outcomes. But from a scientific standpoint, this is an additional assumption that goes well beyond quantum physics—it implies some non-physical agency steering the supposedly lawless quantum events, which starts to look like smuggling in the very thing (free will) that we were trying to explain.

Even if we allow that atomic indeterminacy is real, there is currently no empirical evidence that such indeterminacy in our brains results in violations of the usual statistical laws at the human scale. All our experiments and observations of human bodies (including brains) still show behaviour consistent with the averaged-out, probabilistic laws of traditional physics. In other words, even if your neurons have tiny quantum randomness, your arm generally doesn't move unless a sufficient neural signal—one that is explainable by normal biology—tells it to move. We don't see spontaneous, uncaused large-scale actions in humans that would indicate a quantum trigger at work. Human behaviour, on the whole, remains quite consistent with being caused by prior bodily states (and external influences and internal motivations), without needing to invoke miracles at the atomic level.

In my assessment, Eddington's attempt to reconcile free will with physics, while ingenious and certainly intriguing, does not compel us to rewrite our understanding of human behaviour at this time. It's a possibility that cannot be strictly refuted at present (since we can't peer into a single thought and see if a quantum event was behind it), but it doesn't seem particularly plausible either. It asks us to believe that evolution or design has arranged the brain to utilize quantum uncertainty in just the right way to allow for free will, yet this leaves no obvious trace in how we model or predict neural processes. A more likely scenario, to my mind, is that as science progresses, we may discover new deterministic laws that remove even the limited indeterminacy quantum mechanics currently posits. And even if some atomic indeterminism persists, it might remain irrelevant to higher-level functions like human decision-making, which could still be effectively deterministic through averaging effects. In short, the burden of proof is very much on the idea that quantum physics grants us freedom of the will, and so far that proof is not forthcoming.

The Scientific View of Human Behaviour

While physics was busy challenging the determinism of matter, biology and psychology were quietly reinforcing determinism when it comes to human beings and their minds. Over the last century, research into how our bodies and brains work has increasingly found lawful cause-and-effect processes governing what we think, feel, and do. This doesn't prove that free will is an illusion, but it certainly narrows the gaps where an uncaused will might reside.

25

For instance, studies of physiology and neuroscience have identified specific mechanisms underlying many aspects of behaviour. The discovery of hormones and internal secretions has shown how our moods and actions can be influenced by biochemical causes (like adrenaline triggering a fight-or-flight response, or testosterone potentially affecting aggression levels). Advancements in mapping the brain have linked particular mental functions to distinct regions of the brain: damage to or stimulation of certain areas reliably changes behaviour or experiences in predictable ways. The famous experiments of Ivan Pavlov demonstrated how involuntary behaviours can be conditioned by external stimuli, forming cause-effect links in reflexes (his dogs "learned" to salivate at the sound of a bell due to an associated expectation of food). In psychology, the psychoanalytic approach introduced by Freud (and later refined by others) uncovered how unconscious memories and desires—traces of past causes—can influence our conscious choices and actions, even when we're unaware of those influences.

All these lines of research have something in common: they suggest that human thoughts and actions have causal explanations. They point to antecedent conditions—whether physiological (a neuron firing pattern, a hormone surge), developmental (childhood experiences shaping personality), or environmental (social pressures, education, etc.)—that play a role in producing what we do. None of these findings can disprove the existence of free will, especially if one defines free will in a very metaphysical sense (as something beyond the reach of scientific measurement). However, they do make it seem increasingly unlikely that our volitions occur without any cause whatsoever. If truly uncaused, completely spontaneous choices do happen in the human mind, they would have to be exceedingly rare phenomena that have thus far eluded detection amid the myriad causes we *have* been able to identify.

In everyday terms, it appears that, for the most part, our will is influenced and shaped by prior events—our genetics, our upbringing, our brain chemistry, our past experiences, and the present context. We do not observe a clear "causal gap" where decisions pop out of nowhere. This doesn't mean we aren't making choices—rather, it means the process of choosing is itself part of a web of cause and effect.

Misconceptions About Causation and Free Will

People often fear that if their will or their choices have causes, then they are not truly free. There is a sense that "if my decision was caused by something, then I was forced or compelled, and I'm not really in control." This is a misunderstanding of what causation implies about personal agency. It's important to address some emotional confusions that surround the idea of determinism, because they can make determinism seem more threatening than it actually is.

First of all, having your actions be caused does not mean you are being coerced to do something you don't want to do. The cause of an action, in a psychological context, is often *your own desire or intention*. If you *want* to eat an apple and thus reach out and eat one, the fact that your hunger and liking for apples caused you to do it doesn't make the act any less *yours*. In fact, it's exactly what we mean by acting according to your free will: you did what you wanted to do. If those wants have underlying causes (perhaps you skipped breakfast so you're hungry, perhaps you have a sweet tooth for fruit because of your taste buds or how you were raised), that

27

doesn't negate the fact that you, acting through your wants, performed the action. We naturally conflate "uncaused" with "freely chosen," but they are not the same. An uncaused action would be one that you do for literally no reason at all—not even a reason like a desire or a goal. It's hard to even imagine what that would be; it would feel random, like a twitch. True freedom, one could argue, is not about lacking causes, but about *being able to do what you genuinely want* (without external restraint). By that definition, a caused will is fine as long as the causes align with your own motivations.

Another worry is that determinism makes us powerless or insignificant, that if everything is determined then we're just "slaves of circumstance" and nothing we do matters. This too is a misconception. Power in the human sense means the capacity to achieve intended effects. If I intend to write a book and I succeed in doing so, I have exercised power to bring about an outcome I wanted. Whether my intentions and actions had causes does not change the fact that I wrote the book and can take credit for it. Knowing the causes of our intentions (say, I was inspired by another book, or I have a certain brain chemistry that predisposed me to long focus) doesn't make the accomplishment any less mine. Determinism doesn't mean we sit back and outcomes happen without our involvement—on the contrary, determinism would include *us as part of the chain of causes.* Our choices and efforts are themselves powerful forces that shape what happens in the world. The only difference is that, under determinism, our choices are also outcomes of prior chains. But as long as those prior chains include our character, values, and reasoning processes, we are still *part* of the determination of the future. In short, determinism doesn't strip away our agency or responsibility in the straightforward way people often think. We still deliberate, act, and bring about results, which is exactly what we mean by exercising our will.

It's also worth pointing out that even people who claim to believe strongly in absolute free will in practice behave as if causes and effects govern human behaviour. There's a bit of a psychological compartmentalization here. Someone might insist philosophically that every person has an uncaused free will, but that same person will then go on to educate their children with care, believing that a good upbringing will cause those children to grow into virtuous adults. They will praise the influence of good teachers or moral mentors, implicitly acknowledging that guidance and environment shape a person's choices. They might attend religious services or listen to motivational speakers hoping to strengthen their own resolve or character—again, implying that external inputs can causally affect their will in positive ways. We have entire institutions (schools, legal systems, self-help programs) built on the assumption that people's beliefs and decisions can be influenced by identifiable factors. Laws and punishments, for example, are intended to deter wrongdoing by creating consequences that potential wrongdoers will consider—this only makes sense if we assume that a person's decision to commit a crime can be swayed by anticipation of punishment (which is a causal influence on their will). If someone truly believed that choices are uncaused and completely free in an absolute sense, it would be irrational to bother with education, persuasion, parenting, or any form of social conditioning—none of it should have any effect if wills are entirely independent of causes. But in reality, everyone acts as though psychology and environment matter in shaping human behaviour, which is to say, we all tacitly believe in *causation* when it comes to decision-making.

Thus, there is a kind of inconsistency where people cherish the concept of free will in theory but rely on determinist assumptions in practice. We say to someone "Why did you do that?" expecting a reason (a cause) for their action. If they have no idea why they did something, we find that unusual or concerning. We never truly behave as if actions just happen without cause; when cause is not immediately apparent, we search for one (even if it's hidden in the unconscious). So part of the emotional attachment to free will comes from not fully realizing what a completely uncaused will would entail. It wouldn't actually give us more control or dignity—it would make human action capricious and disconnected from the factors (like beliefs, desires, and experiences) that actually define who we are.

Does Introspection Prove We Are Free?

Another common argument in favour of free will is the appeal to personal experience: when we introspect—when we look inside ourselves during decision-making—we often feel like we are freely choosing among alternatives. "I can sense that I could have chosen otherwise," one might say. If you ask me why I picked coffee over tea this morning, I might reply, "Well, I just felt like coffee, but I *could have* had tea if I wanted; I simply didn't want to." This introspective evidence is taken to show that at the moment of choice, multiple futures were open to me, and *I* determined which became reality.

It's true that when we make a choice, we often imagine that we *could* have done differently. However, this is not proof that our choice was uncaused or independent of antecedent conditions. What introspection reliably tells us is that *if we had wanted* something else, we would have done something else. In other words, we know that our actions follow our *wants* or intentions. But introspection cannot tell us where our wants come from. It's entirely consistent with our inner experience that our wants themselves have causes we're not aware of. If I chose coffee because I "felt like it," that feeling (my preference at that moment) might have been influenced by any number of factors—maybe I smelled coffee brewing, maybe I had a bad sleep and crave caffeine, maybe I've formed a habit of morning coffee over years. None of those causes are directly visible to introspection. All I experience is "I prefer coffee right now."

In situations where we make reasoned decisions, we sometimes do see the causes of our actions: for example, if I consult a map and then decide to turn left to reach my destination, I *know* that this decision was caused by the advice on the map. The cause (the map's information and my desire to get somewhere) is clear and conscious. But in many cases, especially with more spontaneous or subtle choices, the chain of causation isn't fully apparent to us. We might make a snap decision and only later realize, "I think I did that because I was stressed," or we might never quite know why we felt drawn to A over B. We might call those choices "free" in the sense that we weren't *consciously* aware of compulsion, but it doesn't demonstrate that there were no causes. It only demonstrates that the causes did not rise to the level of conscious awareness.

In fact, introspection is a notoriously unreliable method for uncovering the true causes of our behaviour. Psychological experiments have shown that people can often be mistaken about why they did something. We might confabulate a reason after the fact if we're pressed to explain an action that was actually influenced by subconscious cues. For instance, subjects in an experiment might choose one

31

item over another and then give a logical explanation, even if the experiment was rigged to influence them through a factor they didn't notice. This suggests that the feeling of "I chose freely" can sometimes mask the reality that our choice was biased or swayed by unseen factors.

To be clear, none of this is to say we are mindless robots—only that our conscious feeling of freedom is not an infallible indicator of uncaused choice. What we know directly is that we act according to our motivations. Whether those motivations have prior causes (brain processes, upbringing, etc.) is not something introspection alone can decide. It remains a question to be explored through psychology, neuroscience, and philosophy.

It's also worth examining the concept of "will" itself. When we speak of "free will," we often imagine the will as a kind of faculty or entity within us that can initiate actions. But what is the will? The notion is rather fuzzy upon inspection. When I decide to do something, I experience a sense of resolve or commitment to an action. But if I try to *locate* the will, it's hard to pinpoint. Is it a thought? A feeling of determination?

Modern psychology suggests that much of our behaviour does not involve a conscious act of will at all. Most actions are automatic or habitual to a degree. For example, when you get up from a chair and walk to another room, you probably don't consciously will each step. You formed the intention to go to the other room (perhaps to fetch something), and then your body carries it out through a learned sequence of motions without you deliberating on each one. You could say the initial decision was an act of will, but every detail that follows happens almost on autopilot. If someone lacked the ability to perform actions without explicit will (a condition that might be considered a disorder), they would be paralyzed by indecision about every tiny step.

Even in more complex decisions, our choices often emerge from a competition of ideas or desires in the mind, not from a single, unitary "will-power" module. We might feel torn between two options—two sets of reasons or emotional pulls—until one wins out because it appears more attractive or less aversive than the other. The final feeling might be "I willed option A," but one could also describe it as "option A's motivations outweighed option B's." The "will" in that sense is just the tipping point of psychological forces.

When we introspect the moment of deciding, often what we notice is a kind of mental tension or a statement to ourselves: *"Yes, I will do this."* There might even be a slight feeling of mental or muscular effort (like bracing oneself). But if I scrutinize my own mind, I cannot find a separate mental ingredient that is the pure act of will devoid of any reason or desire. It seems rather that will is an expression of our strongest motive at the moment. We call it "will" when we have aligned our mind behind a course of action and push forward with it, especially if there was some resistance (internal or external) to overcome.

I mention this because sometimes free will debates assume there's a clear, singular thing called "the Will" that one can point to. In practice, the concept is murky. A scientifically-minded perspective might say that "will" is not a fundamental feature of the mind but a combination of complex processes (attention, intention, inhibition of alternatives, commitment to a choice, etc.). If that's true, then free will in the absolute sense might be an illusion created by those processes.

33

Even so, we must draw a distinction between voluntary and involuntary acts—a distinction that remains very valid. When I lift my arm intentionally, that's a voluntary act; when my knee jerks from a reflex tap, that's involuntary. Determinism as a concept doesn't deny this difference. It simply states that *both* types of acts have causes: the voluntary act is caused by my decision and desire to lift my arm, whereas the reflex is caused by a direct nerve reaction. The experience is different: one involves a conscious intention and the other doesn't. But determinism can accommodate both by saying: with certain kinds of causes (conscious motives) present, we call the act free; with only direct physiological causes and no conscious choice, we call it unfree or involuntary. The debate is whether those conscious motives themselves are part of a chain of causation or are a special causal fresh start.

Finally, there's the issue of moral responsibility that often entangles itself with free will. People worry that if free will doesn't exist, then concepts of sin, guilt, or punishment lose their foundation. Traditionally, free will has been deemed important for morality: if someone could *not have done otherwise*, how can we blame them? This is a complex issue that this chapter only touches upon. It will be discussed later in the context of ethics. In brief, some argue that you can maintain a coherent system of responsibility even in a deterministic framework (by focusing on changing future behaviour and protecting society, for example, rather than pure blame). But these are delicate questions. The key point here is: the scientific question of whether our actions have causes is separate from the societal question of how we assign responsibility. They influence each other, but one can accept determinism about causes while still holding people accountable in practical ways. We will return to this when we explore how science intersects with our ideas of right and wrong in a later chapter.

Science Between Determinism and Free Will

Looking back at our discussion, it might seem that I have argued first against strict determinism (when considering quantum physics) and then against absolute free will (when considering psychology and the fallacies of introspection). Is this a contradiction? Not really. The fact is that both pure determinism and pure indeterminism (free will being one form of the latter) are, in a sense, metaphysical extremes that go beyond what science can currently establish.

Pure determinism claims that *every single event without exception* is the inevitable result of preceding causes. Pure free-will doctrine (in its most extreme form) claims that *some events (specifically human decisions) are completely independent of prior causes*. Both of these are sweeping assertions that reach outside the realm of immediate empirical verification. Science, by its nature, deals with what can be observed, tested, and evidenced. When neither determinism nor free will can be directly and fully confirmed by evidence, a scientist should be cautious about committing wholly to either.

From a practical standpoint, scientists *behave* as determinists in their work. As we noted, the search for causal laws is the driving force of scientific investigation. A biologist studying a disease will assume there is a cause for its spread or cure; a physicist examining particle interactions will assume there are patterns to be found. This methodological determinism is indispensable—without it, one would essentially give up on understanding phenomena ("there's no reason it happens, it just does"). So, in practice, the scientific

35

attitude is: *assume determinism until proven otherwise.* But this is a hypothesis or approach, not a dogmatic conclusion that determinism reigns everywhere absolutely.

A wise scientist is not obligated to claim that causality exists where it hasn't been demonstrated. We use determinism as a guiding principle to look for causes, but we must also remain open to what we actually find. If we find randomness or lack of a clear cause, we note that honestly. In areas where we haven't yet found laws, it's prudent to say "we don't know the cause" rather than "this has no cause" or conversely "there must be a cause even if we'll never find it." Admitting uncertainty is better than asserting unfounded certainty in either direction.

Likewise, a scientist (or anyone employing scientific thinking) should be wary of assertively claiming that a certain realm *definitely* has no causal laws (which is what an absolute free-will claim would be about the realm of human decision or perhaps atomic events). To declare *"Here, in this corner, causality breaks down entirely"* is a risky stance. It's theoretically and practically unwise because it can discourage further inquiry—if we assume an event has no cause, we won't bother to look for one, and thus we might miss discovering a cause that *is actually there.* History has examples where people thought something was irreducibly random or miraculous, but later research found an explanation. Declaring an area causeless can become a self-fulfilling prophecy of ignorance.

Therefore, one might say that science occupies a middle ground: it operates under the working hypothesis of determinism (seeking causes for events), but it does not endorse a blanket metaphysical determinism without evidence, nor does it embrace a blanket "uncaused events exist" stance without evidence. It remains empirical, pushing neither assertion nor denial of universal determinism beyond what the data support. Where evidence strongly indicates causal connections, science affirms them. Where evidence suggests indeterminacy or lack of a known cause, science acknowledges that and continues investigating or refining its theories.

In the specific debate between determinism and free will, this means science would neither absolutely confirm that *"every thought you have is predetermined"* nor that *"the will is magically exempt from causation."* Instead, science continues to explore how decisions are made in the brain, how randomness in physics works, and so on, refining our understanding step by step. Both extreme determinism and extreme free-willism can be seen as dogmas if asserted without evidence—and dogma is the opposite of the scientific spirit. It's better to collect evidence and remain somewhat agnostic or at least non-committal about the ultimate metaphysical truth until we know more.

The Appeal of Determinism and Free Will

Why has the debate between determinism and free will been so persistent and emotionally charged throughout history? Partly, it's because each side of the debate speaks to deep human desires and fears, and these are in tension.

Determinism, especially in the form of believing the world runs on discoverable laws, has a great appeal because knowledge is power. If we understand the causal laws of nature, we can predict and control outcomes, which vastly increases our ability to survive and thrive. The success of science in giving humanity mastery over many aspects of the environment (curing diseases, engineering technology, predicting weather, etc.) has made us *fond* of deterministic thinking. A world that is orderly and law-governed is comforting in many ways: it means we can plan, we can protect ourselves, and we're not at the mercy of capricious forces beyond our understanding. Think of earlier times when people believed that storms or plagues were the result of angry gods or evil spirits—nature was terrifyingly unpredictable. As we learned natural explanations, these events became less frightening because they were no longer seen as random punishments but as phenomena with causes we could potentially mitigate (e.g. understanding germ theory for diseases, or meteorology for storms).

So, there are strong motives for humans to embrace determinism: it provides a sense of security (the universe isn't fundamentally random or against us), and it provides tangible benefits through applied science and technology. Society's acceptance of scientific determinism grew because it delivered results—electricity, medicine, and countless other advances come from believing in and utilizing consistent natural laws.

On the other hand, people have an equally strong desire to see themselves as autonomous and special, not just cogs in a cosmic machine. We cherish our sense of individuality and the notion that our lives, choices, and efforts have genuine significance. If everything about us was determined from the beginning of time by impersonal laws—if we are just the product of a "blind necessity" churning out outcomes—then some feel that this robs us of our dignity or purpose. It can engender a feeling of futility: *"Why strive or dream if whatever will be, will be regardless of me?"* The idea that you are inevitably saying and doing whatever was pre-programmed into the universe since the start can be quite disheartening. It makes one feel like a puppet of physics, not a creative, self-determining being.

Thus, many people emotionally resist determinism when it comes to human actions. They try to carve out exceptions: for example, a common stance is *"Sure, physics and astronomy might be deterministic, but human beings have free will."* In other words, they grant determinism everywhere except in the domain of the soul or the mind. This reflects the desire to have the predictive power of determinism (for controlling nature) but avoid the personal consequences of being determined (for maintaining a sense of freedom). Others attempt more sophisticated reconciliations: they'll argue perhaps our free choices are somehow compatible with determinism (various philosophical compatibilist arguments exist), or they'll propose dualistic solutions (the mind is outside the physical laws, etc.), or even simply hold contradictory beliefs in different contexts (scientists in the lab, existentialists in personal life).

Neither pure determinism nor pure indeterminism fully satisfies all our desires. Determinism offers understanding and control but threatens meaning and moral responsibility. Free will offers moral dignity and self-importance but at the expense of making our existence less explainable and perhaps less connected to the natural order. It's no wonder, then, that the argument seesaws back and forth over the ages, with people tending to pick the side that addresses whichever worry feels more pressing to them.

However, it's crucial to remember that what we find comforting or disturbing doesn't determine what is true. Reality is not obligated to align with the "agreeable features" of either determinism or free will. We might hope that somehow the truth allows us to have both the predictability and power of determinism and the personal freedom and responsibility of free will. But there is no guarantee the universe will oblige this hope. We have to follow evidence and reason, even if it leads to conclusions that are uncomfortable. It could turn out that the truth is "mixed" or something that doesn't neatly match human preferences at all.

At this juncture, with the knowledge we have, we do not have a final answer to the determinism vs. free will question that satisfies scientific rigor and philosophical scrutiny completely. We see signs that strict determinism may not hold at the quantum level, and we see signs that free will (in the sense of uncaused choices) likely does not hold at the level of human psychology. It may be that the truth combines elements of both, or exists in a framework that transcends the simple dichotomy (some propose, for example, that what matters is not whether choices are caused, but the nature of the causes and how they integrate with our sense of self).

In the end, while it's intellectually interesting and important to debate determinism, we should approach the topic with humility. There is a temptation to side with what aligns with one's emotional inclination—either embracing the cold comfort of a clockwork universe or the warm but perhaps illusory glow of absolute freedom. The scientific attitude advises against making a premature choice driven by desire. Instead, we continue to investigate how the world works, keep an open mind, and be prepared that the ultimate reality might not cater to our wishes. Whatever the truth is— fully determined, partly random, something in between—it likely won't be designed just to make us feel satisfied. Our task is to try to understand the unbroken chain of causes and effects as far as we can, and to understand ourselves within that chain, without succumbing to wishful thinking on either side.

Chapter 2

Origins of the Idea – Historical Perspectives

The philosophical idea that every event is caused and perhaps inevitable has deep roots stretching back to antiquity. Long before the rise of modern science, thinkers grappled with questions of fate, chance, and free will. In this chapter, we journey through key historical eras – ancient, medieval, and early modern – to see how the concept of determinism evolved. We will find vigorous debates at each stage: some philosophers argued that an unbroken chain of causation underlies all of reality, while others pushed back, insisting on contingency or freedom. By tracing these debates from the classical world through the Middle Ages and into the Enlightenment, we'll uncover how determinism emerged as a powerful idea and how it was challenged by alternative perspectives. The progression is not linear, but there are clear threads connecting the centuries. The ancient atomists and Stoics introduced determinist notions of nature's order; medieval theologians struggled to reconcile an all-powerful God with human choice; and Renaissance scientists and Enlightenment philosophers ushered in the image of a clockwork universe governed by laws. Throughout, we will deepen our analysis of key arguments, examine illustrative examples and case studies, consider counterarguments, and draw connections across periods. The goal is to understand how the *idea* of determinism – that events follow inevitably from prior causes – took shape over time, long before it was ever called "determinism." Despite changes in context, many of the core questions remained remarkably consistent: Is the world governed by necessity or is there room for chance? Do we have free will, or are our actions fated by prior causes? How do divine foreknowledge or natural laws fit in? In exploring how various eras answered these questions, we lay the groundwork for the modern concept of the "unbroken chain" described in the previous chapter. The style of this historical survey will mirror that of Chapter 1: clear, rigorous, and engaging, with a structured, book-like narrative that carries the reader forward with logical momentum.

1. Ancient Philosophies of Causation

Ideas about causation and fate first flowered in the ancient world. Greek philosophers in particular were preoccupied with understanding what principles govern nature. Was the universe ultimately ordered and predictable, or capricious and chaotic? Several schools of thought emerged, offering different answers. On one end of the spectrum were the early *materialist* philosophers – notably Leucippus and Democritus, the originators of ancient atomism – who taught that nothing occurs at random and that everything in nature happens out of necessity. On the other end were thinkers who defended the reality of chance or choice – for example, Aristotle, who allowed for contingency in nature, and Epicurus, who introduced randomness to preserve human free will. Between these poles, the Stoics developed a strikingly deterministic cosmology infused with divine reason (the *Logos*), yet they, too, had to explain how human responsibility could coexist with fate. As we will see, the ancient debates already contained many of the key arguments that would resurface throughout history. Let us delve into a few major ancient perspectives on causation: the atomists' doctrine of necessity, the Stoic theory of fate, and prominent alternatives offered by other Greek thinkers.

Atomism and Necessity – Democritus and Leucippus:

One of the clearest early statements of a deterministic worldview came from the atomists of 5th-century BCE Greece. Leucippus, the founder of atomism, asserted a bold principle: "Nothing happens in vain, but everything [happens] from *logos* and by necessity"[2]. In other words, there are no truly random or causeless events; every occurrence has a reason (a *logos*, which can mean explanation or account) and follows necessarily from prior conditions. This surviving fragment of Leucippus' writing is perhaps the oldest explicit formulation of the idea that the world is ruled by causal necessity. His student Democritus built upon this foundation

---

[2] **Leucippus (5th c. BCE)**, *fragment on necessity*, quoted in Aetius 1.25.4. In The Presocratic Philosophers, 2nd ed., edited by G. S. Kirk, J. E. Raven, and M. Schofield (Cambridge: Cambridge University Press, 1983), 410.

to construct a fully materialistic explanation of nature. Democritus taught that reality consists of an infinite number of tiny, indivisible particles – atoms – moving through the void. All that happens in the world, he argued, results from the interactions of these atoms according to fixed laws. Notably, Democritus rejected the notion that events are due to the whims of gods or to pure chance. He "denied the arbitrariness of phenomena" that would exist if things happened by the unpredictable will of deities. Instead, he "replaced that explanation with the idea of deterministic laws governing the behaviour of atoms," which in turn explain all phenomena, "including human beings and their actions"[3]. In Democritus's view, even mental events and decisions are ultimately material processes (movements of atoms) and thus part of the natural chain of causes.

The atomists' commitment to universal causation was so strong that they embraced its logical implications. If only atoms and the void exist, and if atoms obey strict causal laws, then everything that happens – from the falling of a stone to a person's decision to raise their hand – is the inevitable result of prior motions of atoms. Leucippus reportedly put it succinctly: "Nothing occurs at random, but everything for a reason and by necessity". Democritus carried this forward, suggesting that all events are connected in an unbroken causal sequence. One modern commentator summarizes Democritus's worldview by saying that "all the events in the world [are] connected in an eternal deterministic causal chain with a single possible future"[4]. In other words, given the state

---

[3] **Bob Doyle**, "Democritus," (*Information Philosopher*), summarizing Democritus' rejection of arbitrary divine intervention in favour of natural laws.^(1)

[4] **Ibid**. (Doyle, "Democritus," *Information Philosopher*) – describing the "eternal deterministic causal chain" linking all events in Democritus's worldview.

of the atoms at one moment, there is only one outcome that can unfold next – any appearance of chance is an illusion due to our ignorance. This is a stark form of determinism: a belief in a universe where, from the very beginning of time, the course of everything was fixed by the trajectories of atoms.

Why did the atomists adopt such a view? Partly, it was a reaction against earlier mythological and mystical explanations. By positing natural laws and necessity, thinkers like Democritus were moving explanation out of the hands of capricious gods and into impersonal nature. This was seen as a triumph of reason over superstition. Indeed, Democritus and Leucippus "replaced theological and supernatural explanations of phenomena with natural materialist explanations,"[5] seeking lawful regularities instead of divine whims. The idea that even human thoughts and actions have purely physical causes was a radical departure from traditional views that invoked divine agency or an immaterial soul. Yet Democritus appears to have fully endorsed that radical conclusion – famously stating that *by convention* we speak of qualities like sweet or bitter, whereas in reality "there are only atoms and void"[6] moving necessarily.

This thorough going determinism did raise a problem that Democritus was likely aware of: what about human freedom and moral responsibility? If our choices are just the necessary result of atomic motions, can we be praised or blamed for them? Ancient commentators note that Democritus "was no

---

[5] **Ibid**. (Doyle, "Democritus," *Information Philosopher*) – noting that Democritus and Leucippus replaced supernatural explanations with materialist ones.

[6] **Democritus**, fragment 117, in Diogenes Laertius, *Lives of Eminent Philosophers* IX.72, trans. R. D. Hicks (Cambridge, MA: Harvard University Press, 1925). (Democritus: "By convention sweet, by convention bitter; in reality only atoms and void.")

doubt aware of the negative implications for human freedom and moral responsibility". He himself may not have written extensively about ethics (much of his work is lost), but later generations certainly noticed the tension. In fact, the question of free will versus determinism arguably *begins* here in the ancient world as a response to atomism. As we'll see in a moment, one major philosopher, Epicurus, was so concerned about saving free will that he altered the atomist system to reintroduce a bit of indeterminism.

Before turning to Epicurus and other critics, it's worth highlighting that the atomist notion of causal necessity was not just a wild speculation – it became deeply influential. The idea that nature runs according to impersonal laws and that chance is merely a name for unrecognized causes was a legacy passed down through Hellenistic philosophy (e.g. the Stoics) and later picked up by scientists in the Renaissance. Leucippus's fragment about nothing happening in vain was cited for centuries. The Roman poet Lucretius, who much later (1st century BCE) championed Epicurean atomism, still praised Democritus and Leucippus for banishing the "arbitrary fates and capricious gods" from explanations of nature. In short, the atomists established a key theme: the world has an underlying order of causes, and apparent randomness is either an illusion or a result of complexity rather than true indeterminacy.

The Stoic *Logos* – Fate and Providence:

Around a century after Democritus, a very different philosophical school also arrived at a largely deterministic picture of the cosmos. The Stoics (originating in the late 4th to 3rd century BCE with Zeno of Citium and later developed by Chrysippus and others) taught that the entire universe is

48

permeated by the *Logos* – a divine rational principle – and unfolds according to *fate*. Though the Stoic worldview was quite unlike atomistic materialism in its metaphysics (the Stoics were basically pantheists, identifying God with Nature), it was similar in asserting that nothing happens without a cause. The Stoics held a doctrine of universal causation: every event is determined by preceding events in accordance with the logos (rational order or law) of the cosmos. In Stoic physics, even seemingly fortuitous occurrences are governed by this inexorable web of cause and effect, often conceived as a grand chain of *fated* events. As one modern interpreter puts it: "The ancient Stoics were determinists, believing in universal cause and effect". To them, *fate* (or *heimarmene* in Greek) was essentially the sum of all natural causes – sometimes defined as the orderly sequence of events under the providence of the Logos. Cleanthes, a Stoic philosopher, described fate as the "connected series of causes, since it is the reason (*logos*) according to which the cosmos is arranged" – again emphasizing that *reason* and *cause* structure everything.

It's important to understand what the Stoics meant by saying the world is determined by *logos*. This logos was divine in their view – effectively God or Zeus ordering the universe – but it operated through nature's laws, not through arbitrary miracles. The Stoics were impressed by the regularity in phenomena and saw it as evidence of an underlying rational structure. Chrysippus, the great 3rd-century BCE Stoic, wrote extensively on causality to explain how fate works. In his fragmentary writings (preserved by later authors), Chrysippus argues that for anything to happen, there must be a cause; nothing can happen *uncaused*. He even attempted to classify causes and discuss how complex events (like human actions) result from a conjunction of internal and external causes. In effect, the Stoics identified *God or Nature* with *causal law*. Later commentators noted that "the Stoic physicists based physical determinism on the Laws of Nature or the Laws of God, since they identified Nature with God" . In their eyes, saying "X happened by fate" is equivalent to saying "X had a sufficient cause in the natural/divine order."

Despite this strict determinism, the Stoics were very concerned with ethics and moral responsibility. They famously advocated living "according to Nature" – which meant aligning one's will with the inevitable course of events fated by the cosmos. But if everything is fated, a challenge arises: why should we make any effort at all? This was raised in antiquity as the so-called "Lazy Argument" against Stoicism: if it is fated that you will recover from illness or not, then (the argument goes) it doesn't matter whether you call a doctor or not, since fate's outcome will occur regardless . Chrysippus responded by drawing an important distinction: events are *co-fated* with our choices and actions. Fate includes not only the outcomes but the means. For example, if it is fated that you will recover, it may also be fated that you do so *through* consulting a doctor and following treatment. In his rebuttal (cited by Eusebius and Cicero), Chrysippus explained that many outcomes are conditional on our own actions – which themselves are fated parts of the chain. Thus, going to the doctor is part of the cause that fate has ordained for your recovery. In this way the Stoics tried to show that determinism need not lead to inertia or fatalistic apathy; one must still act, because one's actions are the very links that fate uses to produce outcomes.

How did the Stoics view human freedom then? They developed a form of compatibilism – the view that free will (properly understood) is compatible with determinism. A person is free, they argued, when they *will* in accordance with their own nature and with the greater rational order, rather than being impeded or coerced by external forces. In Stoic terms, a sage freely assents to what happens, understanding it as necessary. But this "freedom" is really a recognition of necessity – the Stoic wise person wants events to happen exactly as they inevitably must. Chrysippus reportedly used an analogy: the universe's cause-and-effect chain is like a rolling cylinder; whether it keeps rolling depends on its shape (internal nature) as well as the initial push. Our internal character causes us to respond in one way or another to external stimuli – and that character itself is shaped by prior causes, but when we act according to our own nature without external compulsion, the Stoics call it a *free* act. Still, in modern terms, the Stoic position is strongly deterministic: they did not allow that, given the same preceding circumstances, events *could* have turned out otherwise. Even our "character" that makes choices is ultimately formed by the fated order of things. One might summarize Stoic doctrine by saying "everything is fated to happen exactly as it does, but virtuous people *consent* to fate and thus feel free." The Stoic emperor Marcus Aurelius put it simply: "Accept whatever comes to you woven in the pattern of your destiny, for what could more aptly fit your needs?" That resignation captures the Stoic sense that *Logos* (destiny, nature's law) is inexorable.

To illustrate the Stoic stance with a historical note: the Stoics were so confident in universal causality that they even attempted to defend astrology on deterministic grounds. If indeed everything is interconnected by the chain of causes, then perhaps the configurations of stars (themselves effects of prior causes) could be correlated with earthly events. Stoic thinkers like Posidonius flirted with this idea, treating astrological fate as a piece of the cosmic determinism puzzle (though not all Stoics agreed on astrology's validity). This shows how far they took the notion that *nothing* is left to chance. By contrast, sceptics like the Academic Carneades challenged the Stoics by arguing that we do seem to have a choice, and he attacked their notion of fate. The Stoic response by Chrysippus re-emphasized that every choice has causes (notably one's own disposition) and thus fits into fate's plan.

In summary, the Stoics contributed a theological or providential flavour to determinism: instead of random atoms, it is divine reason that guarantees the universal rule of cause and effect. "Nothing excepted" from this rule – fate works through *all* things. The Stoic universe is a tightly knit web where even the fall of a sparrow or a seemingly chance encounter has its proper cause and place in the grand scheme. This was a compelling vision of cosmic order that influenced later religious and philosophical thought, especially ideas of divine providence and predestination (Stoic ideas were later adopted by some Christian theologians to articulate God's foreordaining plan). Yet, as we noted, not everyone in antiquity found a deterministic cosmos acceptable. Some philosophers valued contingency, spontaneity, or genuine free will and thus offered alternative perspectives.

Alternative Views: Aristotle, Epicurus, and Others – Arguing for Contingency:

The deterministic philosophies of the atomists and Stoics did not go unchallenged in antiquity. Other prominent thinkers argued that not everything is preordained or necessary; there are genuine indeterminacies or freedoms in the world. Two figures stand out as offering influential counterpoints: Aristotle in the 4th century BCE, and Epicurus in the Hellenistic period (3rd century BCE). While very different in approach, both found room for events that are not strictly determined by prior causes.

Aristotle's nuanced causality: Aristotle (384–322 BCE) recognized the importance of causes – indeed he famously analysed four types of causes (material, formal, efficient, final) in his philosophy of nature – but he did not advocate a blanket determinism for all events. Aristotle's worldview allowed for *contingency* and chance. In his work *Physics* (Book II, chapters 4-6), Aristotle explicitly discusses "chance" (*tyche*) and "spontaneity" as real factors. He argues that some outcomes are accidental: they are not *necessary* results of a given set of conditions, but rather the coincidental intersection of independent causal chains. For example, a man goes to the marketplace to buy food (his purposeful action), and by chance he meets a debtor whom he wouldn't normally encounter – resulting in him collecting a debt. The meeting was not necessitated by the man's intention (he didn't go for that purpose) nor by the debtor's intention (the debtor didn't plan to meet him); it was, in Aristotle's term, *accidental*. This analysis shows Aristotle's intuition that not everything that happens is fated by antecedent conditions – some things "happen as chance has it," to use his phrase. He maintains that chance is a real feature of the world, though it only applies in the realm of contingent events (especially human affairs) and is not a fundamental cause itself but a coincidental concurrence of causes.

Perhaps Aristotle's most famous argument relevant to determinism is his discussion of future contingents in *On Interpretation* (De Interpretatione, chapter 9). There he considers the statement: "There will be a sea-battle tomorrow." According to the law of logic (the principle of

53

bivalence), any proposition about the future is either true or false *even now*. But Aristotle realized that if such a statement is already true (or false) in the present, then the future event it describes would seem to be already fixed (determined to happen or not happen). If it's already true now that the battle will occur, then it cannot *not* occur – which implies a form of logical determinism. Aristotle's solution was radical: he denied that propositions about singular future contingents are either true or false at the present time. The truth value is "indeterminate" or as he put it, it is not *necessary* that either affirmation or negation be true. By doing this, he preserved the idea that the future is open: a sea battle may or may not happen tomorrow, and it is *not* already inevitable one way or the other. Only when tomorrow arrives will it become definitively true or false. This stance – basically that the future is not predetermined – was Aristotle's stand against a strict logical determinism that would make all future events necessary. As a modern summary of Aristotle's point explains: the future battle "is neither necessarily going to happen nor necessarily not going to happen; it is *contingent*. Therefore, the proposition 'There will be a sea battle' is neither true nor false today". Aristotle did "doubt that events in the future must be either already true or already false", explicitly to safeguard the reality of alternative possibilities.

Furthermore, Aristotle did not believe that all events have to happen by *necessity*. He distinguished between what happens *always or for the most part* (which suggests underlying causal regularity) and what happens *by chance or rare coincidence*. In Aristotle's biology and ethics, for instance, there is an implicit recognition of variability and contingency – not everything is strictly determined by universal laws. For example, most human actions are for an end (we act for reasons), but we retain the ability to choose among

54

alternatives – otherwise moral responsibility would be undermined. Aristotle was an early proponent of what we might call "soft determinism" or even indeterminism in certain domains: he held that humans have a degree of rational agency that is not simply reducible to physical causation. While he didn't formulate a theory of free will as later ages would, Aristotle did say that many of our actions are "up to us" (in Greek, *eph' hemin*), especially those done with deliberation. He analyses voluntary action in the *Nicomachean Ethics* and implies that praise and blame make sense only if a person could have acted otherwise in a given situation (assuming normal conditions). There is debate among scholars how much Aristotle believed in a robust form of free choice, but it's clear he rejected the idea that human behaviour is fated irrespective of reasoning or decision. By allowing contingency both in nature (through chance) and in human affairs (through deliberate choice), Aristotle carved out conceptual space that a pure determinist like Democritus or Chrysippus would deny.

Interestingly, Aristotle's allowance for chance did *not* mean he thought the world was disorderly. Quite the contrary – Aristotle's philosophy is all about things having natures and purposes (final causes) that produce regularity. He simply had a more complex view of causation: not all outcomes are necessary outcomes of prior conditions; some are conditional or accidental. And he certainly believed that not every event in the cosmos was predictable – especially those involving living beings and their interactions. We might say Aristotle believed in a partially open universe: structured and law-governed, but not a rigid chain of necessity stretching from beginning to end. His stance provided an important counterpoint to the idea of an absolutely preordained history of the world. Many medieval and early modern thinkers

55

would later draw on Aristotle to argue against strict determinism (for example, the medieval debate on "future contingents" and divine foreknowledge was heavily influenced by Aristotle's sea-battle argument).

Epicurus and the Swerve: Perhaps the most explicit ancient attempt to *rescue* free will from determinism came from Epicurus (341–270 BCE), who in effect modified the atomistic physics of Democritus to allow for spontaneity. Epicurus was a great admirer of Democritus – he adopted the atomic theory that Democritus had developed – but he could not accept its deterministic implications for human freedom. Epicurus firmly believed that if every action is necessitated by prior atomic motions, then humans have no control over their fate, which undermines ethics. As a solution, Epicurus introduced the notion of the *swerve* (in Latin, *clinamen*, as described later by Lucretius). He postulated that, at unpredictable times and places, an atom might deviate slightly from its otherwise straight-line motion, *without* a cause. This minute, uncaused swerving of atoms, he argued, could be the physical basis for free will. It "breaks the bonds of fate,"[7] as Lucretius poetically put it, allowing the mind (itself composed of atoms) to not be completely subject to deterministic push and pull.

In essence, Epicurus said: Democritus' determinism *must* be false – he was "arguably the first to make free will a central philosophical issue," explicitly asserting "that determinism must be false"[8]. The atoms' swerve introduces an irreducible

---

[7] **Titus Lucretius Carus**, De Rerum Natura (On the Nature of Things), (Cambridge, MA: Harvard University Press, 1992), 2.251–258. (Lucretius writes that the minute swerve of atoms "breaks the bonds of fate" (fati foedera rumpit), allowing for a degree of freedom.)

[8] **Routledge Encyclopaedia of Philosophy**, s.v. "Epicureanism: Free Will," by (anonymous) (London: Routledge, 1998). (Noting that Epicurus was "arguably the first to make free will a central philosophical issue" and held that determinism must be false.)

element of chance or indeterminacy in the motion of matter. Thus, even though Epicurus kept the idea that natural laws govern most atomic interactions, these occasional random swerves mean the future is *not* entirely fixed by the past. The universe, in Epicurus's account, is not a perfectly predictable machine – there is a built-in source of uncertainty. As one summary of Epicurus' doctrine puts it: "Epicurus deviated from Democritus by proposing the idea of atomic 'swerve', which holds that atoms may deviate from their expected course, thus permitting humans to possess free will in an otherwise deterministic universe"[9]. In other words, if Democritus gave us a universe of atoms and necessity, Epicurus tweaked it to be a universe of atoms, necessity, *and a dash of chance*. That dash of chance was crucial for him to affirm that we are not helpless marionettes dancing to the pull of causal strings – there is the possibility of initiating a new causal chain (through a swerve in the soul-atoms perhaps) that is not predetermined.

How well Epicurus' theory succeeds is a matter of philosophical debate (critics then and now argue that making actions random doesn't really secure meaningful freedom – a point we'll encounter again with modern indeterminism). But historically, the significance is that the free will problem had been clearly identified by the Epicureans. They saw a mechanical determinism as a threat to ethics and responded with a theoretical innovation. The Stoics, interestingly, attacked Epicurus on this very point: Chrysippus argued that Epicurus introduced the swerve arbitrarily, without any

---

[9] **Susanne Bobzien**, "Did Epicurus Discover the Free Will Problem?" Oxford Studies in Ancient Philosophy 19 (2000): 287–337. (Discussion of Epicurus's introduction of the atomic swerve to account for free will in a deterministic universe.)

evidence, just to "escape the necessity of Democritus"[10] – implying it was an ad hoc move. The Stoics themselves, as we saw, had a compatibilist view where determinism and moral responsibility coexist; they didn't think randomness was needed (or desirable) to explain human action. So already in the Hellenistic era we have an explicit clash of perspectives: strict determinists (Stoics) vs. partial indeterminists (Epicureans), with both insisting their view is required for ethics to make sense (the Stoics said fated events can be justly judged because the person *willed* them, the Epicureans said unless there is a break in causality the person has no control).

Beyond Epicurus and Aristotle, a number of other ancient thinkers took nuanced positions. For example, some of Socrates' contemporaries like the sophists raised arguments about responsibility and determinism in nascent form. And much later, academic sceptics and neoplatonists would critique the Stoic causal determinism on various grounds (some invoking a non-material soul with free powers). Even popular thought, as reflected in Greek tragedy, grappled with fate vs. free will: tragic heroes often know their fate yet make choices that lead to it – raising questions about inevitability and responsibility in a dramatic way. The Greek playwrights portrayed an interplay of destiny and character that suggests an early intuition that maybe both fate *and* freedom operate in human life, in tension.

To summarize the ancient scene: By the time of the Roman era, all the main positions in the determinism debate were on the table. Determinists like the Stoics (and arguably Democritus) believed in an unbreakable chain of causation

---

[10] **Chrysippus/Stoics on Epicurus**: the text notes Epicurus introduced the swerve "arbitrarily, without any evidence, just to 'escape the necessity of Democritus'."

fated by reason or nature. Anti-determinists like Epicurus (and arguably Aristotle in some respects) believed that chain could be broken or was not absolute, thereby preserving contingency or free volition. Compatibilists (again the Stoics, and some Aristotelians) tried to have it both ways: a determined world in which moral freedom still exists in a different sense. This lively debate did not produce a consensus, but it laid the foundation for all future discussions. The terminology differed (they spoke of fate, chance, necessity, automata, etc., rather than "determinism" which is a modern term), yet the crux was the same: *Are the laws of cause and effect such that nothing could ever happen otherwise than it does?* The ancients provided a rich variety of answers, and their insights would be absorbed and transformed in later eras.

Before moving on, it's worth noting one ancient development that bridges into the next chapter of history: the influence of Greek deterministic ideas on early Hellenistic and Roman-era religious/philosophical movements. For instance, the idea of a cosmic fate was incorporated into a lot of Greco-Roman thought (even outside Stoicism, many in that era casually believed in Fate or Fortuna controlling outcomes). Conversely, the idea of an atomic swerve influencing events found later echoes in discussions of the unpredictable, and Aristotle's allowance for contingency informed later Christian ideas of free will. In short, the legacy of these Greek debates was carried forward as later cultures encountered them.

2. Medieval and Theological Debates

As we move into the medieval period, the context shifts from pagan philosophy to the religious thought of

Christianity, Islam, and Judaism. The question of determinism in this era most often appears as a theological problem: How do divine omniscience and omnipotence relate to human free will? If God knows and wills everything that will happen, does that mean everything is predestined (a form of theological determinism)? Medieval thinkers grappled with reconciling the belief in an all-powerful Providence – a carryover in part from Stoic fate and the monotheistic creator concept – with the equally strong belief that humans are responsible for sin and moral choices. Thus, the debates often centred on *predestination* vs. *free will*, and on how to understand causation when one of the causes is God. We will explore these discussions primarily in the Christian medieval context (St. Augustine and St. Thomas Aquinas are key figures), but also touch on parallel developments in Islamic and Jewish thought. Despite differences in doctrine, all three monotheistic traditions wrestled with similar issues: some thinkers leaned heavily toward divine determinism (God as the ultimate cause of every action), while others defended human freedom to maintain moral accountability. Along the way, new concepts were introduced – such as the notion of divine concurrence (God cooperating with, but not coercing, secondary causes) – to bridge the gap between an ordained cosmic order and personal agency.

Augustine of Hippo – From Free Will to Predestination:

In the early Christian era, St. Augustine (354–430 CE) stands out for his profound reflections on human will and divine control. Interestingly, Augustine's own views evolved over his lifetime, illustrating the tension between freedom and determinism. In his youth and early career, Augustine was a staunch defender of free will. Writing in the 390s CE against the Manichaeans (a sect that preached a kind of cosmic fatalism and dualism of good vs. evil forces), Augustine argued vigorously that humans have the capacity to choose good or evil and thus are responsible for sin. The Manichaean religion claimed that much evil is due to an evil substance or fate beyond our control, but Augustine countered this by asserting the role of our will in moral evil. In works like *On Free Choice of the Will* (*De libero arbitrio*), he maintains that free will is a good thing granted by God, enabling moral accountability – even though its misuse can lead to sin. He famously reasoned in almost Cartesian fashion that we can be certain of the will's existence and its decisions, using our inner experience as evidence that we are voluntary agents. At this stage, Augustine emphasizes that *nothing* compels the human will from outside; when we sin, it is because we freely chose a lesser good. Free will, for Augustine, was initially the linchpin for explaining the presence of evil without implicating God: God gave us freedom, and we are the ones who turned that freedom toward evil (the classic free-will defence in theodicy).

However, as Augustine's theological battles changed, his stance shifted. By the late 390s and early 400s, Augustine confronted the Pelagian controversy. Pelagius and his followers stressed human free will to such an extent that they downplayed the need for divine grace – they claimed humans could initiate faith or good works on their own. Augustine found this contrary to the Christian doctrine of grace. In opposing Pelagianism, Augustine came to *emphasize the total dependence of the human will on God's grace*. He argued that since the Fall of Adam, human free will has been vitiated ("damaged by original sin" is how he described it) – we still have a will, but it is not capable of choosing righteous deeds without God's healing grace. Increasingly, Augustine taught that those who come to God do so because God *chose* to give them grace, not because they autonomously chose God. Thus enters the idea of *predestination*: that God, from eternity, has chosen certain individuals to be rescued (saved) by giving them grace, while others are passed over. If one carries this idea to its logical end, it can mean that even the eternal fate of each soul is already determined by God's decision. Augustine did indeed lean in that direction, especially in his later works like *On the Predestination of the Saints* and *On Grace and Free Will*. He stops short of saying God causes people to sin (Augustine never denies that our will is involved in sin), but he effectively says that any good we do is due to God's causation (grace) and that the ultimate difference between the saved and the damned is God's choice, not our independent merits.

This was a dramatic shift from his earlier stance that "it is in our power to be good as soon as we will it." Augustine came to believe that statement is true only in the context of already having God's grace move the will. Without grace, our will is *free* in a sense (we still make voluntary choices), but it's not *free* in the higher sense of being able to achieve genuine righteousness, because our nature is corrupted. To the objection that this sounds like fatalism, Augustine answered that humanity exercised true free choice in Adam – but in Adam we fell, and now our will is "weak" or a slave to sin until liberated by God. In a famous metaphor, he said that after the Fall, human freedom is like a lost liberty that only Christ (through grace) can restore. Thus, paradoxically, we must be "freed" by God in order to will the good. Grace does not force us against our will (Augustine insisted that when God changes a person's heart, they follow their reformed will willingly, not by compulsion), but still it is an act of God that ensures someone chooses rightly.

The net effect of Augustine's mature doctrine was a form of theological determinism tempered by complexity: God's *foreknowledge* and *predestination* set the ultimate course of each soul, yet humans still will their actions (they are not puppets, because their choices flow from their own fallen nature or renewed nature). When pressed on whether predestination undermines free will, Augustine's response was that original sin has already undermined our freedom – we are free only to sin, until grace intervenes. He once succinctly stated: "Without God's grace, men either cannot do good, or cannot continue in good" – implying we are determined to stray unless God decides to fix our will.

Augustine's increasingly deterministic view of salvation did draw criticism even in his time. The monk Julian of Eclanum accused Augustine of resurrecting the fatalism of the Manicheans (the very view Augustine fought in his youth), effectively saying Augustine had made God into a new fate and eliminated human freedom. Augustine rebutted that he wasn't denying free will – humans still make voluntary choices – but he did assert that without God's gracious predetermination, those choices will never lead to salvation. The Church after Augustine struggled with this balance. Medieval Catholic teaching tried to temper Augustine's predestinarian streak by maintaining that God's predestination does not negate human freedom (a mystery beyond full comprehension). Catholic interpreters often emphasized that Augustine did *not* teach "double predestination" (the idea that God actively predestines some to damnation); rather, he simply doesn't give grace to some (which is subtly different). Still, the core idea that the course of each life is in God's hands remained powerful.

In sum, Augustine handed down an ambivalent legacy: on one hand, a robust early defence of free will's reality (still cited by Christian thinkers who emphasize liberty), and on the other, a mature doctrine that places the human will under the determining sway of divine grace and predestination. This tension persisted through the medieval era, essentially framing the problem: *if God is sovereign and all-knowing, can any event – including a human decision – be genuinely open or undetermined?* Augustine's answer leaned toward "no" (at least for salvific decisions), but he maintained that we *experience* willing as our own doing, which is enough for moral responsibility. This would later influence Protestant Reformers like John Calvin (who took Augustine's predestination to an even stricter conclusion), but in the intervening medieval centuries, scholars sought more systematized solutions.

Aquinas and Scholastic Synthesis – Divine Concurrence:

By the High Middle Ages, Christian theologians, especially in the Latin West, had assimilated not only Augustine but also Aristotle (whose works became widely known in the 13th century). St. Thomas Aquinas (1225–1274) represents a landmark attempt to reconcile divine determinism with human freedom in a comprehensive philosophical system. Aquinas was deeply Aristotelian in his thinking about causes and also deeply committed to the Christian doctrine of an omnipotent God who is the first cause of everything. His key idea in this realm is the doctrine of *divine concurrence* or *double agency*: every action in the world has both a primary cause (God) and secondary causes (creatures), and these operate on different levels without excluding each other. God is the *first cause* who gives being and efficacy to all secondary causes. Thus, whenever a creature acts (like a human will making a choice), God is simultaneously acting to make that act possible and real. However – and this is crucial – Aquinas insists that God's causation does not violate the nature of secondary causes but rather enables them. In the case of a human free action, God's concurrence "moves" the will to act, but in a manner consonant with the will's own mode of operation (which is to choose freely).

This sounds abstract, so let's unpack it. Aquinas explicitly *rejects* the idea that if God is fully in control, then human free will must be an illusion. He criticizes thinkers who, like some earlier theologians, said that God only gives us the *power* of willing but does not influence our particular choices (those theologians wanted to protect free will by keeping God's hands off our decisions). Aquinas finds this unsatisfactory because it would "place human choices outside of the divine providence" – an unacceptable limitation on God. Instead, Aquinas argues that God is the cause of *all* things, including our act of willing, but in causing our will to act, God causes it to act *freely*. In *Summa Contra Gentiles* (III, ch. 89) Aquinas writes, "no thing can act by its own power unless it acts through [God's] power… Therefore, God is for us the cause not only of our power of willing, but also of our act of willing". This startling statement means that whenever you will something, at the deepest level God is causing you to will it. Yet Aquinas immediately qualifies that this divine causing does not force the will against itself; rather God causes it to act in accordance with its nature (which is a rational appetite for the perceived good). He uses an analogy: an artisan using a tool – the artisan is the cause of the tool's effect, but the tool also truly causes the effect in its own right (for example, a saw cutting wood – the craftsman causes the cutting *through*

65

the saw, but the sharpness of the saw is what directly cuts). Similarly, God uses the human will as an instrument; the will with its freedom is doing the choosing, but God is the deeper cause enabling and actualizing that free choice.

By this model, Aquinas tries to have it both ways: absolutely everything falls under God's causal sovereignty (so determinism at the level of Providence is upheld – nothing escapes God's plan), and yet creatures have real causal efficacy according to their kind (so the human will really does cause our decisions, making them voluntary). Aquinas would say that divine causality and creaturely causality are not in competition, because they operate on different ontological levels – God as the sustaining ground of being and first mover, and man as a proximate mover within the created order. This is often termed *Thomistic compatibilism*, though it is different from modern secular compatibilism. It's not that Aquinas thought free will and determinism are easy to mesh; rather, he redefined "freedom" to mean acting from one's own rational nature (as opposed to external compulsion). As long as nothing external forces the will against reason, the act is voluntary – even if, *behind the scenes*, God's universal causality is "premoving" the will to choose a particular good. In effect, Aquinas's person still *could* have chosen otherwise considered in isolation, but given God's concurrence in this particular choice, that is the choice made. God's timeless plan somehow includes our free choices without nullifying them.

To put it another way, Aquinas believed in *intellectual determinism* in the sense that the will inevitably chooses what the intellect presents as most favourable (the will is not random; it is oriented toward what is perceived as good). But because the intellect can weigh options and no external necessity forces the conclusion, the choice is "free" – it flows from within, from our own judgment. God's role is to give the motion and being to this entire internal process. This is a subtle theory, and not everyone in Aquinas's time or later agreed with it. In fact, late scholastics debated fiercely about how to reconcile grace and free will, with some (the Thomists) favouring a hard line that often sounded like God predetermines the free act, and others (like the Jesuit Luis de Molina with his theory of "middle knowledge") trying to give more leeway to human freedom by saying God foreknows but doesn't cause the free act. Those disputes, however, go beyond our scope.

For our purposes, what Aquinas achieved was a kind of formal framework wherein you could consistently say: *Everything is determined by God's providence, and yet humans have free will.* Aquinas himself doesn't use the word "determined" in a fatalistic way, but he absolutely insists nothing falls outside God's providential order – which is tantamount to saying everything unfolds as God intends (allowing that God's intentions include permitting some to sin, etc.). A later critic might say Aquinas's view "allows the person's act of willing to satisfy the criteria of freedom *even though* it is caused by God". His contemporaries would have phrased it as God's predestination working through, not against, free will.

Beyond Christian Europe, similar debates occurred in the Islamic world and in Jewish philosophy during the medieval period. It's fascinating to see how thinkers in these traditions, often aware of Greek philosophy and occasionally of each other's ideas, tackled the determinism question.

Islamic Perspectives – Averroes and Theological Schools:

In the Islamic intellectual tradition, one major thread was the conflict between the *Qadarites/Mu'tazilites* (who upheld human free will to protect God's justice) and the *Jabrites/Ash'arites* (who leaned toward predestination to uphold God's omnipotence). From the earliest decades of Islam, this issue was hotly debated: if God's will is absolute and He has foreknowledge of all, how can humans be responsible for their actions? The Mu'tazilite theologians (8th–10th centuries) argued that justice demands that humans have genuine freedom; otherwise, holding humans accountable for sin or obedience would be meaningless and God would seem unjust. They thus taught that humans create their own acts (a doctrine of "human agency") – God grants the power, but the decision is from the person. On the other side, the Ash'arite theologians (like al-Ash'ari in the 10th century and later al-Ghazali) asserted that all power and causation belong to God. They developed a doctrine called *kasb* or "acquisition," which says that God creates every human act, but the human "acquires" the act by their intention, making them responsible. This was a delicate compromise that basically made God the real cause of everything while still claiming individuals have some sort of contingent involvement. The Ash'arite view is quite deterministic: nothing, not even the movement of a finger, happens without God's specific causation at that moment. For example, fire does not *by itself* burn cotton – God creates the burning when cotton meets fire; likewise, when you decide to pray or to lie, God creates that motion in you. But because you have a sort of concurrent will to do it (your *kasb*), you can be rewarded or punished. Some modern scholars see this as a form of occasionalism (God is the only cause). Indeed, an extreme Ash'arite perspective was that human "free will" is simply the feeling of choosing, but the choice is efficacious only because God makes it so. Critics said this reduces humans to automatons.

This theological dispute was lively. One side *criticized determinism (jabr) on the ground that it renders religious obligation meaningless* – for if God preordains our acts, why would He command or forbid anything, and how is it just to punish sinners?

The other side feared that asserting too much autonomy for humans compromises God's sovereignty – as one medieval Muslim creed put it, "there is no Creator but God, and the acts of men are created by God." Ultimately Sunni Islam generally took a middle path closer to the Ash'arite view: God is fully in charge, but humans are accountable as though their choices are their own. It's a pragmatic dual affirmation more than a fully rationalized solution.

Within Islamic philosophy (falsafa) which often drew on Aristotle, figures like Ibn Sina (Avicenna) and Ibn Rushd (Averroes) approached the matter from a more philosophical angle. Averroes (1126–1198), known for his commentaries on Aristotle, held a view of nature that was strongly deterministic in the physical sense. He believed, following Aristotle's physics and metaphysics, that every event in nature follows necessarily from prior causes except where chance is merely a name for a hidden cause. One analysis of Averroes notes: "Averroes stresses the strict necessity of natural processes in his commentaries on Aristotle. He views chance as an accidental, not an essential cause. This means whenever we speak of a chance event, there is an essential cause to which the 'casual' element is linked". So in Averroes's Aristotelian worldview, if a rooftop collapses "by chance" on a passerby, in truth there are determinate causes (weak roof structure, timing, the person happening to walk there) that coincided – chance is just our word for a coincident result of definite causal chains. In that sense, he upheld a form of determinism in nature very much like Aristotle (or even a bit stricter).

However, when it came to human acts, Averroes as a philosopher acknowledged the power of human choice in the ethical sphere (being an Aristotelian, he believed in the voluntary character of moral actions). As a Muslim theologian (which he also was to a degree), he likely endorsed the standard view that God's foreknowledge doesn't constrain our will from our own perspective. It's worth noting that Averroes wrote a work *On the Harmony of Religion and Philosophy* in which he argues that scripture and philosophy are not opposed. In Islamic thought, a common idea (also found in some Christian thinkers like Boethius) was that God exists outside of time and knows our choices in an eternal present, thus His foreknowledge doesn't *cause* those choices in time – a way to reconcile omniscience with free will. Whether Averroes explicitly took that line is unclear, but other Islamic theologians like the Mu'tazilites certainly used such arguments.

One medieval Islamic philosopher, Al-Ghazali, while criticizing the philosophers, also leaned heavily on God's direct control of everything, essentially endorsing a deterministic view where cause and effect in nature are just the habitual sequence Allah decrees (he famously said fire does not burn by itself – anticipating Hume's later scepticism of causation). Meanwhile, the mystics (Sufis) would sometimes speak of annihilating one's will in God's will, effectively embracing determinism as a spiritual truth (everything is God's doing). So within Islamic civilization, perspectives ranged from almost predestinarian fatalism in popular piety ("Insha'Allah" – if God wills, it will happen, otherwise not) to more accountability-emphasizing doctrines among rationalist theologians.

Jewish Perspectives – Maimonides on Free Will and Divine Knowledge:

Medieval Judaism also confronted these issues. The Hebrew Scriptures strongly affirm free choice ("I have set before you life and death, choose life," says Deuteronomy) and hold people responsible to divine law. At the same time, the biblical worldview is that God is ultimately in control of history. Jewish philosophers in the Middle Ages, especially Moses Maimonides (1135–1204), sought to reconcile the omnipotence and omniscience of God with the free will evident in the Torah's commandments. Maimonides in his *Mishneh Torah* (a code of Jewish law) makes a clear statement that has become classical in Judaism: *"Free will is granted to all men. If one desires to turn toward the good way and be righteous, he has the power to do so. If one wishes to turn toward the evil way and be wicked, he is at liberty to do so… This doctrine is an important principle, the pillar of the law and the commandment."*. In other words, without free will, the entire edifice of religious obligation (mitzvot) collapses. Maimonides here is unequivocal: every person has the ability to choose good or evil, and that is fundamental.

Yet Maimonides was also an Aristotelian philosopher, and in his philosophical masterpiece *The Guide for the Perplexed* he tackled the thorny issue of God's knowledge of future human acts. If God's knowledge is perfect and unbounded, He must know all our future choices – so how can those choices be free in the sense of being undetermined?

71

Maimonides' answer (Guide III, chapter 20) is somewhat apophatic: essentially, he says the problem arises from imagining God's knowledge as if it were like human knowledge. God is not in time, and His knowledge is not gained the way ours is. The famous resolution he offers is that God's knowledge **is** the cause of things (since by knowing Himself as cause, He knows all effects), but this is an eternal knowing that doesn't nullify our perspective of free will. It's a bit abstract, but basically Maimonides says: *We affirm both God's foreknowledge and man's free will, and we admit we cannot fully understand how they coexist, because God's knowledge is sui generis.* He even says trying to fully grasp it is beyond human intellect. This allowed him to uphold the necessity of free will for law, while not denying any divine perfection.

Moreover, Maimonides and other Jewish thinkers were aware of deterministic philosophies like astrology, which was popular. Maimonides vehemently rejected astrological determinism – the idea that the stars dictate human fate – calling it nonsense. He wanted Jews to steer clear of thinking their choices or outcomes are fated by anything other than their own will and God's providence. The Talmudic rabbis before him had a saying: "Everything is in the hands of Heaven except the fear of Heaven," meaning God governs all the circumstances a person is born into (health, wealth, etc.), but whether a person is virtuous or sinful is their own choice. This encapsulates a compatibilist stance: God determines the framework, humans determine their moral actions. Medieval Jewish scholars like Gersonides even posited that God might not micro-manage or foreknow the specifics of human choices, to preserve freedom (a controversial idea). But the mainstream stayed with Maimonidean moderation: trust in free will as a basic postulate of ethics and law, and leave the reconciliation with

God's omniscience as an article of faith or philosophy that mortal minds cannot fully penetrate.

In summary, the medieval theological scene – whether Christian, Muslim, or Jewish – often arrived at a dual assertion: yes, in some ultimate sense God or Fate governs all, *and yes,* humans possess free will and are responsible. The struggle was to articulate this without contradiction. Augustine shaded toward the side of divine control (especially regarding salvation), Aquinas articulated a model of concurrent causation to have both, Islamic Ash'arites emphasized divine control while formulating a diminished form of free acquisition, Mu'tazilites emphasized free will with God's justice guiding outcomes, and Maimonides affirmed free will strongly as a practical reality while acknowledging God's knowledge is beyond us. Each approach had its difficulties, but all recognized that a pure determinism (that men are like leaves blown by the winds of fate) is hard to reconcile with the ethical and legal core of their religions, and a pure libertarianism (that men can thwart God's will or act outside His plan) is hard to reconcile with their concept of divinity.

One interesting development in late medieval Christian thought worth noting is the rise of *nominalism* with William of Ockham in the 14th century. Ockham emphasized God's absolute power and freedom – God could do things even contrary to what we consider moral (though He wouldn't, being good). Ockham thus leaned on the side that the only reason events follow laws is because God freely wills them so; there is no necessity in God. This actually opened the door to thinking of the world as contingent on God's will, rather than logically determined by divine nature. Some have argued this nominalist shift indirectly laid groundwork for a more open concept of nature that would later allow ideas of contingency (and even early scientific notions of laws as chosen by God, not logically necessary). But that's a tangent.

By the close of the medieval period, the stage was set for new challenges. The Protestant Reformation in the 16th century would revive Augustine's predestination debates in full force (Luther and Calvin versus Erasmus and the Catholic Church), pushing determinism about salvation to extremes. And the Renaissance's recovery of ancient science and philosophy would inject new life into deterministic ideas about nature – leading into the Scientific Revolution. It is to that Renaissance and early modern period that we now turn, to see how the concept of a "clockwork universe" emerged from the convergence of classical ideas and new discoveries.

3. The Clockwork Universe Emerges

By the Renaissance and into the 17th-18th centuries, the conversation about determinism underwent a transformation driven by the rise of modern science. Where medieval debates often revolved around God and the soul, early modern debates increasingly focused on *nature* and *physics*. The rediscovery and publication of ancient scientific works (like those of Archimedes, Hero, and especially Aristotle and Ptolemy) and philosophical poems like Lucretius' *On the Nature of Things* (which expounded Epicurean atomism) gave Renaissance scholars a wealth of material. Coupled with new observations and inventions (telescope, microscope, etc.), this led to the Scientific Revolution. A key outcome of this revolution was the idea that the universe operates according to precise mathematical laws – much like a giant machine. This section explores how deterministic themes from antiquity were revived and amplified during this period. We will see how figures like

Galileo Galilei, René Descartes, and Isaac Newton solidified the concept of lawful causation in the physical world (often explicitly comparing nature to a clockwork). We will also see how Enlightenment thinkers extended these ideas to human behaviour – proposing that even our minds might operate mechanistically – and how other philosophers (like Immanuel Kant) reacted by carving out a special domain for human freedom. The result by the late 18th century was a portrait of reality often called "the clockwork universe": an image of the cosmos as a perfectly ordered system of cogs and gears (causes and effects) ticking along predictably. This era also saw sharper secular debates about determinism versus free will, now framed less in terms of God and more in terms of materialism vs. human agency.

Renaissance Revival of Deterministic Ideas:

The Renaissance (14th–16th centuries) is often characterized by the slogan "ad fontes" – back to the sources. Scholars like Poggio Bracciolini unearthed and studied texts from classical antiquity. Among these was Lucretius' *De rerum natura*, which introduced many to the atomism of Epicurus and Democritus. Although Epicurus included the swerve, Lucretius still describes a world fundamentally made of atoms falling through the void, with everything (including life and mind) arising from their interactions. This implicitly mechanistic view of nature resonated with some Renaissance thinkers. At the same time, the recovery of Stoic and Neoplatonic writings reintroduced ideas of cosmic order and fate. Renaissance intellectuals were a bit syncretic – one finds renewed interest in astrology, hermeticism, and Stoic fatalism in this period. For example, the concept of *astral determinism* (the stars influencing human affairs) enjoyed a vogue in

Renaissance courts (even popes had court astrologers). This was a continuity from medieval times, but with more intellectual backing now from rediscovered Hellenistic works on astrology.

However, the more critical development was in natural philosophy and nascent science. Figures like Leonardo da Vinci and Nicolaus Copernicus began challenging Aristotelian doctrines. Copernicus (1473–1543) moved Earth from the centre of the cosmos, which indirectly suggested that the universe might be governed by uniform laws (if Earth is a planet like others, the same physics could apply everywhere). Copernicus still held some ancient mystical views (like circular motion being "perfect"), but his work triggered questions about how the heavens and Earth could all be part of one system.

In the late 16th and early 17th centuries, the seeds of classical mechanics were sown. A crucial shift was the rejection of Aristotle's idea that objects have natural places and require continuous push to move. Medieval scholars like Jean Buridan had already proposed the concept of impetus (an early form of inertia) – the notion that once set in motion, an object will continue moving without further force (contrary to Aristotle's need for continuous force). Buridan even mused that God could have set the celestial spheres in motion at the start, and they continue by that initial imparted impetus – so God doesn't need angels to keep pushing the planets. This is a clear harbinger of the clockwork idea: *God could give the world a start and then let it run by itself.* Galileo (1564–1642) experimentally and conceptually solidified this principle. Through inclined plane experiments, Galileo found that bodies maintain motion unless acted on – a rudimentary form of Newton's first law. He showed that a ball rolling on a smooth plane will continue rolling (or if going up, loses speed symmetrically – implying if friction were absent, it'd roll forever). This was a deathblow to the Aristotelian physics requiring constant causes for motion, and it supported a view in which *forces and causes can be quantified and predicted*. Galileo's success in describing motion mathematically (e.g., the law of falling bodies: distance $\propto$ time^2) was a triumph of deterministic law finding. It demonstrated that events like a cannonball's trajectory follow precise quantitative rules rather than happening in a haphazard way. His work on projectile motion showed that combining causes (initial velocity and gravity) yields a predictable curved path – the parabola – which matched observation. This reinforced a broader conviction: *nature is written in the language of mathematics*, as Galileo famously wrote, and once we know the laws, we can predict outcomes.

Galileo and his contemporaries also eroded Aristotle's distinction between earthly and celestial physics. With the telescope, Galileo observed mountains on the Moon and satellites around Jupiter, suggesting the same physics applies there. Kepler (1571–1630) gave precise mathematical laws for planetary orbits (though he invoked quasi-mystical forces like a sun emanation), further supporting a lawful cosmos.

By the mid-17th century, the mechanistic philosophy had coalesced. René Descartes (1596–1650) explicitly described the world as a machine. In his *Principles of Philosophy* and other works, Descartes argued that extended matter has no intrinsic purposes or qualities except extension and motion, and that all physical phenomena can be explained by matter in motion according to laws. He pictured even the human body (minus the rational soul) as a complex machine. For instance, Descartes held that animals are purely mechanical – mere "automata" without souls. The motions of animal bodies, he believed, are as determined as the gears of a clock, driven by stimuli and reflex in a pre-set way. This was an extreme view at the time: animals feel pain only as a mechanical response, not as conscious experience, he claimed. While one might cringe at the implications, this view was a direct application of the emerging deterministic science to biology. Descartes' physics itself was somewhat flawed (he believed in corpuscles and vortices rather than Newtonian gravity), but he inaugurated the program of explaining nature (from planetary motion to digestion to nerves) in mechanical terms. "Organisms are machines" is a deterministic stance: their behaviour is governed by physical causes, not free or unpredictable factors. Descartes allowed one exception – the human rational soul (mind) which he considered non-physical and free. This mind-body dualism meant Descartes did *not* extend determinism to human reason or choices (he thought the soul, by virtue of being immaterial, isn't bound by mechanical laws – though how it interacts with the body is a problem he struggled with). But aside from that protected island of mind, his vision was totalizing: the universe is like a giant clock built by God, with every part moving as the laws dictate.

One can see by this point (circa 1650) a full "clockwork universe" conception in place. Indeed, the analogy of God as the master clockmaker became popular. Thinkers like Robert Boyle used the clock analogy to illustrate how God's providence could operate through secondary causes – God made the machine with all its gears and let it run. For many, this bolstered rather than eliminated belief in God: a perfect deterministic universe testified to a perfect designer. By the late 17th century, deism arose – the belief that God set up the world and its laws, and then does not interfere (miracles being unnecessary or even impossible in a law-bound system). The deists embraced a fully law-governed world

78

picture, effectively saying nature's determinism is God's method. Voltaire later quipped that after Newton, God is like a king who only occasionally needs to wind the clock – a nod to the clockwork universe where God's role is mostly initial.

The crowning achievement of this scientific determinism was Isaac Newton's *Principia Mathematica* (1687). Newton (1642–1727) unified celestial and terrestrial physics with his three laws of motion and law of universal gravitation. This mathematical framework allowed, in principle, the prediction of the motion of any object under any set of forces. The success of Newton's laws in explaining the orbits of planets, the trajectory of comets, the tides, and so on was stunning. It was now possible to imagine that *all* physical interactions – the colliding of billiard balls, the flow of the tides, the fall of an apple – followed the same deterministic laws. Newton himself was cautious – he famously said "I feign no hypotheses" about what gravity *is* (just how it behaves). But he provided the predictive toolset. One could plug in initial positions and velocities of objects and compute their future positions. Philosophers quickly realized the implication: if one had perfect knowledge of all particles at one time, one could theoretically calculate the state at any other time, past or future. This is exactly the principle that Pierre-Simon Laplace would articulate a century later. As one historian describes the Newtonian outlook: "The success of Galileo and his successors, particularly Newton, in accounting for motion by pushes and pulls ('forces') gave rise to the thought that everything in the universe capable of measurement could be explained on the basis of pushes and pulls no more complicated in essence than those of levers and gears within a machine". In short, it inspired the belief that nature is fully governed by mechanical laws, making it effectively a gigantic mechanism. This mechanistic view gained favour steadily, dominating Enlightenment science and philosophy.

It's important to note that Newton himself did not say determinism or deny free will – he was deeply religious and left metaphysical questions aside. But the *implications* of his physics were drawn out by others. Newton's friend and disciple, astronomer Pierre-Louis Maupertuis, formulated in 1744 the principle of least action, which gave a teleological veneer to mechanics but still within strict lawfulness. The French mathematician Pierre-Simon Laplace most famously captured the deterministic ideal in 1814, after Newton's physics had proven itself over a century. Laplace posited that if an intelligence knew the exact state of every particle in the universe at a given instant, "nothing would be uncertain, and the future just like the past would be present to its eyes". This hypothetical omniscient calculator (later dubbed "Laplace's Demon") is basically the Newtonian God's-eye-view of a deterministic universe. Laplace confidently asserted that the apparent randomness or probability in phenomena is only due to our ignorance; in principle, the laws fix one outcome given initial conditions. That statement is the epitome of the clockwork universe idea.

During the Enlightenment (18th century), belief in deterministic laws spread beyond physics to other domains. The philosophes in France, many of whom were inspired by Newton and Descartes, started applying mechanism to people. Julien Offray de La Mettrie wrote *L'Homme Machine* ("Man a Machine") in 1747, explicitly extending Descartes's idea (which Descartes had limited to animals) to humans: arguing that even human thought might arise from mere material complexity of the brain, without an immaterial soul. La Mettrie provocatively suggested that our desires, our pleasures, and our actions follow from our bodily mechanisms; thus man is entirely part of nature's mechanical order. This was a radical determinist and materialist view of human beings. It scandalized many, but it found resonance in the growing secular, scientific perspective of the Enlightenment.

Baron d'Holbach (Paul-Henri Thiry) took it further in *The System of Nature* (1770). He presented a thoroughgoing deterministic materialism: humans, like everything else, are subject to necessary causal laws of matter. D'Holbach denied the existence of an immaterial soul and argued that all our thoughts and volitions are the results of physical processes in the brain, which in turn are caused by prior events. In a memorable passage, d'Holbach writes that man's life is like a line that nature commands him to trace, "without his ever being able to swerve from it, even for an instant". He elaborates that a person's organization (body and temperament) is not chosen by him, his ideas present themselves involuntarily, his habits are formed by his environment, and "he is unceasingly modified by causes... over which he has no control, which necessarily regulate his mode of existence, give the hue to his way of thinking, and determine his manner of acting". In short, d'Holbach asserts that everything about a person – character, actions, successes, crimes – is the product of the chain of causality in nature and nurture. Free will, in the sense of an uncaused cause in us, is an illusion, he claims. He wasn't just speculating: d'Holbach drew on the science of his day (like physiology) to argue that the brain is a material entity, so thought must have physical causes.

This deterministic view of human behaviour had important social implications. Some Enlightenment thinkers saw it as grounds for a more compassionate morality: if people are shaped by causes, perhaps reforming society and education can improve outcomes, and punishment should be about deterrence or rehabilitation rather than retribution (since the criminal wasn't ultimately "free" to do otherwise in the moment). Others worried it undercut the basis of morality entirely. But determinists like d'Holbach would respond that morality itself can be naturalized – for example, people can be guided by incentives and disincentives which themselves become causes influencing future actions.

Not everyone in the Enlightenment was a strict determinist. The Scottish philosopher David Hume, for example, offered a nuanced compatibilist view. Hume agreed that every event (including human decisions) has a cause – he thought the idea of an uncaused choice is incoherent and not what people truly want from free will. But he argued that this *causal necessity* in human actions is actually what makes moral responsibility possible. As Hume explained in *Enquiry Concerning Human Understanding* (Section VIII), liberty (freedom) is the power to act according to one's will, without external constraint; and necessity (causation) is the regular conjunction of motives and actions. He believed both are real: our actions flow from our character and motives (necessity), and we act freely when not externally compelled. Thus, he said the dispute about liberty and necessity is just a matter of definitions – properly understood, they are compatible. Hume influenced many subsequent thinkers (including Kant) with this argument. By making free will simply the ability to do what one desires (as opposed to some metaphysical uncaused cause), Hume preserved moral language while fully accepting determinism in nature. He even stated that everyone, in practice, expects human behaviour to be generally law-like; if people truly thought actions were random, we couldn't function or hold anyone accountable.[11]

Immanuel Kant (1724–1804), writing at the end of the Enlightenment, took a different route to safeguard human freedom. Kant was deeply impressed by Newtonian science – so much so that he declared that determinism (or "natural necessity") governs all phenomena in the *sensible* world. In his *Critique of Pure Reason* (1781), Kant argued that causality is a necessary category of human understanding: we cannot experience events except under the rule that every event has a cause. Hence, as far as science and experience are concerned, *determinism is true* – every physical event, including every observable human action, has antecedent causes according to laws of nature[12]. However, Kant did not want to conclude that free will is an illusion, because that would undermine the basis of morality (and Kant was very committed to the idea of moral duty). His ingenious solution was to distinguish between two standpoints: the world of appearances (phenomena), which does indeed follow deterministic laws, and the world of things-in-themselves (noumena), where human beings as rational agents reside in a sense. He suggested that *we can consider ourselves as belonging to both realms*. When we look at ourselves empirically (as psychologists or observers), we see a series of mental and physical states connected by cause and effect – effectively a deterministic process. But when we look at ourselves from the inside, as beings who deliberate about reasons and feel

---

[11] **David Hume**, An Enquiry Concerning Human Understanding (1748), ed. Tom L. Beauchamp (Oxford: Oxford University Press, 1999), 95–99. (Section VIII, "Of Liberty and Necessity," where Hume argues that in practice we all assume the uniformity of human behaviour to ground responsibility.)

[12] **Immanuel Kant**, Critique of Pure Reason (1781), trans. Norman Kemp Smith (London: Macmillan, 1929), A532/B560–A538/B566. (Kant's Third Antinomy: in the realm of appearances, every event is determined by prior causes according to natural laws.)

the pull of duty, we *must* regard ourselves as free – free in the sense that our reason can initiate a new series of events independently of the chain of natural causes. Kant posited that the *noumenal self* (the self as it is in itself) is not bound by time and causality as phenomena are, so it is possible for it to be free[13]. This is admittedly a somewhat mysterious doctrine – Kant basically carved out a metaphysical space for freedom by saying determinism only applies to the empirical world. He famously phrased it: "a free will and a will under moral laws are one and the same" – meaning by adopting the moral perspective, we treat the will as free. For practical purposes, Kant argued, we *must* act as if we have free will (this is a "postulate of practical reason"), even though we cannot prove it theoretically. In fact, Kant considered it a kind of fact of reason that we have an inescapable consciousness of moral obligation, which implies we are free to obey or disobey – because it makes no sense to say you *ought* to do something you have absolutely no power to do. So, in Kant's philosophy, deterministic science and genuine free will coexist, but in different domains: nature versus morality.

Kant's reconciliation was highly influential on subsequent thought. It satisfied neither extreme determinists (who might see it as a sleight of hand to "hide" freedom in the noumenal realm) nor critics of determinism who wanted a more robust, observable freedom. But it set the stage for 19th-century idealists and others to explore freedom in new ways, while science continued largely assuming determinism.

---

[13] **Immanuel Kant**, Critique of Practical Reason (1788), trans. Lewis White Beck (New York: Macmillan, 1993), 28–30. (Kant's doctrine that we must presuppose freedom of the will as a "postulate of practical reason" – the noumenal freedom of the self, necessary for moral responsibility.)

By the end of the 18th century, the momentum was strongly on the side of determinism as a worldview, at least among intellectuals. Laplace's demon encapsulated the zeitgeist of scientific determinism. It was widely believed that Newton's laws – perhaps extended by some yet undiscovered laws for chemistry, physiology, etc. – would eventually explain *everything*. The French Enlightenment, in particular, produced a number of atheist or materialist thinkers (besides d'Holbach and La Mettrie) who saw man as a part of nature to be analysed, not as a special case. Denis Diderot toyed with determinism in dialogues, even suggesting at times a kind of soft determinism where our sense of freedom is itself caused by our ignorance of causes. The deterministic outlook became so pervasive that even those who didn't like it had to acknowledge it as the default scientific assumption.

However, before closing this chapter, it's worth noting that even in the high noon of determinism, there were undercurrents of doubt and alternative views. The poets and Romantic thinkers of the late 18th and early 19th century (like Goethe, Blake, later Coleridge) reacted against a purely mechanistic world-picture, emphasizing organic growth, creativity, and the limits of analysis. And within science itself, there remained puzzles (such as the nature of chemical reactions, or the origin of life) where strict laws were not yet known, leaving room for speculation. But those are stories for later chapters. At the historical point we've reached – roughly the start of the 19th century – the idea of determinism had a long pedigree and had undergone multiple reformulations, but it seemed triumphant. The world could be seen as an "unbroken chain" of causes and effects, from the swirl of galaxies down to the firing of neurons, all governed by discoverable laws. It was an awesome vision of order that promised complete understanding and control.

Little did they know that in the 20th century, with the advent of quantum physics and chaos theory, cracks would appear in this clockwork. But that is to come.

In conclusion, the historical journey of determinism reveals an evolving tapestry of ideas: from Democritus's atoms and the Stoic fate, through theological debates about God's will, to the mechanical philosophy of Descartes and the physical laws of Newton. Each era reinterpreted the notion of an ordered, law-governed universe in its own terms, yet the core intuition remained: to explain is to find a cause. By the Enlightenment, determinism was not just a scientific hypothesis but almost a creed – one that would soon be tested by new discoveries. This chapter has shown the rich intellectual heritage behind the deterministic outlook. Understanding this heritage helps us appreciate why the 19th-century thinkers were so confident that the universe is a predictable machine, and also why challenges to that view in the 20th century were so revolutionary. The idea of determinism, born in ancient philosophy, matured through history into a defining principle of modern thought – setting the stage for the next chapters, where we examine how determinism faced those modern challenges and what the current state of the debate is.

Throughout this exploration, one theme stands out: the tension between our desire for *intelligibility* (which deterministic law provides) and our desire for *freedom* or *meaning* (which deterministic law can seem to threaten). Historical thinkers have never been unaware of this tension. That is why the debate seesaws across ages – when the pendulum swings toward strict determinism (emphasizing order and explanation), a counter-swing often follows to preserve human agency or randomness (emphasizing spontaneity and creativity). Far from being a new dilemma, this is a fundamental human inquiry. The historical perspectives we've surveyed furnish us with arguments and insights that are still invoked today. As we move forward, we will see how contemporary science reframes these age-old questions – but it is striking how many of the essential ideas were already present in one form or another thousands of years ago. The "origins of the idea" of determinism reach back to our earliest attempts to make sense of the cosmos, and they continue to shape our understanding of ourselves and our world. The chain of thought, one might say, is unbroken.

Chapter 3

The Rise of Scientific Determinism –
From Newton to Laplace

By the Renaissance and into the 17th and 18th centuries, the conversation about determinism underwent a transformation driven by the rise of modern science. Where medieval debates often revolved around God and the soul, early modern debates increasingly focused on nature and physics. The rediscovery and publication of ancient scientific works (like those of Archimedes, Hero, and especially Aristotle and Ptolemy) and philosophical poems like Lucretius' *On the Nature of Things* (which expounded Epicurean atomism) gave Renaissance scholars a wealth of material to reconsider old questions. Coupled with new observations and inventions (the telescope, microscope, etc.), this influx of knowledge led to the Scientific Revolution. A key outcome of this revolution was the idea that the universe operates according to precise mathematical laws – much like a giant machine. In this chapter, we explore how deterministic themes from antiquity were revived and amplified during this period. We will see how figures like Galileo Galilei, René Descartes, and Isaac Newton solidified the concept of lawful causation in the physical world (often explicitly comparing nature to a clockwork mechanism). We will also see how Enlightenment thinkers extended these ideas to human behaviour – proposing that even our minds might operate mechanistically – and how other philosophers (like Immanuel Kant) reacted by carving out a special domain for human freedom. By the late 18th century, the result was a portrait of reality often called "the clockwork universe": an image of the cosmos as a perfectly ordered system of cogs and gears (causes and effects) ticking along predictably. This era also saw sharper secular debates about determinism versus free will, now framed less in terms of God's predestination and more in terms of materialism versus human agency.

Renaissance Revival of Deterministic Ideas

The Renaissance (14th–16th centuries) is often characterized by the slogan *ad fontes* – "back to the sources." Scholars like Poggio Bracciolini unearthed and studied texts from classical antiquity, reviving old ideas. Among these was Lucretius' *De rerum natura*, which introduced many readers to the atomism of Epicurus and Democritus. Although Epicurus had included the unpredictable "swerve" of atoms to allow for some indeterminacy, Lucretius still described a world fundamentally made of atoms falling through the void, with everything (including life and mind) arising from their interactions. This implicitly mechanistic view of nature resonated with some Renaissance thinkers. At the same time, the recovery of Stoic and Neoplatonic writings reintroduced ideas of cosmic order and fate. Renaissance intellectuals were often syncretic – one finds, for example, a renewed interest in astrology, Hermeticism, and Stoic fatalism during this period. The concept of astral determinism (the idea that stars and planets influence human affairs) enjoyed a vogue in Renaissance courts; even popes had court astrologers. This was largely a continuation of medieval astrological traditions, but now with greater intellectual backing from rediscovered Hellenistic sources on the subject.

More crucial to the development of determinism, however, were changes in natural philosophy and nascent science. Figures like Leonardo da Vinci and Nicolaus Copernicus began challenging certain Aristotelian doctrines. Copernicus (1473–1543) moved Earth out of the centre of the cosmos, placing the Sun at the centre instead. This heliocentric model indirectly suggested that the universe might be governed by uniform laws: if Earth is a planet like the others, perhaps the same physics applies everywhere. (Copernicus himself still held some ancient mystical notions – for instance, he believed circular motion was "perfect" and thus fundamental – but his work opened the door to thinking of the heavens and Earth as one system governed by common principles.)

In the late 16th and early 17th centuries, the seeds of classical mechanics were sown. A crucial shift was the rejection of Aristotle's idea that objects have natural places and require continuous pushing to keep moving. Medieval scholars like Jean Buridan had already proposed the concept of *impetus* (an early foreshadowing of inertia) – the notion that once set in motion, an object will continue moving without further force (contrary to Aristotle's view that constant force is needed to sustain motion). Buridan even mused that God could have set the celestial spheres in motion at the beginning of time and then left them to continue by that initial imparted impetus – so God wouldn't need angels to keep pushing the planets along. This was a clear harbinger of the clockwork idea: God could give the world a start and then let it run by itself.

Galileo Galilei (1564–1642) experimentally and conceptually solidified the principle of inertia. Through his famous inclined-plane experiments, Galileo found that bodies maintain motion unless acted upon by another force – a rudimentary form of what would later become Newton's first law of motion. He showed that a ball rolling on a smooth horizontal plane will keep rolling indefinitely (and if the ball rolls up an incline, it loses speed in a way that mirrors how it gains speed rolling down – implying that if friction were completely absent, the ball would roll forever). This was a deathblow to the old Aristotelian physics that required constant causes to sustain motion. Galileo's findings supported a view in which forces and causes can be quantified and predicted with mathematical precision.

Importantly, Galileo achieved great success in describing motion mathematically. For example, he discovered the law of falling bodies, which states that the distance an object falls is proportional to the square of the time it has been falling. This was a triumph of finding deterministic laws in nature. It demonstrated that events like the trajectory of a cannonball follow precise quantitative rules rather than occurring in arbitrary ways. Galileo's study of projectile motion showed that combining causes (an initial horizontal velocity with the constant downward acceleration of gravity) yields a predictable curved path – a parabola – matching what we observe. This reinforced a broader conviction that Galileo himself famously articulated: nature is "written in the language of mathematics." Once we know the laws governing a system, we can in principle predict the outcomes.

92

Galileo and his contemporaries also eroded Aristotle's old distinction between earthly physics and celestial physics. Using the newly invented telescope, Galileo observed mountains on the Moon and moons orbiting Jupiter – evidence that the heavenly bodies are material and perhaps subject to the same kind of processes we find on Earth. Around the same time, Johannes Kepler (1571–1630) formulated his three precise mathematical laws of planetary motion (elliptical orbits, equal areas in equal times, and the harmony between orbital period and distance). Kepler's laws described how planets move in elegant quantitative terms, though Kepler himself still invoked quasi-mystical forces (imagining the Sun exerting a sort of motive influence on the planets). Together, however, the work of Galileo and Kepler powerfully supported the idea of a lawful cosmos unified across heaven and earth.

Galileo's championing of the Copernican system – the idea that Earth moves around the Sun – and his insistence on physical explanations for celestial phenomena did bring him into conflict with the religious authorities of his day. This culminated in his famous trial by the Inquisition in 1633, which saw Galileo placed under house arrest. Yet despite such resistance, the long-term trend was clear. The methods of careful observation and mathematical analysis were rapidly unlocking an understanding of nature in terms of universal laws, undermining the older reliance on Aristotle's explanations or theological doctrine in scientific matters. What Galileo and others set in motion could not be stopped: the clockwork universe was beginning to emerge.

The Mechanical Philosophy and Newton's Clockwork Universe

By the mid-17th century, the mechanistic philosophy of nature had fully coalesced. René Descartes (1596–1650) explicitly described the world as a kind of machine. In his *Principles of Philosophy* and other works, Descartes argued that matter has no intrinsic purposes or qualities; the only properties of physical matter are those that can be quantified – essentially extension (size, shape) and motion. All physical phenomena, he claimed, can be explained by matter in motion following basic laws, like the collisions and interactions of particles. He even pictured the human body (apart from the rational soul) as a complex mechanism. For instance, Descartes held that animals are purely mechanical – mere "automata" without immaterial souls. The motions of animal bodies, he believed, are as determined as the gears of a clock, driven by stimuli and reflexes in a pre-set way. This was an extreme view at the time: Descartes went so far as to claim that when an animal appears to express pain, it is simply a mechanical reaction, not a sign of conscious experience. While one might cringe at such implications, his stance was a direct application of the emerging deterministic science to biology.

Descartes' specific physics had flaws (for example, he believed the space between planets was filled with invisible "vortices" of swirling subtle matter that pushed them in their orbits, a hypothesis that was later superseded by Newton's theory of gravity). Nonetheless, Descartes inaugurated a program of explaining nature – from the motions of planets to the beating of the human heart – in strictly mechanical terms. The bold slogan of this new approach was essentially that organisms are machines. This represents a deterministic stance because it implies that an organism's behaviour is

94

governed by physical causes just like a clock's behaviour is governed by its gears, leaving no room for unpredictable or supernatural influences in the realm of life. Descartes did allow one important exception to this universal mechanism: the human rational soul, or mind, which he considered non-physical and genuinely free in its decisions. This famous mind-body dualism meant Descartes did not extend determinism to human reason or moral choice – he thought the soul, by virtue of being immaterial, isn't bound by mechanical laws (even though how this non-material mind interacts with the physical brain remained a problem he struggled to explain). Aside from that one protected island of free mind, however, Descartes' vision was comprehensive: the universe at large, and almost everything in it, was like a giant clock built by God, with every part moving as the laws of nature dictate.

Other thinkers of the mid-17th century similarly pushed deterministic ideas. In England, the philosopher Thomas Hobbes (1588–1679) insisted that even human thought was a purely material process and that our choices result from internal motives that are as mechanically determined as the motions of clockwork. In Hobbes' view, when we appear to choose freely it only means we are not externally impeded – not that our will escapes causation. He famously argued that "liberty" simply means the absence of external obstacles to action, not some magical inner spontaneity. Such ideas, published in his *Leviathan* (1651), were shocking to many of his contemporaries, but they prefigured arguments about free will that would resurface with force in the Enlightenment. Meanwhile on the European continent, Baruch Spinoza (1632–1677) put forward an even more radical vision of a determined cosmos. Spinoza famously proposed that God and Nature are one and the same underlying reality (a kind of pantheism), and that everything in nature follows from this reality with strict necessity. In his *Ethics* (1677), Spinoza argued that every aspect of existence – including human thoughts and actions – unfolds from prior causes according to the immutable logic of the universe. He even mused that if a stone hurtling through the air had consciousness, it would imagine that it was moving of its own free will[14], when in reality it is being propelled by forces beyond its control. This analogy was Spinoza's way of suggesting that humans feel ourselves to be free, even though our desires and decisions are in fact determined by prior causes (just as the stone's trajectory is fixed by the throw). Spinoza's uncompromising determinism (and his identification of God with the deterministic order of nature) shocked many in his time – he was denounced as an atheist by religious authorities – but his philosophy laid down a profound challenge. He essentially said: to truly understand ourselves, we must recognize that we are part of Nature's inevitable order, not exempt from it.

Another great intellectual of that age, Gottfried Wilhelm Leibniz (1646–1716), offered his own version of a determined universe. Leibniz introduced the principle of sufficient reason – the idea that for anything that happens, there is a reason why it is so and not otherwise. In essence, this principle rejects the notion of events without cause or explanation. Leibniz's universe was one in which God, in his infinite wisdom, had pre-established a harmonious order so perfect that nothing occurs without purpose or rational necessity. He famously argued that we live in "the best of all

---

[14] **Baruch Spinoza**, Letter 58 to G. H. Schaller (October 1674), in The Collected Works of Spinoza, vol. 2, ed. and trans. Edwin Curley (Princeton: Princeton University Press, 2016), 499. (Spinoza's analogy: if a thrown stone had consciousness, it would believe its motion was voluntary—illustrating human illusion of free will.)

possible worlds," meaning God chose this world's initial conditions and laws to maximize goodness and rationality. In Leibniz's metaphysics, the fundamental units of reality were "monads" (sort of indivisible points of spiritual force), each programmed by God to unfold its states in a pre-ordained way. While Leibniz did believe in a form of freedom, it was a carefully constrained one: for him, human freedom meant that we act according to our own internal principles – but those principles and our circumstances are ultimately part of God's pre-established plan. The key point is that both Spinoza and Leibniz reinforced the 17th-century trend of seeking complete explanations. Whether through Spinoza's impersonal Nature or Leibniz's rational divine plan, the thinking of the time was that nothing happens without a cause and a rule – a truly deterministic vision of reality.

By the late 17th century, a full "clockwork universe" conception was in place. Indeed, the analogy of God as the master clockmaker became popular in this era. Thinkers like Robert Boyle – a pioneer of the new chemistry and a devout Christian – used the clock metaphor to explain how divine providence might operate: God designed the cosmic clock and set it ticking, so His continuous involvement wasn't needed for the day-to-day running of the world. For many, this idea actually bolstered belief in God rather than undermining it. A perfectly law-governed, deterministic universe was seen as an eloquent testimony to a perfectly intelligent creator. By the late 1600s and early 1700s, a religious philosophy called Deism arose. Deists believed that God set up the world and its laws at the beginning of time and then did not interfere thereafter – miracles or divine interventions were unnecessary (and, in the strict view, impossible) in a system governed by God's flawless laws. The deists thus embraced a fully law-governed picture of nature, effectively saying that determinism was God's chosen method of running the universe. Voltaire later quipped that after Newton, God could be thought of as a king who "only occasionally needs to wind the clock" – a nod to this clockwork universe concept where God's role is mostly to create the mechanism, not to constantly adjust it.

The crowning achievement of the scientific revolution – and the single work that did the most to cement belief in a lawful, deterministic cosmos – was Isaac Newton's *Philosophiæ Naturalis Principia Mathematica* (1687), usually known simply as the *Principia.* Newton (1642–1727) succeeded in unifying celestial and terrestrial physics with three simple laws of motion and a universal law of gravitation. This mathematical framework allowed, in principle, the prediction of the motion of any object under a given set of forces. The success of Newton's laws in explaining the orbits of planets, the trajectories of comets, the ebb and flow of ocean tides, and so on was stunning to Newton's contemporaries and successors. For the first time, it was possible to imagine that virtually all physical interactions – the collision of billiard balls, the rising of the Sun, the fall of an apple – followed the same basic set of deterministic laws. Newton himself was cautious about overstepping what his equations could tell him. He famously wrote "I frame no hypotheses" in response to questions about what gravity *is* – he did not propose any cause or mechanism for gravity itself (such as Descartes' vortices or some emanation from the Earth), contenting himself with describing how gravity behaves mathematically. In essence, Newton provided the world with the predictive tools needed for a deterministic outlook while steering clear of metaphysical pronouncements. With Newton's equations in hand, one could plug in the initial positions and velocities of objects and then compute their future positions and motions with arbitrary accuracy.

Philosophers quickly realized the sweeping implication of Newton's system: if one had perfect knowledge of all particles and forces at a given moment in time, one could – at least in theory – calculate the state of the universe at any future time, and indeed at any past time as well. The entire history of the cosmos would be an open book to such an intelligence. Newton himself did not publicly declare this in such terms or attempt to apply it to questions like human free will; as noted, he tended to leave metaphysical questions aside and was personally a very religious man. But others were happy to draw out these implications. Newton's friend and disciple, the French mathematician Pierre-Louis Maupertuis, introduced in 1744 the principle of least action – the idea that in physical processes, a quantity called "action" is minimized, almost as if nature is being efficient or economical. This principle gave a subtle, teleological spin to mechanics (it's as if nature has a goal of economy), yet it still lay within a deterministic framework (it could be derived from Newton's laws). More directly, another French scholar, Pierre-Simon Laplace, famously captured the deterministic ideal in unabashed form a few decades later. By 1814, after Newton's physics had been vindicated by more than a century of spectacular successes, Laplace put forth a bold vision of causal determinism: if an intelligence (often referred to as *Laplace's Demon*) knew the exact state of every particle in the universe at one instant, then "nothing would be uncertain, and the future, just like the past, would be present before its eyes."[15] In other words, with perfect information

---

[15] **Pierre-Simon Laplace**, A Philosophical Essay on Probabilities, (New York: Dover, 1951), 4. (Laplace's articulation of causal determinism: if a vast intelligence knew all forces and positions, "nothing would be uncertain, and the future, like the past, would be present to its eyes.")

and enough calculating power, the entire course of the universe could be foreseen. This hypothetical omniscient calculator is essentially the Newtonian God's-eye view of a perfectly deterministic universe. Laplace asserted confidently that any appearance of randomness or chance in phenomena is only a reflection of our ignorance; in principle, the laws of nature together with the initial conditions ensure only one outcome is possible. Such a statement is the very epitome of the clockwork universe idea.

Laplace's confidence in a self-sufficient, law-governed cosmos was famously illustrated by an anecdote involving Napoleon. The story goes that Napoleon, having read Laplace's treatise on celestial mechanics, remarked that it was strange to see no mention of God in the book. Laplace coolly replied, "Sir, I had no need of that hypothesis."[16] Whether or not those were his exact words, the tale captures the prevailing attitude: the new physics appeared so powerful and complete that one did not require supernatural agencies to explain the workings of the world. The clockwork universe, in the Laplacean vision, ran smoothly on its own, governed entirely by the ironclad rule of natural law.

Enlightenment Extensions: Determinism Beyond Physics

By the 18th century, Newton's system had proven its worth so thoroughly that the belief in deterministic laws spread far beyond the bounds of physics. During the

---

[16] **Pierre-Simon Laplace**, reply to Napoleon on omitting God, in Correspondence of Laplace, 1802, quoted in Roger Hahn, Laplace: Enlightenment, Revolution, and the Rise of Modern Physics (Chicago: University of Chicago Press, 2005), 128. ("Je n'avais pas besoin de cette hypothèse-là" – "I had no need of that hypothesis.")

Enlightenment (the intellectual movement of the 1700s), thinkers in many fields – especially in France – began applying the same mechanistic, law-seeking principles to living beings and even to human thought and society. Many of the French *philosophes*, inspired by the success of Newton and the earlier ideas of Descartes, sought to explain people as they would explain a machine.

One striking example is Julien Offray de La Mettrie, who in 1747 wrote a provocative little book titled *L'Homme Machine* (*Man a Machine*). In it, La Mettrie explicitly extended Descartes' idea (which Descartes himself had cautiously limited to animals) to human beings. He argued that even the human mind might arise purely from the complex organization of matter in the brain, without need for an immaterial soul. All of our feelings, he suggested, are essentially products of our physiology. La Mettrie provocatively wrote that our thoughts, desires, and pleasures follow from the configurations and movements of our bodily organs – thus, man is entirely a part of nature's mechanical order. This was a radical form of determinist and materialist philosophy. It scandalized many in its day (earning La Mettrie both outrage and a degree of exile), but it also found a receptive audience among those who were pushing for a thoroughly secular and scientific understanding of everything, humans included. By the Enlightenment's later years, the notion that human beings could be studied like any other natural object – that we might not be exempt from deterministic laws – was gaining traction.

Baron Paul-Henri Thiry d'Holbach took the deterministic philosophy even further. In his massive work *The System of Nature* (1770), published under a pseudonym to avoid persecution, d'Holbach presented a comprehensive, unabashedly materialistic and deterministic view of reality.

According to d'Holbach, human beings – just like animals, plants, planets, and everything else – are wholly governed by physical laws. He denied the existence of any immaterial soul, insisting that the mind is merely the brain in operation. All our thoughts and volitions, he argued, are the results of physical processes in the brain, which are themselves caused by prior events (inputs from the senses, the state of our body, etc.). In a memorable passage, d'Holbach writes that a person's life is like a line that nature commands him to trace "without his ever being able to swerve from it, even for an instant." In other words, at every moment, the state of our body and brain has been shaped by all the causes leading up to that moment, so we cannot do otherwise than what those causes dispose us to do. He elaborates that a person's physical organization (one's body, temperament, genetic makeup, we might say) is not chosen by the person; one's ideas and thoughts present themselves involuntarily in the mind; one's habits are formed by education and environment; and man is "unceasingly modified" by the various causes impinging on him, which "necessarily regulate his existence, give the hue to his way of thinking, and determine his manner of acting." In short, everything about a person – character, actions, even feelings and aspirations – is the product of the chain of cause and effect in nature. What we commonly call free will, in the sense of a choice that could have been otherwise or that is entirely independent of prior causes, is, for d'Holbach, an illusion born of our ignorance of the full causes behind our actions.

D'Holbach and his allies did not present these views as mere abstract speculation; they marshaled the best science of their day to back them up. For instance, studies of physiology were beginning to show correlations between physical processes (like brain injuries or chemical substances) and mental states, suggesting the dependence of mind on matter. The overall thrust of Enlightenment science was to find lawful explanations everywhere, and human behaviour was increasingly being examined in that light.

This thoroughgoing deterministic view of human behaviour had important implications for society and morality, and Enlightenment thinkers themselves were divided on how to feel about it. Some saw it as grounds for a more compassionate and rational approach to human affairs. If people are wholly shaped by causes beyond their control, then punishing someone for a crime as if they could have chosen differently starts to look questionable. Instead, one might focus on rehabilitating criminals or changing social conditions – in other words, treating the causes of crime – rather than exacting revenge on "evil" free agents. Similarly, understanding that behaviour has causes could encourage improvements in education, moral instruction, and social institutions to promote better outcomes. Determinists like d'Holbach actually argued that morality could be *naturalized*: society could use knowledge of causes to encourage good behaviours (through education, laws, incentives) and to discourage harmful behaviours (through deterrents, rehabilitative efforts, etc.), thereby weaving morality into the chain of causality.

Other thinkers, however, worried that this kind of determinism undermined the very basis of morality and responsibility. If no one has genuine freedom to choose their actions, how can we hold anyone accountable or praise and blame people for what they do? Would concepts like duty, justice, and rights even make sense in a fully predetermined world? These counterarguments didn't so much disprove determinism as express a deep concern about its consequences. The debate was lively and would continue into modern times.

Philosophical Reactions: Resisting or Reconciling Determinism

Not everyone in the Enlightenment embraced strict determinism. Some philosophers sought to resist it or find a middle ground. The Scottish philosopher David Hume (1711–1776), for example, offered a nuanced position that attempted to reconcile causation with a meaningful notion of freedom. Hume essentially argued for what we now call compatibilism – the view that free will and determinism can both be true, properly understood.

Hume agreed with the determinists on a key point: every event, including every human decision and action, has a cause. In fact, Hume contended that the very idea of an uncaused, spontaneous choice is incoherent – it isn't what sensible people should even *mean* by "free will." (If actions were truly random or uncaused, how would that be an improvement? It would make our choices erratic and inexplicable.) But, Hume argued, this causal necessity in human actions does not undermine morality or the sense of freedom. Instead, he claimed, it is precisely what *allows* us to hold people morally responsible.

In his *Enquiry Concerning Human Understanding* (1748), Hume draws a distinction between *liberty* and *necessity*. "Liberty," as he defines it, is the power to act according to one's will – to do something if you want to do it, without external constraint stopping you. "Necessity," in the context of human behaviour, is the consistent conjunction of similar motives and similar actions – basically, the observation that people's actions follow from their character and desires in a regular way (just as one billiard ball striking another in the same way under the same conditions will produce the same result). We all expect a degree of necessity in behaviour; if human actions were utterly unpredictable and capricious, society couldn't function. What Hume argues is that when we properly understand these definitions, we see no conflict: we have freedom when we can do what we desire (without someone chaining us up or otherwise physically preventing our action), and at the same time our actions can be determined by our desires and dispositions (which is what makes us who we are and makes our actions intelligible). Thus, for Hume, "free" actions are those that proceed from the internal motivations of the person (rather than external coercion), and such actions can still be completely caused by prior events like one's upbringing, genetic temperament, current mood, etc. In fact, Hume suggests that if actions weren't connected to motives in a law-like way, we'd have no basis for assigning praise or blame. We praise or blame people precisely because we assume their good or bad actions flowed from their character – a reliably connected cause – and are not just flukes.

Hume's resolution of the free will problem was influential. By reframing free will as the freedom to act according to one's determined will (as opposed to some kind of spooky uncaused will), Hume preserved the language of freedom and moral responsibility while fully accepting determinism in nature. He even noted that everyone, in practice, expects human behaviour to be law-like to some extent. When we navigate the world – making choices, forming friendships, enforcing laws – we rely on the predictable relationship between intentions and actions. If people truly behaved in a random manner from moment to moment, social life would be impossible and the notion of responsibility meaningless. So, argued Hume, both philosophers and laypeople actually agree on the matter once terms are defined clearly: causal necessity and human freedom (properly understood) coexist. The longstanding argument was, in his view, largely a dispute over words.

Another towering figure, Immanuel Kant (1724–1804), took a very different route in grappling with determinism. Kant was profoundly impressed by Newtonian science – to him, the success of physics demonstrated that determinism (what he called "natural necessity") governs all phenomena in the observable world. In his *Critique of Pure Reason* (1781), Kant argued that causality is a fundamental category of human understanding. This means that whenever we experience events, our mind cannot help but interpret them as having causes. In other words, as far as the phenomenal world (the world of appearances, what we can sense and measure) is concerned, every event we observe – including every human action insofar as it is an event in space and time – has a determinate cause and follows natural laws. So Kant grants the determinists their point when it comes to science and empirical observation: yes, the entire natural world operates deterministically.

However, Kant was not willing to conclude that *free will* is therefore an illusion. To do so, in his view, would destroy the basis of morality – and Kant was deeply committed to the idea that humans are moral agents. His strategy was to carve out a special philosophical space for free will. He did this by drawing a distinction between two standpoints from which we can consider events: one is the standpoint of phenomena (the world as we experience it), and the other is the standpoint of noumena (the world "in itself," which we cannot directly observe). This is often described as Kant's two-world or two-aspect view.

When we look at human beings from the outside – say, as a scientist observing a person's behaviour or a psychologist analysing decision-making – we are viewing them as phenomena, and thus we see a chain of cause and effect. From that perspective, a person's choices seem determined by prior events: genetic influences, upbringing, current stimuli, brain states, and so forth. However, when we consider human beings from the inside – as conscious agents who deliberate and experience moral obligation – we feel that we are more than just links in a chain of events. Kant argued that we are entitled to think of our own selves as belonging also to the noumenal realm, where the strict causality of time-bound phenomena might not apply. In the noumenal realm (which we can think about through reason but cannot see or measure), it is at least possible that the will is free. Kant suggested that our noumenal self (sometimes called the transcendental self) is not bound by the chain of natural causes, even though our empirical self (the one that can be studied scientifically) is fully part of that chain.

This is admittedly a rather abstract and philosophically complex solution – Kant essentially said that determinism is true of everything science examines, but freedom can still hold for the things science cannot examine (namely, things-in-themselves, which include the soul or the will as it is in itself). He famously phrased the reconciliation by saying: "a free will and a will under moral laws are one and the same." By this he meant that if we adopt the moral perspective – treating ourselves as responsible agents – we must *presuppose* that our will is free (otherwise the notion of moral laws that we choose to follow would make no sense). This is a kind of practical assumption rather than a theoretical proof. In

Kant's philosophy, one does not *prove* free will; rather, one acts on the unavoidable conscious sense that one ought to do certain things, which implies one *can* do them. For practical purposes, then, Kant says we must act *as if* we have free will (this is a "postulate of practical reason"), even though when we do science we proceed *as if* everything is deterministic.

Kant's reconciliation was highly influential on subsequent thought. It satisfied neither extreme side entirely – hardcore determinists might have seen it as a clever but untestable escape hatch, and ardent free-will defenders might have found it unsatisfying to banish real freedom to a noumenal realm beyond investigation. But by carefully delineating the domains of science and morality, Kant allowed both the law-governed order of nature and the intuition of personal freedom to coexist in his system. This move set the stage for 19th-century idealist philosophers and others to further explore concepts of freedom, while mainstream science continued on largely assuming determinism in practice.

By the end of the 18th century, momentum was strongly on the side of determinism as the worldview of educated thinkers, at least in scientific contexts. Laplace's thought experiment of a supreme intelligence that could predict the future became an emblem of the age's confidence in reason and science. It was widely believed that Newton's laws – perhaps extended by some yet undiscovered principles for areas like chemistry or physiology – would eventually explain everything in nature in a complete mechanistic way. The French Enlightenment, in particular, produced a number of atheist or materialist thinkers (besides d'Holbach and La Mettrie) who treated man as nothing more than a part of nature to be analysed and understood, not as a special case outside of nature's laws. Denis Diderot, the chief editor of the great French *Encyclopédie*, flirted with deterministic ideas in some of his writings. In one of his dialogues, he even suggested a kind of "soft" determinism in which our very sense of having freedom comes from our ignorance of the countless causes acting upon us – if we knew all the causes, we'd see that our actions are necessary, but because we don't, we *feel* free. By 1800 or so, even those who disliked the deterministic outlook had to acknowledge that it had become the default assumption in scientific and philosophical circles.

Triumphs of the Clockwork Universe

The early successes of the "clockwork universe" paradigm were so impressive that they encouraged ever bolder applications of deterministic thinking. In astronomy, for instance, Newtonian theory scored triumph after triumph during the eighteenth and early nineteenth centuries. Perhaps the most famous early example is the case of Halley's comet. Edmond Halley, using Newton's laws of gravitation and motion, calculated that a certain bright comet observed in 1682 was the same object that had been recorded in 1531 and 1607. He predicted this comet would return again in late 1758. Indeed, right on schedule (though Halley himself had died by then), the comet appeared in the skies as predicted. This was hailed as a dramatic confirmation that even some of the most spectacular and seemingly capricious events in the heavens were in fact governed by precise, predictable laws. No longer was a comet an omen from the gods; it was now a periodic object following a computable path.

In 1781, the astronomer William Herschel discovered a new planet – later named Uranus – in the outer solar system, further extending the known clockwork of planetary motion. Initially, Uranus' orbit, as it was tracked over the decades, showed small deviations from what Newton's law would predict. Rather than seeing this as a failure of determinism, astronomers postulated an extra cause: perhaps an unseen farther planet was perturbing Uranus's motion. In a now-legendary episode, two mathematicians – Urbain Le Verrier in France and John Couch Adams in England – independently calculated where such a planet should be located to account for the deviations. In 1846, observers pointed their telescopes to the predicted spot in the sky, and there was Neptune, a new planet discovered essentially by Newtonian mathematics. The discovery of Neptune by calculation was perhaps the most stunning vindication of Newton's deterministic model of the solar system: it showed that even without direct observation, one could infer the existence and position of a hidden object purely from the requirement that the laws hold true. The message was loud and clear: the celestial machine was reliable and complete, and if something ever seemed off, the solution was to look for more causes, not to abandon the laws.

On Earth, too, engineers and physicists made advances that demonstrated the explanatory power of deterministic science. The burgeoning understanding of mechanics and thermodynamics in the eighteenth and early nineteenth centuries led to new inventions and predictions. For example, the behaviour of gases came to be understood in terms of quantitative laws: Robert Boyle discovered in the 1600s that the pressure and volume of a gas are inversely related (Boyle's law), and later Jacques Charles found the proportional relationship between temperature and volume of a gas (Charles's law). Such laws proved invaluable in the development of steam engines, a driving force of the Industrial Revolution. The operation of a steam engine – pressure pushing a piston – was nothing mystical, it was hot gas following predictable rules. In chemistry, Antoine Lavoisier around 1789 formulated the law of conservation of mass, showing that even when substances undergo dramatic transformations (like metal turning to rust or liquids fermenting into alcohol), the total amount of matter remains the same. This strongly suggested that chemical processes were not magic but lawful rearrangements of particles. In the early 1800s John Dalton proposed the atomic theory of matter, which held that each chemical element consists of fundamental units (atoms) that combine in fixed ratios. Dalton's theory explained why elements react in consistent proportion by weight, reinforcing the idea that if you know the ingredients (atoms) and the rules of combination, you can predict the outcome of any chemical reaction – a deterministic view of chemistry. Later in the 19th century, Dmitri Mendeleev created the periodic table of the elements (1869), organizing elements by atomic weight and properties. This table not only brought order to chemistry but even allowed scientists to predict the existence and properties of elements that hadn't yet been discovered, as if nature had been following a logical blueprint. Meanwhile, advances in electricity and magnetism led to James Clerk Maxwell's equations in the 1860s, which unified those two forces and even described light as an electromagnetic wave. Maxwell's equations are deterministic (they allow one to predict how electromagnetic fields will behave and propagate), extending the mechanical philosophy into the realm of fields and waves.

By the late 19th century, many scientists felt that the edifice of knowledge was nearly complete. The successes of deterministic science were everywhere. Precise astronomical tables allowed sailors to navigate by the stars and predict eclipses and transits years in advance. Reliable timetables could be set by the regular motions of celestial bodies. In technology, machines built on mechanical principles were transforming society, and the chemistry of materials was well on its way to being understood. It seemed that the fundamental forces of nature were identified and mathematically described (gravity, electromagnetism, and the forces governing heat and thermodynamics). A famous remark attributed to the physicist Lord Kelvin in 1900 expressed the sentiment that physics had discovered everything important and there were only some minor "clouds" on the horizon – little details to be resolved. In essence, the clockwork universe vision had reached a zenith of prestige: if the universe was a machine, it was a machine that we were increasingly mastering and comprehending in full.

However, before closing this chapter, it is worth noting that even at this high noon of determinism, there were undercurrents of doubt and alternative perspectives. Not everyone was comfortable viewing the universe as a soulless machine, or humanity as just another set of cogs within it. The Romantic movement, which flourished in the late 18th and early 19th centuries, pushed back against a purely mechanistic outlook. Poets and thinkers like Johann Wolfgang von Goethe, William Blake, and Samuel Taylor Coleridge emphasized aspects of reality that they felt the clockwork analogy missed: organic growth, creativity, emotional depth, and the irreducible uniqueness of the individual. They celebrated nature's beauty and mystery, and they often portrayed strict rationalism and determinism as something that could "disenchant" the world and rob it of meaning. In their view, the universe was not *just* a dead machine; it was also alive with spirit, inspiration, and unpredictable vitality. This wasn't a scientific refutation of determinism so much as a cultural and philosophical counter current, reminding the age that man does not live by reason and logic alone.

Within science itself, there remained a few recognized puzzles where strict laws were not yet known, leaving room (at the time) for speculation that maybe the laws of nature had limits. The nature of chemical reactions, for instance – why certain substances have an affinity to combine with certain others – was not fully understood around 1800, and some scientists entertained the idea that there might be special "vital" forces at work in living chemistry. The origin of life and the inner workings of living organisms were similarly mysterious; many in the early 19th century still thought that life could not be explained solely by physics and chemistry (this was the doctrine of vitalism). Likewise, the workings of the human mind and consciousness remained deeply puzzling – even if philosophers like d'Holbach proclaimed the brain to be a machine, scientists had not come close to explaining how thoughts and consciousness arise. So, even as determinism triumphed in celestial mechanics and classical physics, questions at the frontiers of knowledge provided humble reminders that much remained to be understood. Hardline determinists tended to assume these were merely temporary gaps in our knowledge that would eventually be filled by deterministic explanations, while others wondered if something fundamentally new might be required.

By roughly 1900, the idea of determinism had a long pedigree and had undergone multiple reformulations, but it seemed to be utterly triumphant in the realm of science. The world could be conceived as an "unbroken chain" of causes and effects, from the swirling of galaxies down to the firing of neurons, all governed by discoverable laws. It was an awe-inspiring vision of cosmic order that promised complete understanding and, with that understanding, perhaps complete control over nature. Little did anyone suspect that in the 20th century, with the advent of revolutionary new physics (from quantum mechanics to chaos theory), cracks would begin to appear in this majestic clockwork. But that is a story for later chapters.

In conclusion, our journey from the Renaissance through the Enlightenment has revealed an evolving tapestry of determinist ideas. We have seen how ancient notions of atoms and fate were reborn in the mechanical philosophy of Descartes and the physical laws of Newton. Each era reinterpreted the notion of an ordered, law-governed universe in its own terms, yet a core intuition remained constant: to explain an event or phenomenon is to find its cause. By the Enlightenment, determinism was not just a working hypothesis for scientists – it had become almost a creed, a defining principle of educated thought. One theme that emerges from this history is the tension between our desire for intelligibility (the assurance that events have reasons and follow rules) and our desire for freedom or meaning (the feeling that we are more than gears in a machine). Time and again, when the pendulum of thought swung strongly toward strict determinism (emphasizing order and explanation), a counter-swing followed to preserve some space for human agency or spontaneity (emphasizing creativity and individual purpose). Far from being a new dilemma, this back-and-forth is a fundamental human inquiry that has played out over millennia. The arguments and insights formulated in these historical debates are still invoked today; indeed, it is striking how many of the key issues we wrestle with now were already being discussed in some form hundreds or even thousands of years ago.

Understanding this rich intellectual heritage helps us appreciate why 19th-century thinkers were so confident that the universe is a predictable machine – and also why the challenges to that view in the 20th century were so revolutionary and unsettling. The idea of determinism, born in ancient philosophy, grew and matured through history into a central doctrine of modern science, setting the stage for the profound questions and upheavals that would come when the limits of the clockwork universe finally came into view. The chain of thought – one might say – was unbroken, linking distant eras in a continuous quest to understand whether the cosmos follows a fixed, calculable order or allows for some measure of spontaneity. As we move forward to the next chapters, we will see how determinism faced those modern challenges, and how contemporary science has reframed these age-old questions in light of new discoveries.

Chapter 4

Cracks in the Clockwork – Chaos and Quantum Uncertainty

In the early 20th century, the once unshakable vision of the universe as a perfectly predictable clockwork began to show signs of strain. Two revolutionary developments in science—chaos theory in classical mechanics and quantum mechanics in atomic physics—introduced new kinds of unpredictability into our understanding of nature. These were the "cracks in the clockwork" that challenged the deterministic creed established by Newton and Laplace. In this chapter, we will explore how small causes can lead to enormous effects in chaotic systems, and how at the microscopic level chance itself enters the picture. Along the way, we will illustrate these ideas with real-world examples, delve into the historical reactions of scientists who first encountered these phenomena, and consider the philosophical implications for the age-old debate about determinism and free will.

117

The Challenge of Chaos: When Predictability Breaks Down

Imagine trying to predict the weather a month from now. Even with modern supercomputers, detailed physics equations, and tons of data, such a long-range forecast is nearly impossible. We experience this limit all the time: a weather report beyond a week or two becomes highly uncertain. Why should this be, if weather follows the same laws of physics that govern a clock pendulum or the motion of the planets? The answer lies in chaos theory—the discovery that small differences in initial conditions can lead to wildly different outcomes in certain systems. This phenomenon is often summed up by the famous phrase "the butterfly effect." The idea is that something as small as the flap of a butterfly's wings might ultimately set in motion forces that change the course of a tornado weeks later. In a chaotic system, tiny changes get magnified over time, so that predictability breaks down even though the system is still following deterministic laws.

To make this more concrete, consider a simple example from everyday life: a double pendulum. A single pendulum (like a weight on a string) swings back and forth in a very regular, predictable way. But if you attach a second hinged arm to the first pendulum, creating a pendulum-on-a-pendulum, the motion can become chaotic. Start two identical double pendulums with nearly the same starting position—so close that you'd need careful instruments to tell the difference—and within a short time their swings will diverge dramatically. One might be flipping end over end while the other is fluttering in a completely different pattern. The slight initial difference (maybe one was released a millimetre higher than the other) grows with each swing until the two pendulums bear almost no resemblance in behaviour. This sensitive dependence on initial conditions means that unless you know the exact starting state perfectly (an impossible demand), you cannot predict the long-term behaviour. The system is still deterministic—if you *did* have the perfect information, the laws of motion would dictate each swing without mystery—but *practically* speaking, the outcome is as good as random because any tiny uncertainty gets explosively amplified.

Weather is a classic real-world chaotic system. In the 1960s, meteorologist Edward Lorenz discovered the butterfly effect while running weather simulations. He found that rounding off the input numbers—changing them only in the slightest decimal places—led to completely different weather patterns in his computer model. At first, he thought it was a mistake, but it turned out to be a fundamental property of the equations governing fluid flow in the atmosphere. Weather obeys Newton's laws and other physical principles, yet it's so complex and sensitive that a minuscule difference (too small to measure, like the heat from a butterfly's wings) could make the difference between a sunny sky and a storm two weeks down the line. In practical terms, this is why meteorologists can only reliably forecast weather a short time into the future; beyond that, the accumulated uncertainty from countless small factors overwhelms the prediction.

The recognition of chaos was a significant crack in the deterministic worldview. Classical scientists in the 18th and 19th centuries believed that if you understood the laws of nature and had enough information about the present, you could calculate the future with arbitrary accuracy—Laplace's demon could, in principle, predict the entire course of the universe. Chaos theory complicates that vision by showing that knowing the laws is not enough; you also need impossibly perfect knowledge of the present. Any tiny uncertainty or rounding error will grow exponentially in a chaotic system. In essence, Laplace's demon might still know the future *if it had infinite precision and infinite computing power*, but no real observer can achieve that. For all practical purposes, certain processes in nature are unpredictable. The "clockwork universe" metaphor loses some of its shine: the gears might be turning according to rules, but we can't always tell what time it will be in the future because the gears sometimes slip in inscrutable ways.

Early Clues and the Birth of Chaos Theory

The idea that small causes could have large effects didn't fully emerge until the 20th century, but there were early clues. In the late 19th century, the French mathematician Henri Poincaré stumbled upon the seeds of chaos theory while studying a seemingly straightforward problem: the motion of planets. Newton's laws can predict the gravitational dance between two bodies (say, the Sun and Earth) exactly. However, add a third body (like the Moon or another planet) and the equations become much harder to solve. Poincaré tackled the three-body problem and made a startling realization: the gravitational interactions in a three-body system can exhibit sensitive dependence on initial conditions. He noted that small differences at the start could lead to vastly different trajectories over time. In a famous passage, Poincaré wrote that it "may happen that small differences in initial conditions produce very great ones in the final phenomena." This was a hint that even a deterministic system (the planets following Newton's law of gravity) might not be as predictably clockwork-like as previously thought if you tried to project its behaviour far into the future.

Poincaré's insight was largely theoretical and ahead of its time. In the early 20th century, scientists were more preoccupied with the coming revolution in quantum physics (which we will discuss shortly) than with revising their view of classical mechanics. It wasn't until the 1960s that chaos theory truly came into focus, thanks to advances in computers and the work of researchers like Edward Lorenz. Lorenz's accidental discovery during weather simulations in 1961 is often marked as the birth of modern chaos theory. He demonstrated quantitatively how a tiny alteration in initial conditions could dramatically reshape the evolution of an entire system. Over the next few decades, other scientists started finding chaos in various systems: from the dripping of a leaky faucet, to fluctuations in wildlife populations, to the beat of the human heart. By the late 20th century, "chaos" had become a recognized field of study in mathematics and physics, revealing a whole new class of behaviour in deterministic equations.

It's worth emphasizing how counterintuitive this was for the scientific community. Determinism had been equated with predictability. If you know the causes, you should know the effects—that was the mantra. Chaos theory forced a distinction between determinism (the existence of definite causes and laws) and predictability (our ability to forecast outcomes). A system can be completely deterministic and yet effectively unpredictable. This taught scientists a bit of humility: even if the universe follows exact laws, we might not always be able to pin down what will happen next. The clockwork universe, it turned out, could generate inscrutable patterns on its own, without any external randomness, simply by virtue of complexity.

Everyday Analogies of the Butterfly Effect

The butterfly effect, as dramatic as it sounds, has analogies we can relate to everyday life. Think of a snowball rolling down a hill. If you nudge it slightly to the left or right at the start, that small deviation can determine which side of a tree the snowball passes and whether it picks up more snow or breaks apart. By the time it reaches the bottom, the outcomes (where it ends up, how big it is) could be completely different for two almost identical starts. A tiny push at the top means a huge difference at the bottom. Or consider pool (billiards): after the break shot, balls carom around the table, colliding several times. If the break is even minutely different— impossible for a human to repeat in exactly the same way— the sequence of collisions changes. After a few hits, the configuration of balls on the table will be nothing like it would have been with the other break. The first slight difference got amplified with every collision. By the end of the game, one version of the break might leave the balls scattered randomly, while another (almost identical) break might result in a neat cluster in a corner pocket area. This is a kind of chaotic behaviour in a familiar setting: microscopic differences lead to macroscopic divergences.

These analogies underscore why chaos was called a "crack" in the clockwork. The machinery of cause and effect can produce irregular, hard-to-predict outcomes without any supernatural interference or true randomness. In a fully deterministic world, one might have expected that better measurement and better computation would eventually iron out all unpredictability. Chaos theory says there is a deeper limitation: even with the best measurement, you cannot eliminate all uncertainty, and in certain systems that residual uncertainty will balloon.

Importantly, chaos does not mean "utter disorder" in the sense of complete lawlessness. There is structure in chaos—often chaotic systems have beautiful underlying patterns known as "strange attractors" that govern the overall behaviour. But those patterns are not simple formulas you can use for straightforward prediction; they're more like statistical or geometric portraits of how the system behaves in general. For example, while we cannot predict the weather on a particular day a year from now, we do know the climate (the broad patterns): summer will be warmer than winter, the tropics will be wetter than the deserts, and so forth. Chaos typically doesn't destroy all order; it mixes unpredictability with a higher-level order. This realization led scientists to refine how they make predictions: instead of exact long-term forecasts, they focus on probabilities, ranges of outcomes, or qualitative behaviours.

Coping with Chaos: Science in an Uncertain World

The emergence of chaos theory prompted a rethinking of scientific methodology in systems where it applies. If long-term precision is impossible, how do scientists proceed? One approach is ensemble forecasting. In weather prediction, for instance, meteorologists don't rely on a single forecast. They run dozens of simulations with slightly varied initial conditions (since the true initial state can never be measured perfectly) to see a spread of possible outcomes. If all the simulation runs show a similar trend—say, all of them produce a storm in a certain region—then forecasters can be confident in that outcome. But if the runs diverge widely, the forecast will be correspondingly cautious, perhaps saying there's only a moderate chance of rain. This is a direct response to chaos: you acknowledge the uncertainty and try to quantify it, rather than pretending you can eliminate it.

Another strategy is focusing on statistical properties rather than exact outcomes. For example, while you cannot predict exactly what the stock market will do on a given day (the market dynamics have some chaotic attributes, influenced by countless small factors), you might predict statistical trends or probabilities of certain fluctuations. In physics experiments with chaotic systems, researchers often repeat the experiment many times to gather an average picture. They might not predict each run in detail, but by looking at patterns over many runs, they can understand the system's characteristics. In a chaotic chemical reaction (yes, chemical reactions can be chaotic under certain conditions), a scientist might not be able to say "at 10 minutes, the concentration of X will be exactly Y." But they might learn that the concentration will oscillate in a certain range in a chaotic fashion, and they can characterize how big those oscillations typically are.

The key point is that science adapts. The deterministic ideal of predicting everything exactly gave way to a more nuanced view. Scientists came to accept that uncertainty is an inherent part of nature's complexity. This doesn't mean science loses its power—on the contrary, understanding chaos has *increased* our power in many ways. By respecting the limits of prediction, we have improved certain technologies and strategies. For instance, airplane engineers realized that airflow over a wing can enter chaotic regimes; knowing this, they design wings to avoid those regimes or account for them. Heart surgeons and medical researchers study chaotic rhythms in the heart to better understand arrhythmias. Ecologists recognize that animal populations might fluctuate chaotically, and thus they plan conservation strategies that are robust to unpredictable swings. In all these cases, acknowledging chaos leads to *better* outcomes than assuming strict predictability where it doesn't exist.

Philosophical Reflections on Chaos

What does chaos theory mean for our broader philosophical perspective? At first glance, one might think chaos undermines determinism completely, but that's not quite right. Chaotic systems are still deterministic in the strict sense: if you had Laplace's demon to know all initial conditions to infinite precision, the demon's equations would still churn out one outcome. There's no roll of the dice by an outside hand; cause and effect still reign. However, chaos teaches us that determinism does not guarantee human knowledge or control. This resonates with a philosophical position that has been around for a long time: *epistemological humility*—the idea that there are limits to what we can know, even in a lawful universe. For centuries, philosophers and theologians debated whether humans, with finite minds, could ever know the mind of God or the full plan of the universe. Chaos provides a concrete scientific example where even though there is a "plan" (the laws of physics), we might not be able to discern it in full detail for certain systems.

To a person concerned about free will, chaotic dynamics offer an interesting angle: even if, in principle, your brain were a deterministic machine, it might be such a complex and chaotic machine that no prediction could pre-empt your choices. In other words, your actions could be *unpredictable* even if they aren't fundamentally *uncaused*. Some have argued that this kind of unpredictability at least *feels* like what we associate with free will—we don't experience our decisions as pre-programmed outputs, and indeed if the brain has

125

chaotic processes, no outside observer (not even a hypothetical super-neuroscientist) could perfectly forecast our next thought. However, others point out that unpredictability alone isn't the same as true freedom. A roulette wheel is unpredictable, but we don't think of it as "free." It just follows mechanical chaos. Likewise, a purely deterministic but chaotic brain might produce spontaneous-seeming behaviour, yet one could argue it's still mechanistic at its core.

The philosophical debates that chaos touches are subtle. Some philosophers suggest that chaos leaves room for human creativity and innovation in a deterministic world— since outcomes aren't pre-ordained in a way we can see, there's genuine novelty. Others maintain that nothing fundamentally changes: the universe could still be predetermined in theory, and chaos only underscores our ignorance. One clear impact of chaos was to weaken the hard determinist position that every event is not only caused but also, in principle, perfectly predictable. After chaos theory, the educated view had to acknowledge that even a Newtonian clockwork can have surprises. The dominoes of cause and effect can tumble in extraordinarily complex ways.

Now, as profound a challenge as chaos theory posed, an even deeper crack in the clockwork view came from a completely different quarter: the realm of the very small. While chaos still operates within Newton's overall paradigm (just with complexity that frustrates prediction), quantum mechanics threw out the old paradigm altogether when it came to fundamental events. Here we move from the merely unpredictable to the truly probabilistic or random. Let us now turn to quantum uncertainty—the second great challenge to determinism.

Quantum Uncertainty: Physics Enters the Realm of Chance

By the early 20th century, physics encountered phenomena that simply could not be explained by classical deterministic laws. When scientists probed the atom and the subatomic world, they found nature behaving in ways that defied the clear cause-and-effect picture. The result was the development of quantum mechanics, a theory that has been astoundingly successful at predicting atomic-scale events—but only in terms of probabilities, not certainties. This was a radical departure from everything that came before.

In classical physics, if you know how a system is set up and you know the forces at work, you can, at least in principle, calculate exactly what will happen next. Think of a simple case: if I throw a ball, and I know the angle, speed, air resistance, etc., I can calculate precisely where it will land. Classical physics prided itself on this predictive power. Quantum physics, on the other hand, says something different: if you fire a single electron (a tiny subatomic particle) at a screen, you cannot say exactly where it will hit. You can only calculate a spread of probabilities for where it might land. Do the experiment many times, and the pattern of hits will follow those probabilities—perhaps forming an interference pattern if there are two slits in the way (as in the famous double-slit experiment)—but each individual electron's landing spot is, as far as we can tell, *fundamentally random*. There is no further information in our equations or knowledge that would allow us to predict "this particular electron will go here." We can only say "there is a 30% chance it will land in band A, 70% chance in band B," and so on.

This shift was not made lightly. The early 20th-century physicists were dragged kicking and screaming into abandoning determinism at the micro level. The seeds were planted around 1900 when Max Planck found that energy exchange in matter seemed "quantized" (happening in discrete packets) to explain the spectrum of light from hot objects. Einstein in 1905 showed that light itself sometimes behaves like particles (later called photons), with energy quantized, to explain the photoelectric effect. These were startling findings, but they didn't fully break determinism yet—they just introduced the idea that at small scales, things come in lumps. The real assault on determinism came in the 1920s. Experiments with atoms and electrons (like those examining how atoms emit light, or how electrons scatter) led to puzzling outcomes that defied classical prediction. In 1927, Werner Heisenberg formulated the uncertainty principle, which basically said you can't simultaneously know certain pairs of physical properties (like a particle's exact position and exact momentum) beyond a certain precision. This wasn't just a statement about the limitations of our instruments—it was a statement that nature itself doesn't allow those quantities to be pinned down at the same time. If you can't even *know* the full state of a system, how can you predict its future with certainty? The uncertainty principle hinted that nature might not have a single, definite outcome in mind for certain measurements.

Around the same time, the mathematical formulation of quantum mechanics by Heisenberg, Erwin Schrödinger, and others made it clear that the theory inherently produces probabilistic results. Schrödinger's wave equation could tell you the "wave function" of a particle, which would give you the probabilities of finding the particle in various places or states. Max Born interpreted the wave function as a probability wave. So, for example, an electron in an atom doesn't have a definite orbit like a planet around the sun. Instead, it has a cloud of possible positions—when you look (measure it), you get a single position, but the theory only gives the likelihood of finding it here or there.

This was a bitter pill for many physicists. Albert Einstein, one of the founders of early quantum theory (with his photon idea), became its most famous critic in terms of interpretation. He quipped, "God does not play dice with the universe," expressing his discomfort that fundamental events would be left to chance. To Einstein and others of his mindset, it was more palatable to think that maybe the theory was incomplete—that there were some hidden variables or causes we hadn't found yet, which, if known, would restore determinism. Niels Bohr, leading the opposing camp (often called the Copenhagen interpretation of quantum mechanics), responded to Einstein with a respectful yet firm admonishment to accept nature as experiments reveal it—supposedly saying, "Stop telling God what to do." Bohr and his colleagues argued that asking for a definite outcome beyond the probabilities wasn't meaningful: the theory gives everything that can be observed, and that includes an irreducible element of chance.

At first glance, one might hope that quantum indeterminacy is just a sign of our ignorance—maybe our instruments disturb the system when we measure it (indeed, measuring a quantum system invariably changes it), or maybe there are hidden details. However, as the decades went on, experimental evidence increasingly supported the view that the randomness is fundamental. A crucial series of insights came from John Bell in 1964. Bell derived a theorem showing that if you assume certain types of hidden deterministic variables, you get mathematical constraints (Bell's inequalities) that quantum mechanics predicts will be violated in specific experiments. When those experiments were finally done (notably by Alain Aspect and collaborators in the 1980s), the results agreed with quantum mechanics' predictions and violated the hidden-variable constraints— strongly suggesting that there aren't local hidden variables restoring determinism. While debates continue about philosophical loopholes (like whether causality could be non-local or whether we need to accept many parallel universes as in the many-worlds interpretation), the mainstream scientific view accepts quantum mechanics at face value: on the micro level, nature appears to make some choices randomly, with only the probabilities fixed by the laws.

The World of Probability: From Atoms to Large Numbers

Now, how does this quantum randomness manifest in the world we see? It turns out that for large-scale objects, the quantum indeterminacy often averages out, giving the appearance of classical determinism. This is why Newton's laws and other classical principles work so well for big things even though, underneath, at the atomic level, there's randomness. We touched on this idea already when discussing chaos versus statistical behaviour, but in the quantum realm it's even more pronounced: the laws we once thought were fundamental (like precise conservation of energy-momentum in each interaction) are replaced by statistical laws (like exact conservation on average, but individual interactions can fluctuate as long as they respect uncertainty constraints).

Let's illustrate with an analogy introduced by Sir Arthur Eddington, a leading astrophysicist who was also an interpreter of the new physics. Imagine a giant who observes human civilization from high above, so high that individual people are invisible and only large flows are noticeable. This giant sees, every morning, a great mass of "stuff" moving into a city, and every evening a great mass moving out. Day after day, this pattern repeats with consistency: inflow in the morning, outflow in the late afternoon. The giant, not seeing the individual people, might hypothesize a deterministic law: perhaps he thinks the sun's rising causes matter to be drawn into the city, and the sun's setting causes it to leave, much like the tides. Indeed, the pattern correlates with day and night, so it seems plausible. But of course, we know the truth: each individual person is choosing to go to work or school in the morning and go home in the evening. The overall flow is statistically regular because of the coordinated habits of millions of individuals, not because of a fundamental physical law of sun and city. If the giant later gets a closer look (resolving individuals), he'd discover a mess of varied behaviours—people oversleeping, taking days off, leaving early—tiny irregularities that were invisible in the big picture but show that the precise timing and number of commuters can vary day to day. The "law" of mass motion in and out of the city was an emergent, statistical regularity.

Eddington used this story to explain how quantum events might underlie classical laws. Each atom or particle might have a bit of spontaneity or unpredictability, just as each commuter has personal reasons and could deviate from routine. But with zillions of atoms, their individual deviations mostly cancel out or blur into a stable average. Temperature, for instance, is a measure of the average energy of trillions of molecular motions. At the microscopic level, each molecule in a gas is whizzing around, colliding, maybe swapping energy in unpredictable ways. But take the aggregate, and you

131

get smooth, reliable laws like the ideal gas law or the laws of thermodynamics. In fact, even before quantum mechanics, 19th-century scientists like James Clerk Maxwell and Ludwig Boltzmann had introduced statistical mechanics to explain how the seemingly deterministic laws of heat and gas pressure emerge from fundamentally probabilistic behaviours of molecules. They knew that, in principle, if you had all positions and velocities of gas molecules you could apply Newton's laws to get the next state—but with $\sim 10^{23}$ molecules, that's hopeless to do exactly. Instead, they showed that the average behaviour can be predicted using probability, and this gives us laws like entropy increase and pressure calculations. They also realized that these laws are statistical: it's not impossible for all the air in a room to spontaneously shuffle so that one corner has all the oxygen and another has none; it's just fantastically unlikely and has *never* been observed because the odds are astronomically against it.

Quantum mechanics took this notion to a more fundamental level. It isn't just that we have too many particles to track, but that each particle doesn't necessarily have a predetermined path at all—only a range of probabilities. So, the classical laws are like the commuting pattern seen by the giant: emergent regularities born from a haze of underlying possibilities. A large chunk of radioactive material, for example, will decay in a very predictable way in bulk: if it has a half-life of 10 hours, then in 10 hours roughly half of the atoms will have decayed, in 20 hours about 3/4 will have, and so on. This bulk behaviour is so reliable that doctors use radioactive isotopes to measure kidney function or treat tumours, knowing exactly how much radiation will be emitted over time. But no one can say which particular atom will decay in the next minute. Each atom's decay is, as far as we can tell, uncaused and random—yet in aggregate, the behaviour follows a precise exponential decay law. This is analogous to how each person's decision to leave work might be somewhat independent or "random" from the city's-eye view, but collectively we get consistent rush hours.

Does Probability Mean "No Cause"?

This new quantum perspective raises a profound question: Are these probabilities just a convenient description because we're ignorant of deeper causes, or are they telling us that chance is woven into the fabric of reality? Determinists, naturally, lean toward the former: throughout history, whenever something looked random, it was often because we hadn't found the cause yet. The motion of dice or roulette wheels is unpredictable to us in practice, but we know it's due to complicated but deterministic physics. The weather seemed capricious until we understood meteorology (and, as we saw, even then it's chaotic rather than truly random). So, a determinist might argue, quantum randomness is just another temporary placeholder—a sign of our current ignorance. They might say: "Give us time, we'll find the hidden variables or deeper laws that determine when an atom will decay or how an electron chooses its path." Indeed, this was a common sentiment among many 20th-century scientists. Einstein was not alone; physicists like Erwin Schrödinger and Louis de Broglie also felt uneasy with accepting pure randomness. There were numerous attempts to formulate underlying deterministic theories that would reproduce the results of quantum mechanics—so-called "hidden variable" theories. One of them, proposed by David Bohm in 1952, actually succeeded in making a deterministic model of quantum phenomena, but at the cost of reintroducing mysterious, faster-than-light connections between particles. Bohm's theory remained a minority pursuit, as most physicists favoured the standard quantum theory which, while weird, was simpler in its weirdness: it just said "this is how it is."

Let's consider the arguments on both sides of this debate more systematically. On one side, defenders of determinism often cite historical precedent: "In the past, everything that looked random eventually got an explanation. Why should quantum physics be the exception?" For example, before we understood genetics, the inheritance of traits seemed like a random lottery—then genes were discovered, and patterns emerged. Before germ theory, catching a disease might have seemed bad luck—then we found the microbes causing them. Following this line, a determinist will say: sure, right now the atom's behaviour looks random, but maybe tomorrow we'll discover some sub-quantum mechanism that decides things. They also argue that quantum theory still has *something* causing the statistics to be stable. If truly nothing was determining individual events, why do probabilities themselves often look so precise? For instance, an electron in a certain state might have precisely a 50% chance to go through one channel and 50% through another. If each event were completely free and undetermined, how do they conspire to obey that 50-50 split so perfectly over many trials? It's as if thousands of coin flips all collectively obey the law of large numbers exactly—one might suspect the coin has a design ensuring that balance. This intuition says: behind the scenes, maybe each electron has some internal "coin" it flips that is biased exactly to those percentages, and if we knew that internal mechanism, we'd see a cause for each outcome.

On the other side, the champions of indeterminacy respond that probability doesn't need a deeper cause—it could just be a fundamental element of nature. They point out that mathematicians have long studied random processes as *primitives*. And importantly, they argue that quantum experiments have been extraordinarily successful using probability as the fundamental tool. For many scientists, the proof is in the pudding: by treating quantum events as inherently probabilistic, we have been able to invent transistors, lasers, MRI machines, and predict the outcomes of particle collisions with stunning accuracy. If there were hidden deterministic factors and we were ignoring them, it's puzzling that none of our predictions have ever stumbled over them. Every test of quantum randomness (like tests of Bell's inequalities) has thus far come out in favour of genuine randomness (or at least, against a broad class of deterministic explanations). As such, a pragmatic physicist might say: "Whether or not you're philosophically comfortable with true chance, the universe behaves *as if* it is truly random at the microlevel, so that's what we'll go with."

To draw an analogy, consider coin tossing in a slightly altered universe. In our real world, if you flip a fair coin, it's deterministic (in principle) because the outcome is fixed by how you flip it; we just can't calculate it easily without detailed information. But imagine a magical coin where each flip truly has no predetermined outcome, only a 50% chance of heads or tails by the coin's nature. Now suppose you flip this magical coin millions of times and you get very close to 50% heads and 50% tails. The determinist in our debate finds it hard to believe that each flip had no cause and *still* ended up producing perfect statistical regularity—so they suspect an unseen mechanism ensuring the balance. The indeterminist says, no, that's just how probability works with large numbers; no hidden hand is needed, just like how in mathematics random independent events naturally fall into a distribution with high probability. Both perspectives struggle with conceptual challenges: the determinist must accept that any hidden mechanism might involve phenomena outside classical intuition (like Bohm's nonlocality or parallel universes), while the indeterminist must accept that at rock bottom, the universe might "just happen" in certain ways without further reason.

From a metaphysical perspective, this is deeply unsettling or exciting, depending on your inclination. It essentially asks: can we live with the idea that not everything happens for a reason, at least not a reason we can pinpoint beyond "quantum chance said so"? In the history of thought, many found that idea disturbing. It flies in the face of the principle of sufficient reason (the idea that everything has an explanation) that philosophers like Leibniz championed. But the 20th century forced thinkers to at least consider it as a live possibility.

The Current State of Play: Determinism on the Defensive

As things stand, determinism is no longer the default, taken-for-granted worldview in science that it was in the 19th century. Modern physics has introduced areas where unpredictability and probability rule, and we have had to incorporate those into our understanding of the universe. However, the story is nuanced. Determinism is *down*, but not necessarily *out*. Many scientists and philosophers adopt a sort of pragmatic agnosticism: they use quantum mechanics as a tool (which is indeterministic in its standard interpretation) because it works, but they remain open to the possibility that a deeper deterministic theory might one day emerge. Others are convinced that quantum randomness is here to stay and perhaps even underlies the apparent determinism of the classical world, making randomness more fundamental than law in some sense.

Let's summarize the key points so far: Chaos theory showed that even classical laws can lead to unpredictable outcomes due to sensitivity to initial conditions, placing limits on our predictive power but not necessarily violating determinism. Quantum mechanics went further, suggesting that at a microscopic level nature might not follow a strict script at all, only a statistical one. Both developments cracked the confidence in a strictly deterministic, clockwork cosmos. As a result, the doctrine of determinism, once a near-article of faith for many scientists, became an open question. Does the universe run like a precise machine, or does it incorporate genuine spontaneity? The answer now seemed to be: it depends on how you look at it, and we're not entirely sure.

It's ironic that physics—the very field that cemented determinism through Newton—became the field that most strongly challenged it. By mid-20th century, anyone claiming the universe was 100% predictable in principle had to reckon with the twin spectres of chaos and quantum uncertainty. While neither gave license to pure whimsy or magic, both showed that the Laplacean ideal had cracks: some due to complexity, some perhaps due to nature's fundamental dice-playing.

Free Will in the Light of Chaos and Quantum Mechanics

All these scientific findings loop back to a question very close to home: What about us? If the laws of physics do not inexorably predetermine every event in the cosmos in a straightforward way, does that reopen the door for human free will? Or conversely, do chaos and quantum randomness actually make free will any more plausible than before?

This question has generated passionate discussions across disciplines. Let's break down a few key perspectives:

Eddington's "Free Will Leverage" Hypothesis

One of the earliest thinkers to draw a connection between quantum indeterminacy and free will was Sir Arthur Eddington, whom we've already met in analogy. Eddington proposed what we might call a "free will leverage" hypothesis: perhaps the mind (or brain) takes advantage of microscopic indeterminism to exert macroscopic control. Here's the essence of his idea: The brain is made of atoms, and if some of those atoms behave in a way that isn't strictly determined, then maybe an act of volition (a decision) could influence which way an atom goes at a critical juncture. That tiny influence could then be amplified by chaotic or sensitive processes in the brain, eventually resulting in a neuron firing or not firing, and thus affecting our actions. In more colourful terms, if a single quantum event in one neuron is the proverbial butterfly, the thought or action that results is the hurricane. So when you choose to raise your arm, perhaps at some microscopic level your "will" nudged a few quantum events that tipped the balance.

This notion tries to give substance to free will without violating physics, by inserting the will at the one place physics

138

might allow a little wiggle room: the indeterminate quantum jump. Eddington and others pointed out that living organisms might be particularly well-suited to magnify small effects. Biological systems can be extremely sensitive; for instance, just a couple of molecules can trigger a cascade in a cell that leads to a big response. If somewhere in the brain there was a neuron (or a molecular switch in a neuron) finely poised on the edge of firing, then a single electron's movement or a single ion channel's random opening (quantum effects could influence both) might be enough to set it off. That neuron might then trigger a whole network, eventually leading to muscular contraction and a bodily action. In such a scenario, the action wasn't pre-determined—there was a point where it could have gone one way or the other—and if the person willed it, perhaps that will could bias the outcome.

It's a fascinating idea, and it gave hope to those who felt squeezed by the deterministic picture of humans as automatons. However, even Eddington admitted it was speculative. There are some significant challenges to this hypothesis. For one, how exactly would the "will" interface with a quantum event? If we imagine the will as something non-physical (like a soul or mind-stuff), then we're invoking a kind of dualism where the non-physical can poke the physical at the quantum level. That's a huge assumption, and it basically inserts free will as a cause without explaining it—some would say it's sneaking in the very mystery we're trying to solve. If instead the will is just the brain itself, then we haven't explained anything—we're just saying the brain might have random triggers, but that's not wilful control, that's chance.

This leads to a crucial insight: randomness is not the same as freedom. If your decisions were completely random, you wouldn't be exercising free will in any meaningful sense. We generally think of free will as *intentional* and *reasoned*: you choose based on your desires, goals, or values. A random event has no regard for those; it's just a dice roll. So even if quantum indeterminacy means your next action isn't predetermined, if it were merely because of a random atom flip, that doesn't make *you* in control. It would be bizarre to say "Hooray, I have free will because a radioactive decay in my brain might make me do something unexpected!" That sounds more like lack of control than freedom.

Eddington was aware of this and thus implied that the mind would have to *direct* the quantum event toward a desired outcome. But as mentioned, that becomes essentially a mystical claim: a non-material mind influencing matter at the quantum scale. Science has not found evidence for such a directed influence. All experiments to date show that even in the brain, quantum events obey the same statistical laws as anywhere else. If you could somehow watch the atoms in a neuron, you'd presumably see them behaving like atoms in a test tube—sometimes tunnelling, sometimes not, following quantum probabilities, not suddenly all aligning to the dictates of a person's will.

Modern neuroscience, in fact, has found that a lot of brain activity underlying a decision happens before we are even conscious of making a choice. Famous experiments by Benjamin Libet in the 1980s showed that the brain's motor regions can become active *fractions of a second before* a person feels they've made a conscious decision to move. Some have over-interpreted those results to "disprove" free will (that's a debate for another time), but importantly, none of that research has indicated any special exemption from physical causation. The brain seems to be operating as a complex biological system. If quantum randomness plays a role, it's buried under layers of biochemical processes. No obvious "quantum jumps" show up in human behaviour that would scream "aha, a miracle happened here."

Compatibilism: Free Will Without Cosmic Uncertainty

Given the issues with trying to pin free will on quantum randomness, many philosophers lean towards compatibilism. Compatibilism is the idea that free will and determinism are not actually in conflict, properly understood. Classical compatibilists (like David Hume in the 18th century) argued that free will is about being able to act according to your motivations and reasoning without external coercion or constraint, not about being uncaused. In other words, what we really want when we want free will is the capacity to make choices in line with who we are (our character, desires, values) and to have those choices effectual—resulting in actions. Whether the process that leads from desire to action is deterministic or has some randomness isn't what makes it free or not. In fact, randomness could undermine it: if I decide to order chocolate ice cream but a random neuron firing makes me say "vanilla" at the last second, that wasn't a free choice—that was chance overriding my intention.

Many modern thinkers take this line: even if physics had turned out 100% deterministic, we could still have a meaningful notion of free will as long as our actions flow from our internal deliberations and we are not externally forced. And now that we know physics isn't fully deterministic, that doesn't automatically grant us some new kind of freedom—it just adds unpredictability. The compatibilist stance is basically that human freedom is a higher-level phenomenon, somewhat independent of the nuts and bolts of particles. It has to do with how our brain processes information, makes plans, and self-regulates, not with quantum coin flips. So, a compatibilist would say: "Sure, the clockwork universe idea was scary because it imagined every thought of mine was set in stone since the Big Bang. Quantum mechanics shows that's not exactly the case—there were some genuine forks in the road at the micro-level. But even so, that doesn't solve anything for free will. What matters is how decisions are made, not whether they could have turned out differently by a roll of the dice."

Interestingly, if one adopts the compatibilist view, chaos and quantum uncertainty become less about free will and more about human unpredictability. Compatibilists can even celebrate chaos and indeterminism as aligning with our intuition that the future is open in some sense, but they will quickly add that true freedom comes from acting *because you want to, because you decided to*, not because of random disturbances. So, one might say chaos and quantum chance save free will from the nightmare of strict predestination—there's no cosmic script that inevitably leads you to steal that cookie or choose that career; there were many possible outcomes given the starting conditions of the universe. However, to actually have *free will*, it's not enough that the universe isn't strictly fated—you also need the capacity to consciously shape your actions. That's a capacity that might be perfectly compatible with a mostly deterministic brain, as long as the determinants are your own thoughts and desires.

Existentialism and the Philosophy of an Open Universe

In the mid-20th century, while scientists were absorbing chaos and quantum theory, philosophers in Europe were exploring human freedom from a very different angle. The Existentialists, like Jean-Paul Sartre and Albert Camus, were less concerned with physics and more with the human condition in a seemingly indifferent or absurd universe. Yet, there's an interesting resonance: existentialists asserted that there is no preordained meaning or purpose given to us—we must create our own meaning and define ourselves by our choices. Sartre famously said that we are "condemned to be free," highlighting the burden that, in the absence of a divine plan or a fixed human nature, each of us must decide what to make of our life.

Although Sartre wasn't writing about quantum mechanics, the notion of an open universe (not scripted by fate or divine will) harmonizes with a universe that is not fully deterministic. If even the laws of physics allow for uncertainty and multiple possible futures, then certainly on the human scale there is no fixed destiny written in the stars. Existentialists would likely caution, however, that physics alone doesn't grant you meaning or moral freedom. Whether or not atoms swerve unpredictably, you still face choices and the responsibility for those choices. Camus wouldn't say "because quantum mechanics is indeterminate, you have free will"; rather, he'd say "regardless of whether the universe has underlying uncertainty, you are free in the sense that you must choose, there's no escaping that freedom."

In a way, the breakdown of the clockwork universe was culturally and philosophically encouraging to those who believed in human creativity, novelty, and responsibility. It removed the chilling vision of a future that's already written. But it also introduced a new kind of angst: if the universe has elements of randomness, does that mean things can happen for no reason at all, that our lives are subject to pure chance? This was a theme Camus touched on: the absurdity of a life that can be upended by a chance encounter or a random accident. Modern literature and philosophy absorbed the quantum-age understanding that certainty is an illusion; no perfectly ordered script governs our lives. We often use "chaos" in a colloquial sense to talk about life's unpredictability—little do people realize it also reflects a precise scientific concept!

Scientific Determinism, Revisited

So, where do we stand now, after chaos theory and quantum mechanics, in terms of scientific determinism? The picture we have is neither a simple clockwork nor a complete dice game, but a layered reality. At the human scale and everyday experience, things still often behave in regular ways. You turn the steering wheel in your car and it reliably changes direction; you mix vinegar and baking soda and you get a predictable fizzy reaction; planets still orbit the sun in a manner that NASA can plot years in advance for space missions. The classical deterministic laws are *not wrong*—they are just not the whole story. Underneath, there are chaotic systems and quantum events where prediction and determinism hit their limits.

Scientists handle this by effectively using a hybrid view: For systems where deterministic models work (like engineering a bridge, or computing an orbit), they use them. Where randomness has to be accounted for (like in quantum chemistry or nuclear physics), they incorporate probabilities. Often, both aspects come into play. Take modern electronics: the microchips in your phone rely on quantum physics (electron tunnelling, semiconductor band theory) to function. Engineers design them using quantum principles that are probabilistic. Yet, they create circuits that behave very reliably by the time you use the phone—so reliably that you never have to think "maybe my phone will spontaneously not follow its programming because of a quantum accident." How is that? It's because the design is robust to the underlying randomness; signals involve billions of electrons, so they average out to very stable outcomes (with some safety margins). In essence, technology has domesticated quantum mechanics to an extent—using the laws of probability to get deterministic behaviour when summed over large numbers.

In scientific practice, determinism now is often about deterministic chaos vs. stochastic (random) models. Researchers ask: should we model this system with a purely deterministic set of equations, or do we need to introduce randomness? For example, modelling the climate might use deterministic fluid dynamics equations (which are chaotic) combined with random perturbations to simulate unpredictable events like volcanic eruptions or small-scale cloud formation noise. Stock market models might treat price movements as having a random component (a "stochastic" term) because the myriad of human decisions effectively behaves like a random process, even if each decision has a reason.

Conclusion: A Universe with Wiggle Room

Chaos theory and quantum mechanics have taught us that the universe has wiggle room—it is not the rigid, unyielding machine that 19th-century determinists imagined. There are cracks in the old clockwork image. Through those cracks, we see complexity and uncertainty filtering in. But we should be careful in our conclusions: the laws of nature still hold true;

what's changed is our understanding of what those laws can guarantee us.

Determinism, in the classical sense, guaranteed certainty if you had complete knowledge. Now we know we can never have complete knowledge of a chaotic system's present state (not to infinite precision), nor complete knowledge of a quantum system's future state (because the theory itself forbids it). The philosophical implication is a more open future, one that is not strictly pre-scripted by the past. However, an open future is not the same as one we can freely shape to our whim—our freedom, whatever it may be, operates within a framework of laws and randomness.

As we move forward in this exploration of determinism and free will, the lessons of chaos and quantum physics will stay with us. They caution us against easy answers. They show us a cosmos that is orderly in many ways, yet not a monolith of order. The cosmos allows for spontaneity, whether in the flutter of a butterfly leading to a storm, or in the decay of an atom without cause. The debate now is how to interpret that spontaneity: is it just a veil over deeper order, or is it an irreducible feature of existence? Different scientists and philosophers answer differently, and the discussion continues.

One thing is certain: the advent of chaos theory and quantum mechanics was a turning point. It forced a re-examination of ideas that had been taken for granted and invigorated age-old debates with new content. The clockwork universe was not overthrown outright, but it was irrevocably changed. We now envision a clockwork with fuzzy gears and probabilistic cogs, a magnificent machine that sometimes behaves like an improvisational jazz player rather than a strict metronome.

In the chapters to come, we will examine how these cracks in the clockwork influence other fields—biology, neuroscience, and our understanding of human behaviour. We will see how the tension between determinism and uncertainty plays out when we consider life and mind. The journey from Laplace's demon to Lorenz's butterfly and to Heisenberg's uncertainty has prepared us to ask deeper questions about ourselves: Are we just another complex part of this semi-chaotic, semi-lawful universe, and if so, how do we find meaning and agency? With the stage set by physics, we turn next to the realm of life and consciousness, to see whether they too are governed by iron laws or if they harbour their own forms of unpredictability and freedom. The story of determinism is far from over—these cracks in the clockwork are where the light gets in, illuminating new paths of inquiry into the nature of reality and our place within it.

Chapter 5

Mind Under the Microscope – Neuroscience and Determinism

As we turn our focus from the broad strokes of physics and philosophy to the intimate workings of the human brain, a new perspective on the age-old free will debate comes into view. In the previous chapter, we saw how modern physics introduced uncertainty into an otherwise law-bound universe, and we explored how our own introspections about choice can be misleading. We now arrive at the crux of the matter: the human mind itself. If free will resides anywhere, it would be in the mind – in our thoughts, intentions, and decisions. But neuroscience increasingly treats those very thoughts and decisions as products of electrochemical processes in the brain. Can a lump of biological tissue following the laws of chemistry and electricity truly be the seat of freedom? Or does it render our sense of volition just another link in the causal chain? In this chapter, we will peer into the "black box" of the brain to see what light it sheds on the question of determinism. We'll examine the idea of the brain as a causal machine, review groundbreaking experiments on decision-making that measure the mind in action, and wrestle with how to interpret those findings. We'll see how psychology and behavioural science reveal hidden influences on our choices, and reflect on historical perspectives about the mind-body relationship that have shaped this debate. Finally, we'll take a detour into the realm of artificial intelligence and cognitive science to see what man-made decision-makers can teach us about our own. Each step will bring us closer to understanding whether our mental life is an enclave of freedom or simply the most complex example of determinism at work.

The Brain as a Causal Machine

For centuries, the brain was a mystery. Today, we understand it as an organ made up of billions of neurons, each firing electrical impulses and releasing chemicals that influence other neurons. From this frenetic electrical storm emerges our every thought, feeling, and action. On a physical level, the brain can be seen as an incredibly complex machine — a biological computer of sorts — that processes inputs (sensory information, hormones, memories) and produces outputs (decisions, behaviours, speech). This viewpoint leads to a profound philosophical implication: if the brain is a machine following the laws of nature, then our mental states and decisions might be fully caused by prior physical events. In other words, if we had complete knowledge of a person's brain state and all the inputs affecting it, could we in principle predict that person's next thought or choice? Determinism in neuroscience suggests that, yes, given enough information, the next move of the "mental gears" could be anticipated as surely as sunrise.

This idea can be unsettling because it clashes with our intuitive sense of being free agents. We don't experience ourselves as cogs in a machine; we experience making choices, deliberating, weighing reasons, and sometimes genuinely feeling torn between alternatives. However, neuroscience asks us to consider that what we experience as the will — our choosing self — is itself an emergent property of physical events in the brain. The brain, on this view, isn't just a passive vessel that a soul or mind controls; the brain is the thing doing the decision-making, through and through. The neurons firing in specific patterns *are* the decision happening. To many neuroscientists and philosophers, saying "my brain decided" is not different from saying "*I* decided" — because *I am my brain*, in large part. But notice the shift in perspective: instead of thinking of the will as an immaterial commander that can override physical causality, this outlook suggests that the will is what it feels like to have complex neural circuitry execute a choice.

Consider a simple example of the brain's causal power. If a certain area of your brain is directly stimulated (by a surgeon's electrode, say), you might suddenly laugh or move your arm or recall a long-forgotten memory, depending on where the electrode is placed. You didn't "will" these actions or memories — they happened because the underlying neural circuit was artificially triggered. Conversely, damage to a particular brain region can remove your ability to do something. A stroke in the motor cortex might paralyze your right arm, not because "you" decided never to move it again, but because the neural machinery required is broken. These examples illustrate a key point: the content of our mind and the occurrences of our will correspond to physical events in the brain. Change the physical events, and you change the thought or action. We are used to this idea when it comes to drugs and behaviour: alcohol, for instance, can lower inhibitions and lead to actions one wouldn't consider while sober. We rightly attribute those changes to alcohol's chemical effect on the brain. Yet, if a chemical can alter your decision-making, it implies those decisions had a biochemical basis to begin with.

The brain-as-machine model suggests that, in principle, every decision we make is the result of antecedent causes. Those causes might include the firing of a cluster of neurons that encode a preference, the release of neurotransmitters that signal pleasure or aversion, or the strengthening of certain synaptic connections due to past learning. Each of these events follows naturally from prior events: genes that built certain neural pathways, past experiences that shaped neural connections, current environmental stimuli provoking a response, and so on. The brain integrates all this information and at some point produces an output we recognize as a decision. If all these contributing factors were exactly the same, it's assumed the brain would produce the same decision every time — a hallmark of determinism.

One might wonder, where is "free will" in this picture? If my thoughts arise from neural firings, and those in turn are prompted by prior causes, it feels like I, the conscious me, am not in charge in the way I thought. Some have gone so far as to describe the conscious mind as a mere spectator to the brain's workings — like a person watching an automated factory and believing they are controlling it because they happen to witness what's happening. That view might be too extreme for many, but it underscores a worry: if the brain is a causal machine, maybe our sense of actively willing our actions is an elaborate cognitive illusion.

It's important to clarify that saying the brain operates by cause and effect does not automatically negate *all* concepts of free will. It depends on what one means by "free." If by free will one means a magical ability to cause events without any prior cause (a truly spontaneous, acausal origination of action), then a causal brain leaves little room for that. But if one means the ability to act according to one's internal desires and reasoning (which themselves have causes), then the brain can be both fully causal and still the vehicle of our agency. This latter position is often called *compatibilism* — the idea that free will can coexist with determinism, because what matters is that our actions are the result of *our* internal states (even if those have prior causes), rather than external coercion. We will return to such interpretations later. For now, the main takeaway is that modern neuroscience conceives of the brain as a natural object, obeying natural laws. This perspective lays a foundation on which researchers have probed the very moments of decision to see if they can catch the brain in the act of "deciding" — and what they've found raises fascinating questions about the nature of will.

Experiments on Decision-Making

To investigate how our brains make decisions, scientists have devised clever experiments that allow them to monitor brain activity in real time while a person is making a choice. Perhaps the most famous of these are the pioneering studies by neuroscientist Benjamin Libet in the 1980s, which have become a cornerstone of the free will debate. Libet wanted to know: if we measure the brain's electrical activity and also know the exact moment a person consciously decides to do something, which comes first — the brain activity or the conscious decision?

153

Libet's experiment was elegantly simple in design. Participants were asked to perform a very basic voluntary action: flick their wrist whenever they felt like it, a spontaneous movement with no pre-planned timing. While they did this, Libet recorded their brain's electrical activity using EEG (electroencephalography, which detects the collective firing of neurons). He also had participants watch a special clock with a dot sweeping around it and report the position of the dot at the exact moment they *felt the intention* to move arise. This allowed Libet to time, with reasonable accuracy, when the conscious decision occurred in the subject's mind ("I'm going to flick my wrist now!"). The EEG, on the other hand, could detect a well-known signal called the *readiness potential* — a gradual ramping up of neural activity in the motor cortex (the brain region that controls movement) that typically precedes a voluntary movement.

The results were striking and a bit unsettling: Libet found that the brain's readiness potential began to increase **a** fraction of a second *before* the person reported deciding to move. On average, the EEG showed the brain "gearing up" about 300 milliseconds (0.3 seconds) before the person was aware of their intention to act. The sequence of events looked like this: first, the unconscious buildup of neural activity (as if the brain was starting to initiate the action), and only later, the conscious awareness "I've decided to move now," followed almost immediately by the movement itself. It was as though the brain had already started the process of flicking the wrist, and the conscious mind came in at the end and noted, "Yes, I've decided to do this now," taking ownership of an action already underway.

Libet's findings seem to imply that the conscious will might not be the originator of our voluntary actions, but rather a witness to a decision that has already been made by neural processes behind the scenes. This was a provocative suggestion. After all, we usually feel *certain* that our conscious choice causes our action. If I decide to stand up and then I stand up, I naturally believe the conscious decision was the driver. Libet's experiment challenges that certainty: maybe the decision was actually initiated unconsciously, and my consciousness only became aware of it at some point, mistakenly believing it was in charge.

It's worth noting a few details and subsequent developments. First, the time differences in Libet's experiment were on the order of tenths of a second. This is a very small window, and some have argued that 0.3 seconds is plenty of time for the conscious mind to still veto or adjust an action. In fact, Libet himself, while interpreting his results as evidence that unconscious brain processes start actions, suggested that consciousness might still have a role in approving or aborting the action in that brief interval. He called this idea "free won't" — maybe we don't initiate our decisions freely, but perhaps we have a capacity to stop or modify them once we become aware of what's happening. For example, your brain might unconsciously gear up to scratch an itch on your face, but then you consciously decide not to because you're in polite company. That veto power, Libet proposed, could be a remaining vestige of free will.

After Libet, many other studies have probed the timing of decisions with increasingly sophisticated technology. In the 2000s, researchers used functional MRI (fMRI) brain scanning to delve deeper. In one notable study, participants were asked to press a button with either their left hand or right hand whenever they chose, and to indicate when they had made their decision. The fMRI data was analysed with computer algorithms to see if patterns of brain activity could predict which hand the person would choose, before they themselves knew. Astonishingly, the researchers found signals in certain brain regions that predicted the choice up to several seconds before the subject became conscious of their decision. In some trials, about 7–10 seconds prior to the person reporting a decision, there were subtle patterns in frontal and parietal cortex activity that, when decoded, could indicate with better-than-chance accuracy which button they eventually would press. Think about that: an outside observer reading a brain scan could foresee a person's decision long before the person consciously made that decision. It's as if the brain was "preparing" or leaning toward a particular option well in advance, even though the person only felt the urge to act much later.

These findings further reinforce the notion that a lot of what goes into a decision is happening under the hood, outside of our awareness. By the time we consciously "choose," the choice may have already been largely determined by prior brain activity. This calls into question the classic image of free will as a moment of pure, independent choice by the conscious self.

Another fascinating line of evidence comes from studies of people with split brains or neurological conditions that affect conscious awareness. In split-brain patients (individuals who have had the connection between the two hemispheres of the brain severed, usually to treat severe epilepsy), the two halves of the brain cannot directly communicate. This leads to a situation where the left hand, controlled by the right hemisphere, might perform an action that the left hemisphere (which controls speech and is typically where the conscious narrative "voice" resides) did not initiate. In laboratory tests, a split-brain patient might, for example, draw a shape with their left hand in response to a command shown only to their right hemisphere (via the left visual field). The speaking left hemisphere wasn't aware of the command. Yet when the patient is asked why they drew that shape, the left hemisphere — lacking the real information — often *confabulates* a reason, inventing an explanation that sounds plausible. The patient might say, "Oh, I just felt like drawing something," or some story to justify the action. This happens smoothly, with the person completely unaware that the true cause was a visual instruction seen by the other half of their brain. Such experiments highlight how our minds can generate a feeling of intent and a retrospective explanation for actions, even when the real cause is hidden from conscious awareness. It's a dramatic illustration that our sense of volition can sometimes be detached from the actual causal process. If one half of the brain can trick the other half into thinking "I meant to do that," it suggests that within a single intact brain, a similar dynamic could occur: unconscious processes initiate an action, and the conscious mind takes note and tells itself, "I chose to do this," not realizing the choice was already set in motion.

Yet another set of experiments in psychology has people make a choice and then manipulates the outcome without them realizing. For instance, in a "choice blindness" experiment, participants might be asked to choose which of two pictures of faces is more attractive. They point to their choice. Then, through a sleight of hand, the experimenter *switches* the photos and shows them the one they did *not* actually choose, asking, "Why did you find this face more attractive?" Amazingly, a large fraction of participants don't notice the switch and proceed to give explanations for why they chose that face — even though, in reality, they did not choose it. They might say, "I liked the shape of her eyes," rationalizing a choice they never made. This demonstrates

157

how our brain is adept at fabricating a coherent story of our own decision-making, even if that story is false. It's not that people are foolish; rather, the brain's narrative centre is a master storyteller that always has an explanation for what "we" do, whether or not it has access to the true causes.

All these experiments on decision-making, from Libet's timing studies to fMRI predictions to psychological sleights of hand, converge on a surprising revelation: our subjective experience of willing an action may not always reflect the true causal sequence behind that action. The brain seems to be doing a lot behind the scenes, and our conscious awareness may be the last to know. For those who argue that free will is an illusion, these findings are prime evidence. They suggest that what we call a conscious decision is the end product of a chain of events, not the beginning.

Interpreting the Data – Neuroscience vs. Free Will

Do these scientific findings truly mean that free will is an illusion? Many thinkers have jumped to that conclusion, while others urge caution and nuance. The interpretation of what neuroscience tells us about free will is as contentious as the experiments themselves. Let's unpack the arguments on both sides and see where they leave us.

On one hand, the case that free will is an illusion gains support from the idea that our brain is calling the shots behind our back. If my brain has effectively "decided" to do something before I'm even aware of wanting to do it, then in what sense did *I* freely choose it? To some, this paints a picture of consciousness as a sort of public relations manager: taking credit for decisions and actions that are actually made by unconscious processes. The conscious mind might be rationalizing and narrating a story ("I chose to do X because..."), while the real determinants of behaviour are electrochemical signals responding to prior causes (genes, environment, neural noise, etc.). This viewpoint can be disturbing because it suggests that the feeling of deliberate control is a kind of necessary fiction our brain generates. Just as our brains construct our visual world (we don't see raw sensory data; we see an interpreted, constructed image), perhaps they also construct a sense of being an autonomous agent, which might not hold up under scrutiny.

Supporters of this hardline interpretation often point out that even complex decisions might be influenced by unconscious biases and brain activity patterns long before we consciously weigh in. They might say: try as we might, we never asked for the preferences, personality, and inclinations that we have – those emerged from our biology and experiences. So when we "choose according to our preferences," we are still acting out a script that we didn't ultimately write. In this view, each of us is like a very sophisticated AI, programmed by a combination of our genetic code and life's inputs. We respond to stimuli according to that programming. The program may be so advanced that it includes a module that thinks it's in charge (our conscious ego), but in reality, that module isn't free in the metaphysical sense; it's just another piece of the clockwork.

However, many neuroscientists and philosophers push back against the conclusion that free will is simply a myth. First, they argue, we must be careful about what aspect of free will these experiments are testing. Take Libet's experiment: flicking one's wrist at a random moment is hardly a paradigm case of a significant, reasoned decision. It's a trivial act with no consequence or deliberation. Does it

159

capture what we really mean by a free choice of moral or personal importance? Perhaps not. It could be that for a toss-away action with no stakes, our brain can and will initiate it without bothering our conscious mind until the last moment. But consider a more complex decision, say, choosing which college to attend or whether to change careers. Those decisions often involve extended deliberation over days or weeks, consideration of pros and cons, a weighing of values, discussion with others, and so on. It's not a quick, spontaneous flick of the wrist. Critics of the "free will is an illusion" stance ask: are the same neural precedents and delays present in such cases? It's much harder to measure brain activity for decisions that unfold over long periods. The current neuroscience is far from able to predict *days* in advance which college you'll pick based on your brain activity. In fact, one might argue that the brain's decision in those cases *includes* the conscious deliberation as part of the causal process, rather than happening hidden from consciousness.

Another point of interpretation is what we consider "the decision." In Libet's work, one could argue that the brain activity building up is part of the decision process, and what the subject reports as the moment of deciding is just the point at which the decision crosses a threshold into consciousness. Imagine a kettle heating on a stove: it simmers for a while (unnoticed), and then eventually it starts to whistle (now you notice it's boiling). The boiling was underway before the whistle, but the whistle is a result of it reaching a certain point. Similarly, maybe our brains "simmer" on a decision, and only when it reaches a certain level does it enter awareness as a formed intention. From this angle, conscious will might still play a role: it's the integrated result of many factors, and perhaps once aware, we can still change our mind or adjust. The key disagreement is whether consciousness is just a passive observer or an active participant in the decision process. The experiments show it might not be the initiator, but they don't conclusively show it has zero influence.

There's also the philosophical stance we touched on earlier: *compatibilism*. Compatibilist philosophers would say that these findings don't undermine free will at all, depending on how you define it. If free will means that your actions are the result of your own motivations, desires, and intentions (as opposed to someone else forcing you), then even a fully determined brain can have free will. Under determinism, your decisions have causes, but they are *your* causes — your brain states, your character, your values (which in turn have their own causes, certainly). Compatibilists often emphasize that the opposite of free will is not causation but *coercion or compulsion*. From this view, the fact that a decision can have unconscious neurological precursors is not fatal to free will. It just means our subconscious mind is part of the decision-making team — which we already knew, in a sense, because we often act on intuitions or gut feelings that we can't fully articulate. As long as the action aligns with our overall self (and isn't something like a seizure or an external manipulation), we can still consider it "freely chosen" in a practical sense, even if it was caused.

However, those who are sceptical of compatibilism will respond that this seems to redefine free will away from what people historically meant. It's true that *if* you redefine free will as "my actions flow from my internal states without external interference," then a determined mind fits that bill. But traditionally, many have thought free will requires something more: the genuine ability to have done otherwise under identical conditions — a kind of ultimate origin of choice that isn't fully accounted for by prior events. This is often called *libertarian free will* (not related to the political ideology, but in philosophy meaning a free will that is not determined by prior causes). The neuroscience findings, if taken at face value, are quite at odds with libertarian free will. If every decision we make can be traced back to earlier brain activity and influences, then it doesn't seem we have this causa sui (self-caused) ability that some imagine. In short, neuroscience bolsters the idea that our will is *caused*; whether or not that robs us of freedom depends on what you think freedom fundamentally is.

Another line of counterargument to the sweeping dismissal of free will is to question the gap between correlation and causation in these experiments. Yes, readiness potential precedes the conscious intention, but does that readiness potential *cause* the action, or is it just a reflection of subthreshold thinking/planning? Some researchers note that the readiness potential isn't a deterministic predictor of movement — people can have a buildup of it and not move (perhaps they changed their mind last second). Additionally, participants might be feeling an urge that grows and only when it's strong enough do they say "now"; in that case the "decision" is a gradual process, not an instantaneous spark. The recorded brain activity could just be the physical signature of that gradual process. It's not so much the brain "deciding for you" as it is "you, via your brain, deciding slowly." From this perspective, the fact that we can detect it earlier than awareness is interesting but not conceptually earth-shattering — it just means the unconscious parts of our cognition are doing their job before handing off to consciousness.

Perhaps an even deeper question is: Even if our decisions are fully caused by brain processes, why should that make them *not ours?* If I *am* a brain (plus body), then its states are my states. This touches on personal identity. If one is hoping that free will means some immaterial soul stands apart from the brain and drives it freely, then indeed determinism in the brain is a problem for that view. But if one identifies with one's brain, then the fact that your brain operates by causal laws doesn't alienate you from the decision — it just describes how you (as an organism) function. For example, suppose a neuroscientist could predict I will choose chocolate over vanilla ice cream because they see that I have a "sweet-tooth pattern" in my brain and certain neural pathways light up at the sight of chocolate. If I then indeed choose chocolate, did I lack freedom? From my perspective, I chose what I wanted. The prediction didn't force me; it just accurately anticipated my desire. One might say I was *going* to choose chocolate all along, but how is that different from saying I really wanted chocolate? This subtlety is important: a completely determined will can still align with what the person wants and cares about, which is arguably what we actually experience as acting freely. The tricky part is that our wants and cares are themselves determined by other factors… and around we go in circles.

In sum, the neuroscience data undeniably challenge a naive view that our conscious mind is a sovereign, uncaused cause. They invite us to see ourselves as deeply integrated into the natural order of causes and effects. We don't stand apart from nature, magically pushing it around; rather, nature (through our brains) is pushing *us* around — or, more charitably, *operating through us.* For those inclined to a deterministic worldview, this is vindicating evidence. For those inclined to believe in a special human power of free will, this is a call to either refine that concept or find some

163

way to accommodate these findings (perhaps by looking for some break in the chain that science hasn't discovered yet).

The jury is still out on a final verdict because, fundamentally, the question of free will is partly empirical and partly philosophical. Empirically, neuroscience can show us the mechanisms of decision-making in ever greater detail. But philosophically, society must decide what to make of that knowledge. Do we conclude that people aren't responsible for their actions because "their brain made them do it"? Or do we conclude that responsibility still makes sense because the brain *is* the person, and when the brain acts, the person acts? These are questions we will explore later in the book when looking at ethics and responsibility. Before that, let's broaden our perspective beyond neuroscience into the realm of psychology and behaviour in general. There, too, we find a wealth of evidence that our choices are shaped by factors outside our conscious control, further tightening determinism's grip on the will.

Psychology and Behavioural Determinants

Long before we could peer inside the skull with brain scanners, psychologists were uncovering patterns in human behaviour that suggested our choices are far from the sovereign, uninfluenced whims we imagine them to be. In everyday life, we readily accept that people's decisions are affected by their upbringing, their mood, their habits, and their surroundings. Modern psychology has gone a step further, demonstrating in controlled experiments just how powerful and sneaky these influences can be. The accumulated findings of psychology and behavioural science paint a picture of human decision-making that is laden with subconscious biases, conditioned responses, and situational influences — in a word, *determined* by various factors we often aren't aware of.

Consider the phenomenon of priming. Priming refers to the effect that subtle cues can have on our behaviour and choices. You might think you choose and act based solely on your own thoughts at that moment, but it turns out prior exposure to certain stimuli can bias those thoughts dramatically. For example, in one classic study, people who were incidentally exposed to words related to old age (like "Gray," "Florida," "Wrinkle") during a word puzzle later walked more slowly when leaving the lab, as if they had been subconsciously influenced to act "older." In another experiment, simply having a briefcase in sight (versus a backpack) during a negotiation made participants more competitive and less cooperative — the briefcase subconsciously primed the concept of business and aggression. There have even been studies where participants primed with the idea of money (say, by seeing images of cash or unscrambling sentences about finances) became less likely to help others or ask for help, as if the idea of self-sufficiency had been triggered. What's remarkable is that in all these cases, people are typically unaware of any influence; if asked why they did something (why they walked slower or acted stingy), they'd likely give some reasonable-sounding personal rationale, not "because I saw some words that made me think of old people" or "the briefcase in the room put me in a competitive mindset." The priming phenomenon underscores that our environment can activate mental associations that shape our behaviour without any conscious assent or even awareness.

Hand in hand with priming come biases – systematic tendencies in our thinking that skew our decisions. Decades of research in cognitive psychology have revealed that

165

humans, for all our intelligence, rely on mental shortcuts (called heuristics) that can lead us astray in predictable ways. For instance, the *availability heuristic* makes us judge events as more likely if they come easily to mind (which is why many people fear plane crashes more than car crashes – plane crashes are more dramatic and memorable, so we think they're more common than they are). These biases can influence decisions big and small: an investor might put too much money in a stock simply because it's been talked about a lot (availability again), or a juror might be swayed by how evidence is framed rather than its factual content (the *framing effect*). In the framing effect, people will make different choices depending on how the same information is presented. Tell patients that a surgery has a 90% survival rate, and most will opt for it; tell another group it has a 10% mortality rate (identical meaning, just phrased negatively), and fewer want the surgery. The information is the same; only the frame differs, yet it significantly alters the decision. Such biases operate beneath the hood of our rational mind — we often only realize they influenced us in hindsight, if at all.

Then there are emotional and physiological factors that sway our choices. We all know the advice "Don't make important decisions when you're angry (or hungry, or tired)." A fascinating study found that judges were more likely to deny parole just before lunch and more likely to grant it just after lunch — suggesting that a full stomach (or better blood sugar levels) made them more lenient. It wasn't the merits of the cases that changed, but an irrelevant factor: hunger. Likewise, being in a state of fear or joy can dramatically change what we decide in a given moment. People in a happy mood tend to be more optimistic and may take more risks; people in a sad or anxious mood might play it safe or perceive more negatives. These mood swings correspond to chemical changes in the brain (neurotransmitters like serotonin, dopamine, and hormones like adrenaline or cortisol). When you're stressed, cortisol levels rise and your brain shifts into a state geared for quick, defensive decisions, perhaps at the cost of careful deliberation. When you're attracted to someone, a cocktail of dopamine and oxytocin might flood your system, colouring your decisions about that person (you might overlook red flags or agree to things you normally wouldn't). We often later rationalize these choices in terms of reasons ("It seemed like a good idea because of X, Y, Z"), but often our reasons are back-filled to explain what our biochemically swayed self wanted in the moment. The takeaway is that factors like hormones, neurotransmitters, and general bodily states can push our decision-making in particular directions, all without consulting our conscious permission.

A huge influence on our choices is our past conditioning and learned habits. The field of behavioural psychology, starting with Ivan Pavlov and later B.F. Skinner and others, demonstrated how animals (including humans) can be conditioned to respond in certain ways through rewards and punishments. Pavlov's dogs, famously, were conditioned to salivate at the sound of a bell because it had been repeatedly paired with food. While humans are not as mechanically simple in their behaviours, we are not exempt from conditioning. If you've ever found yourself automatically reaching for a snack at a certain time of day, or checking your phone whenever you hear a notification sound, you've experienced the power of conditioned habits. We develop likes and dislikes, routines and reflexes, based on what we've been taught or what consequences we've experienced. A child raised with consistent encouragement to read books may develop a genuine love for reading; one raised with harsh criticism might avoid challenges for fear of failure. As adults, those early conditioned patterns play out as seemingly free choices ("I choose to read a lot" or "I choose to stay in my comfort zone"), but they have clear causal roots in one's personal history. Even at a subtler level, much of our day-to-day decision-making is habitual. We might choose the same route to work every day without really deciding anew — it's a settled disposition. Breaking out of a habit requires effort precisely because you're going against the grain of prior conditioning.

Social psychology adds another layer: social pressure and context profoundly shape decisions. In groundbreaking studies by psychologists like Solomon Asch, people would conform to a group's obviously wrong judgment about the length of a line, just to fit in. In Stanley Milgram's famous experiments, a majority of participants were willing to deliver (simulated) painful electric shocks to another person because an authority figure calmly instructed them to continue. These experiments highlight that our choices can be heavily influenced by authority, peer behaviour, and context cues. We like to think we'd always do the right or the rational thing according to our own agency, but in practice, situational forces often override personal resolve. The environment – who is around us, how options are presented, what the "norms" seem to be – can steer our decisions without us fully realizing it.

What do all these psychological findings have in common? They show that our behaviour is, to a large degree, explainable and manipulable by external and internal causes that don't appear to involve a conscious "act of will." Of course, we *experience* ourselves as making choices, but those choices are shaped by so many prior and present factors: the

168

sights and sounds we've been exposed to, the way a question is framed, our current mood, our ingrained habits, our social environment, and even our level of fatigue or hunger. None of this is mystical or random. It's quite systematic, which is why psychologists can document these effects and even predict behaviour in controlled settings.

Neuroscience ties into these findings by providing a mechanism. For each of the influences above, there is a neural correlate. Priming works because networks of neurons that represent related concepts get subconsciously activated, making them more likely to influence behaviour. Biases arise partly because of how our brains have evolved to process information (e.g., the amygdala may hype up fear responses, the cortex might economize by using heuristics). Emotions and hormones change the neurotransmitter levels in synapses, tipping neural circuits toward certain patterns of activity (a stressed brain literally operates differently than a calm brain). Habits are encoded in strengthened connections in the basal ganglia and other habit-learning circuits – literally "wired in" by repetition. Social influence registers in brain regions associated with pain and reward; for example, resistance to group opinion can activate conflict/pain centres (it *hurts* to be the odd one out), while conforming can give a reward signal. In short, modern neuroscience is mapping out the decision-making process in the brain, and finding that it is lawful and causally linked to both prior brain states and external stimuli. We are beginning to see the pathways by which a suggestion or a hormone leads to a change in neural firing, which leads to an action. It's like watching dominoes fall, except the pattern is immensely complex and multi-layered.

Does this deterministic picture completely rule out free will? The pattern is certainly that of cause and effect. But some may argue, again, that many of these influences become part of *our* will. For instance, I might realize I'm being influenced and then make a conscious effort to counteract it (that, too, would have its own causes, perhaps knowledge of psychology acting as a cause!). Or I might reflect on my upbringing and decide to change a habitual pattern, exerting what feels like independent effort to do so. Even if that effort is brain-based, to the person experiencing it, it feels like pushing back against causes to assert oneself. A hard determinist would say even that pushback was caused by some prior condition (maybe you read a book that inspired you, etc.). And indeed, around and around it goes.

The emerging consensus in behavioural sciences is that there's no clear "gap" in which a freely willing agent could operate outside of causal influences. Every time we identify a factor, it seems to play a role. This doesn't mean people are mere puppets with no sense of self; rather, it suggests that the self *is constructed by these influences*. Your preferences, values, and personality are largely a result of your genetics and life experiences (neither of which you chose initially), and those in turn guide your decisions. In a fully causal universe, even the act of resisting your bias or changing your life path has an explanation in prior causes (maybe a formative conversation, a dramatic event that "opened your eyes," etc.). For many, this realization is enough to conclude that what we call "free will" is simply the feeling of choosing among options, even though that choice is determined by who we are and the situation we're in. For others, it's a call to refine what freedom means, perhaps viewing true freedom as something like acting in accordance with one's deeper values and reasoning, even if those have origins.

One might ask, if our choices are so influenced by subtle factors, can we do anything about it? Knowledge is power:

being aware of biases and influences can sometimes help mitigate them. But even that awareness works through brain processes, perhaps setting up new cues and counter-influences. It becomes a bit like trying to pull yourself up by your bootstraps; you can change yourself, but only using tools and motivations that themselves come from somewhere. The big-picture implication is that psychology reinforces the deterministic interpretation of human behaviour: give enough information about someone's mind and context, and you could in principle explain why they did what they did (and perhaps even predict what they will do). We're obviously not perfect at prediction yet, because people are very complex systems, but the fact that we can systematically tilt behaviour with experiments shows that it's not magic — it's mechanism.

As we digest this view of ourselves coming from neuroscience and psychology, it's useful to step back and see how we arrived at this point. The idea that the mind might be subject to laws just like the body is a product of a long intellectual evolution. To better understand the significance of these modern findings, let's travel back in time briefly and examine how people have thought about the mind and brain through history. This will give context to why the notion of determinism in human thought has been both fascinating and controversial across the ages.

Historical Perspectives on the Mind-Body Relationship

The relationship between mind and body — between our conscious self and the grey matter in our skull — has puzzled humankind for millennia. How people have viewed this relationship has profound implications for belief in free will or determinism. If the mind is something ethereal and independent of physical causality (like an immortal soul), then it's easier to imagine it having free will, unbound by material constraints. If the mind is essentially what the brain does, then it likely follows that the mind's workings are as lawful as any physical process. Let's trace a rough history of ideas about the mind and brain to see how we arrived at the modern neuroscientific viewpoint.

In ancient times, explanations for human thought and action were often spiritual or mythological. Many early cultures didn't even recognize the brain as the seat of the mind. For example, ancient Egyptian embalmers famously removed the brain and discarded it during mummification, while carefully preserving the heart — because they believed the heart was the centre of intelligence and emotion. Similarly, in the Bible and other ancient texts, the heart or the breath is associated with the soul or mind, not the brain. This suggests that the linkage between the squishy organ in our heads and our personality was not obvious to early observers. If anything, the mind was often equated with a soul or spirit that animated the body.

The philosophical inquiry into mind and determinism can be traced back to ancient Greece. One of the earliest deterministic thinkers was Democritus (5th century BCE), who imagined that everything in the universe, including human beings and their thoughts, consisted of atoms swerving through the void. Democritus was a strict materialist: in his view, the soul itself was made of fine atoms. This is a remarkably prescient stance — essentially anticipating a universe governed by physical laws and removing special exemption for the mind. If one takes Democritus's approach, free will is hard to justify, because all events (including mental ones) are the inevitable interactions of atoms. However, this was not the dominant view in the ancient world. Far more influential were ideas separating the mind from the material realm.

Plato (4th century BCE) saw the soul (of which mind or reason is a part) as an immaterial entity distinct from the body. In his famous analogy, the soul is like a chariot driver guiding the horses of passion and spirit — it is something that can exert control. Plato's dualism (separating soul and body) set the stage for thinking of the mind as something potentially independent of deterministic physical laws. If the soul comes from a realm of eternal Forms (as Plato thought) and is only temporarily in the body, one could imagine it not being bound by the clockwork of matter. However, Plato also believed in a kind of cosmic order and in reason's rule, so it's not exactly a libertarian free will model either. Nonetheless, Plato's influence, and later Aristotle's, cemented the notion that there is something special about human reason and will. Aristotle himself had a more integrated view: he considered the soul the "form" of the body (meaning it's essentially the organizing principle of a living being, not a separate substance). Interestingly, Aristotle located different faculties in different body parts; he wrongly believed the heart was the seat of thought and that the brain's function was to cool the blood. This error shows how far we were from understanding the brain's true role. Still, Aristotle's idea that the soul is the form of the body meant that for him, the soul (and by extension the mind) wasn't something that floated free of physical reality — it was tied to the organism. Yet, when it came to the rational soul (the intellect), even Aristotle entertained the possibility that it might be a special case, capable of existence apart from the body (a point of ambiguity that later commentators, including medieval scholars, would debate).

173

Moving into the Hellenistic period, the Stoics (3rd century BCE onward) introduced one of the clearest early statements of determinism. The Stoic philosophers, like Chrysippus, believed in *logos*, a rational order or divine reason that permeates the universe. They argued that everything unfolds according to fate or providence — a web of cause and effect willed by the cosmic order. Human beings, being part of this universe, are also subject to fate. However, the Stoics tried to preserve a notion of human responsibility by distinguishing between internal assent and external events. In other words, while events are fated, how we mentally respond to them is up to us. A Stoic would say we can't control external circumstances, but we can control our attitudes. Some interpret this as a form of compatibilism: our character is part of the causal chain, so if we act according to our character (aligned with nature), we are in a sense "free" even though everything is fated. Others see Stoics as straightforward determinists who happen to emphasize acceptance and virtue. Either way, in Stoicism, the mind was not outside the causal order; it was emphatically *in* it, though a virtuous mind aligns itself willingly with fate.

In contrast, Epicurus, a contemporary of the early Stoics, took a different approach to preserve free will. He was also a materialist like Democritus (believing everything is atoms and void), but he recognized the challenge that pure determinism poses to the idea of personal agency. Epicurus proposed that atoms occasionally swerve randomly, an indeterministic "swerve" that breaks the chain of determinism just enough to allow for human free will. This was a remarkable instance of a philosopher introducing randomness to solve the free will problem — a foreshadowing of sorts to the quantum randomness discussion in modern times. Epicurus basically said: if all atoms moved in fixed paths, everything would be predetermined; so atoms must have an inherent unpredictability to allow human beings to be in charge of our decisions. Critics, then and now, question if randomness actually grants meaningful free will (after all, a random swerve isn't the same as a conscious choice). But it shows that the tension between determinism and free will was keenly felt in antiquity.

Medieval thought, heavily influenced by Christianity (and to some extent Islam and Judaism in their own spheres), reintroduced a strongly dualistic and free-will-affirming perspective. The mind was equated with the soul, a God-given immaterial essence. Free will in the Christian context was vital: it justified moral responsibility, sin, and the need for divine grace. Thinkers like Augustine (4th-5th century CE) wrestled with how to reconcile human free will with an all-knowing God (if God knows what you will do, can you do otherwise?) and with the doctrine of original sin (how freedom operates under a fallen nature). Augustine ultimately affirmed free will but argued that without God's grace, our will is inclined to sin — a sort of middle ground acknowledging influences (sinful nature) but still requiring voluntary choice for moral accountability. During the high Middle Ages, Thomas Aquinas (13th century) synthesized Aristotelian philosophy with Christian theology. Aquinas saw human beings as having rational souls that are the form of the body (following Aristotle), and he strongly defended free will — seeing it as part of our rational nature. However, Aquinas also believed that divine providence ordains everything; his view was that God's causation works in harmony with human free will rather than against it (a mystery he felt the human mind can't fully comprehend). The key point is that medieval thinkers, by and large, placed the mind/soul in a special category, not bound by the deterministic physical order in the way mere matter is. This provided a bulwark for the concept of free will: our choices might be influenced by temptation or grace, but ultimately the soul can choose, for which it can be praised or blamed.

The late medieval and early modern period ushered in new scientific thinking that began to chip away at the special status of the mind. René Descartes (17th century) is a pivotal figure here. Descartes famously declared, *"Cogito, ergo sum"* ("I think, therefore I am"), and identified the mind (res cogitans, the thinking thing) as fundamentally distinct from matter (res extensa, the extended thing). In one stroke, Descartes reinforced a strong mind-body dualism: the mind is an immaterial substance, and the body (including the brain) is a material machine. He even conjectured that the two interact in the pineal gland of the brain. For Descartes, the body could be deterministic (he thought animals, lacking souls, were mere automata), but the human mind/soul had free will and was not subject to mechanical laws in the same way. This dualistic view influenced Western thought for a long time — the idea that *we* (as thinking souls) are somehow separate from and riding within our bodies, able to make choices independent of the deterministic machinery. Many people even today intuitively feel this way (as if the "real me" is a spirit or soul controlling the body). However, the very same era produced thinkers who challenged this view.

Thomas Hobbes, a contemporary of Descartes, took a radically different stance: he was a materialist about everything, including the mind. Hobbes argued that thoughts are just the motions of matter in the brain. To Hobbes, the concepts of will and appetite could be explained in terms of physical processes. He saw no need for an immaterial soul to account for human behaviour. As for free will, Hobbes redefined it in a compatibilist way: he said a free action is simply one that isn't externally constrained[17] – basically, if I'm not locked up or coerced, and I do what I want, that's free, even if my wants have causes. This pragmatic definition sidesteps the metaphysical issue and would later become a staple of compatibilist philosophy. But the critical move Hobbes makes is explaining the mind in natural terms. Similarly, Baruch Spinoza (17th century) took determinism to its logical extreme. He asserted that everything that exists is one substance (which you can call God or Nature), and everything follows from the necessity of its nature. Spinoza famously argued that free will is an illusion; in his view, even our thoughts and desires are determined by prior causes. His oft-quoted line is that humans think themselves free because they are conscious of their actions but ignorant of the causes that determine them – a statement uncannily similar to the conclusions of modern psychology and neuroscience. Spinoza believed that if we understood all the forces impinging on us, we'd see that we couldn't have done otherwise. Our sense of freedom comes from not seeing the full picture.

As science progressed through the Enlightenment, the successes of mechanistic explanations in physics and biology increasingly suggested that maybe we are fully part of nature's machine. La Mettrie, an 18th-century French physician and philosopher, wrote *Man a Machine* (L'Homme Machine), explicitly arguing that man is just a more complicated animal, and that even mental faculties are just complex bodily functions. He pointed to examples like how taking opium can alter thoughts or how illness can change

---

[17] **Thomas Hobbes, Leviathan** (1651), ed. Edwin Curley (Indianapolis: Hackett, 1994), 136–37. (Chapter 21, where Hobbes defines a free act as one not hindered by external constraints—"liberty" being "the absence of external impediments.")

personality, to argue that the state of the body (and brain) determines the state of the mind. La Mettrie's view was shocking to many at the time because it left no room for an immortal soul or for free will in the traditional sense. Around the same time, David Hume, the empiricist philosopher, while not denying the existence of mind, argued that our idea of causation and necessity should apply equally to human actions as to any other events. He was also a compatibilist, thinking that necessity (causation) and freedom (meaning voluntary action) are compatible. To Hume, seeing human behaviour as caused didn't undermine morality or responsibility — it enabled them, because if actions were random or uncaused, we couldn't connect them to character or motives.

The 19th century continued this trajectory. Discoveries in physiology and neurology started pinning down that specific parts of the brain had specific functions. For example, in 1848, the famous case of Phineas Gage provided dramatic evidence that brain injury can alter personality and self-control. Gage, a railway worker, survived an accident in which an iron rod pierced through his skull, damaging his frontal lobes. He went from being a responsible, mild-mannered man to irreverent and impulsive, "no longer Gage," as his friends said. This case strongly suggested that aspects of personality and decision-making (the very stuff of will and character) depend on the physical integrity of the brain. If a mere accident can so change a person's will, it implies the will is grounded in brain circuits. Throughout the 1800s, the rise of fields like neuroscience (though it wasn't called that yet) and experimental psychology brought more and more of human nature into the realm of natural laws. Researchers like Pierre Flourens and Paul Broca identified areas of the brain responsible for language and other faculties

178

by studying stroke patients and doing animal experiments. The message was clear: the brain is the organ of mind, and its processes underlie mental activities.

By the late 19th and early 20th century, the deterministic view was ascendant in science. Charles Darwin's theory of evolution (1859) placed humans firmly within the natural order, suggesting our behaviours and even our moral sense could be products of gradual adaptation (and thus governed by hereditary and environmental factors). Sigmund Freud around 1900 proposed that our actions are driven by unconscious drives and childhood experiences. Freud's model was not exactly mechanistic in a simple physical way, but it was deterministic in a psychological way: our so-called free choices are significantly shaped by unconscious urges and by how we were raised. Even if Freud's specific theories have been contested, the general idea of unconscious motivation has been validated by later psychology (as we've seen with biases and priming). Meanwhile, behaviourists like John Watson and B.F. Skinner in the early to mid-20th century took a very strict determinist stance: they argued that psychology should only concern itself with observable behaviour and its environmental causes. To a behaviourist, talk of free will or inner decision is meaningless; what matters is that given a certain stimulus history, an organism will respond in predictable ways. Skinner even wrote a book titled *Beyond Freedom and Dignity* (1971), contending that our ideas of freedom are outdated and that we should instead focus on controlling variables to shape behaviour beneficially.

Against this backdrop, some thinkers tried to rescue free will by looking for new kinds of indeterminism. The advent of quantum mechanics in the early 20th century (as discussed in the previous chapter) gave a scientific basis for randomness in nature. A few scientists and philosophers,

179

such as Arthur Eddington or later Karl Popper and John Eccles, speculated that maybe the brain could amplify quantum indeterminacies to allow a bit of true randomness that the will could "use" to be free. Eccles, a neurophysiologist, even proposed that the mind might influence which synapses fire by exploiting quantum uncertainties at the neuronal level. However, these ideas remain speculative and contentious, as there's no strong evidence that quantum effects in the brain are significant enough or orchestrated in any meaningful way. Moreover, as we noted, randomness alone doesn't solve the philosophical problem of free will — it might just insert noise, not agency.

In the big sweep of history, we've gone from a time when the mind was a total mystery and often regarded as a gift from the gods, to a time now where the mind is studied as a natural phenomenon. Ancient and medieval views gave the mind/soul a high degree of independence from physical causation, thereby giving philosophical room for free will (and also aligning with moral and religious notions of responsibility). Over centuries, evidence accumulated that mental processes correlate with brain processes. Each new finding — that a chemical affects mood, that an injury affects character, that electrical stimulation elicits a memory, and so on — chiselled away at the idea that the mind stands apart from the physical order. The historical trend lines point to increasing acceptance of materialism (the idea that only physical things exist, so the mind is ultimately physical) and determinism (the idea that physical laws govern all events, including thoughts).

But we should also note that there has always been resistance and alternative perspectives. Even in the face of today's neuroscience, some philosophers and theologians maintain that consciousness might be more than just brain activity — that there might be something irreducible about subjective experience that leaves room for free will. This view is known as dualism (in modern forms, sometimes called "non-reductive dualism" or invoking concepts like an immaterial mind or soul). They would point to the so-called "hard problem" of consciousness (the challenge of explaining why and how brain activity produces subjective experience) and suggest that if consciousness is not fully explained, maybe free will isn't either. Yet, the dominant trend in science leans toward a monistic view: mind and brain are one reality described at different levels, and no new non-physical ingredient is needed.

Understanding this history, we see that the debate over free will versus determinism is not just about today's experiments; it's a continuation of a very long dialogue between different conceptions of what a human being is. The current neuroscience and psychology findings can be seen as the latest chapter in a story that started with mystical explanations, moved through philosophical speculation, and is now in an empirical, data-driven phase. From souls to neurons — that's the trajectory. And as we stand on the shoulders of historical giants, our generation's contribution is to incorporate the rapid advances in brain science into this philosophical puzzle.

AI and Cognitive Science – Insights into Human Decision-Making

As if studying the human brain weren't challenging enough, humans have also embarked on building artificial minds — or at least artificial decision-makers that mimic some aspects of our intelligence. The fields of artificial intelligence (AI) and cognitive science (the study of mind and intelligence, both natural and artificial) provide a unique mirror for examining our own decision-making. By creating machines that can perform tasks requiring choice, inference, or learning, we can test ideas about how those processes might work in us. And, crucially for our discussion, AI systems are essentially deterministic (or algorithmic) in how they operate. If something akin to "free will" were to emerge in an AI, it would force us to ask whether free will is compatible with being a programmed machine — because that's what an AI ultimately is. Alternatively, comparing AI behaviour to human behaviour might highlight differences that point to something we have (perhaps unpredictability or consciousness) that current machines lack. Let's explore how AI and cognitive science shed light on human decision-making and what that means for determinism.

From the earliest days of AI research in the mid-20th century, scientists like Alan Turing and Herbert Simon conceived of thinking as a form of computation. Turing's famous question, "Can machines think?" led to the idea that maybe the human brain itself is, in essence, a kind of computer — albeit an organic, massively parallel one. Cognitive science in the 1950s and 1960s adopted the "mind as information processor" metaphor enthusiastically. Researchers began to model aspects of human decision-making using algorithms. For example, one could model logical reasoning with formal rules, or model simple decision behaviour with if-then statements and utility calculations. The successes in this realm were telling: computers proved capable of performing logical tasks, solving mathematical problems, and eventually even beating human champions at games like chess (Deep Blue defeated Garry Kasparov in 1997) and Go (Google's AlphaGo beat the world champion in 2016). These victories were achieved by machines that followed strictly defined algorithms — essentially long chains of deterministic rules and calculations (sometimes incorporating randomness in a controlled way, but nothing like a wilful choice).

When Deep Blue contemplates a chess position (we anthropomorphize here — it actually just analyses possible moves via brute-force search and heuristics), it doesn't "freely decide" what move to make. It evaluates millions of possibilities according to a programmed value system (pieces and positions have certain weights, etc.) and chooses the move that maximizes its chances of winning based on those calculations. If you reset the machine to the same state and give it the identical situation, it will (barring any random tie-breaking element in its program) make the same decision every time. It is a deterministic decision-maker. And yet, watching it play, one might describe its moves as "brilliant" or "creative" or "unexpected." We use mentalistic language because the machine's behaviour in the context of a game exhibits qualities we associate with human thought. But there's no ghost in Deep Blue's shell — no consciousness directing the play from inside. It's all algorithm.

This invites an analogy: could it be that *we*, when making decisions, are doing something similar? Perhaps not with the cold calculation of a chess computer (humans use intuition and experience in chess more than brute force search), but maybe our intuition is itself a kind of algorithm honed by evolution and learning. Indeed, modern neural network-based AI provides an even closer parallel to human decision-making. Inspired loosely by the brain's structure, artificial neural networks "learn" from examples and adjust the connections between simulated neurons. After training, such a network can perform tasks like recognizing faces, understanding speech, or recommending movies. The

183

network doesn't follow a simple set of human-written rules; instead, it develops an internal model through many iterations of adjusting weights. This is reminiscent of how humans learn from experience: our synaptic connections strengthen or weaken with practice and feedback. What's intriguing is that neural networks can end up making decisions or judgments in ways their creators don't explicitly understand line by line — they operate as a black box to some extent, just as the human brain does. Yet, at the lowest level, each "artificial neuron" is just multiplying inputs by weights and summing them up — basic arithmetic. That's deterministic math. The network's complexity (millions of parameters) makes its behaviour hard to predict in detail, but given the same input, it will produce the same output (again, unless some randomness is intentionally introduced).

One might argue, then, that modern AI demonstrates how complex, seemingly autonomous decision-making can arise from deterministic processes. If an AI can recognize a face or drive a car, tasks that involve making decisions based on perception, it's following a cause-effect process (cameras take in light, sensors record data, the program processes it, and outputs a steering command). There's no little decision-maker homunculus inside the computer pulling levers — the process *is* the decision-making. Similarly, in humans, despite how it feels from the inside, perhaps the process (neurons firing, signals propagating) *is* the decision, with no extra agent required.

There are also AI systems designed to mimic human-like decision strategies. For instance, cognitive scientists have written programs that simulate how people solve problems or even how we might get distracted or make errors. By adjusting parameters, they can make the AI mimic human reaction times and mistake patterns. When such models align with human data, it suggests that the underlying assumptions about processing might be on the right track. Many of these models treat decision-making as an accumulation of evidence. A popular model in psychology and neuroscience is the drift-diffusion model, which imagines that we accumulate evidence for option A vs. option B over time until a threshold is reached and we decide. This model can predict how long decisions will take and how accuracy trade-offs work if you change the threshold. Significantly, it portrays deciding as a kind of mechanical process — like water filling two buckets until one overflows. There's randomness in the evidence (like noise), which can explain variability in decisions, but nothing "freely willed" in the sense of breaking from the process. The model can be implemented as a computer simulation, and it will produce decisions with similar patterns to humans in certain tasks. This is another example of how we can capture aspects of choice in algorithmic terms.

AI also forces us to clarify what we mean by "unpredictable" or "spontaneous." We often equate unpredictable behaviour with free or spontaneous behaviour. However, unpredictability can come simply from complexity or hidden information. A chaotic system, like the weather, is extremely hard to predict in detail, yet we don't think the weather has free will — it's just very complex and sensitive to initial conditions. A human brain, with its billions of neurons, is enormously complex. Even if it were completely deterministic, an external observer (or even the person themselves) might not be able to predict its actions easily, especially not far in advance. That kind of unpredictability is not magic, it's just complexity. AI systems, particularly those using random elements or those that are very complex, can also be unpredictable. For example, some generative AI might come up with a sentence or image that even its programmers couldn't have specifically foreseen, but it's still following rules and patterns from its training data. If in the future we create an AI as complex as a human brain, it might be as unpredictable to us as another person is — but both the AI and the person could nonetheless be deterministic in principle.

There is a counterpoint here: current AIs, as impressive as they are, lack consciousness (at least, we have no evidence they possess subjective experience). Some argue that free will is intimately tied to consciousness — the conscious deliberation and feeling of choosing. So one could say, "Sure, an AI is deterministic, but it doesn't have free will. We humans might operate under similar principles but with an added element of conscious awareness that could allow a different kind of control." This is a fair point for discussion. However, note that adding consciousness doesn't obviously add indeterminism; one could have a conscious AI that still operates via cause and effect (if we managed to engineer that). And if the idea is that consciousness is something non-physical that could override physical processes, that veers into the dualistic territory which, as we saw, is not the direction the evidence has been heading. Nonetheless, the absence of a clear understanding of consciousness leaves a sliver of a gap in which some might place free will as a sort of currently inexplicable feature of complex brains.

From a determinist standpoint, one could argue that consciousness is a mental state like any other, arising from brain activity, and it doesn't escape the causal web. If we someday fully understood how to program consciousness, we might see it play out in machines too. At that point, if the machine claimed "I feel free to choose" just as we do, would we regard its decisions as free or as programmed? Likely, many would say "programmed," because we know we built it. But then, from a scientific perspective, one could say *we* are also "programmed" by evolution and upbringing, albeit not by a designer in our case. The AI comparison forces us to confront that double standard: We see a machine making choices and we're comfortable saying it's following its code. We see ourselves making choices and we *feel* like it's something more. Is that feeling telling us something true, or is it an illusion of complexity?

Another angle is that AI can sometimes highlight how *mechanical* our own decisions can be. For example, researchers have developed AI that can predict human decisions in certain scenarios. One AI might predict, based on your browsing and clicking history, what product you're likely to buy or what video you'll watch next — and it can be eerily accurate. That's basically pattern recognition and statistical determinism at work: you are predictable because your past behaviour and the context strongly indicate what you'll do. Or consider psychological profiling AI that, given enough of your social media data, can estimate your personality traits and preferences, then predict choices (like whom you might vote for). Again, this is not reading your soul; it's just crunching data about you. The fact that this can be done to any degree of accuracy underscores how our decisions flow from definable patterns — patterns which an algorithm can detect and use.

On the flip side, sometimes AI fails in ways humans don't, pointing out differences. For instance, AI might lack the common sense or generalization that humans have, leading it to make absurd mistakes outside of its training distribution (like misidentifying an image because of a weird noise pattern that fools it, whereas a human wouldn't be tricked). Some might use this to argue that humans have something extra —

perhaps our brain's complexity or our embodied experience gives us an edge that isn't just more computation. However, many AI researchers would say these are just issues of degree and data; with more advanced architectures and more comprehensive training, machines could overcome those shortcomings. The trend so far supports that: tasks once thought uniquely human (like language translation or intricate strategic games) have fallen to AI capabilities one by one.

In terms of cognitive science, studies of human decision-making often proceed by analogy to machine processes. For example, economists and cognitive scientists developed the field of bounded rationality, seeing humans not as perfect rational agents, but as limited information processors who use shortcuts (some of which correspond to the biases we discussed). They sometimes simulate this with computer models to see how an agent with certain limitations would decide and compare it to human data. The successes of such models reinforce that we can often understand human decision patterns without invoking any mysterious free will — we can get a lot of explanatory power just by assuming humans have certain goals, certain knowledge, and certain processing strategies. None of that requires an uncaused cause; it just requires a sufficiently rich model.

All these points lead to a provocative question: If we did create an AI that is as cognitively sophisticated as a human, would it *deserve* the same consideration as a free agent? If we say no, because it's just a machine following code, we must then ask, in what way are we different? Is it that our "code" is self-written (it isn't, mostly), or that our code is biological rather than electronic (irrelevant to the logic of free will), or that we have a soul (a belief which isn't scientifically substantiated)? It could force a reckoning either by granting that such an AI would also have what amounts to free will (if one is a compatibilist, one might say yes, if it has desires and can act on them without external force, it has free will in the same way we do), or by admitting that our own sense of freedom is built on a computational platform not fundamentally different in concept from an AI's, just immensely more complex and refined by evolution.

In summary, the advances in AI and cognitive science provide a strong analogy that intelligent decision-making behaviour can, at least in principle, be achieved through deterministic or rule-governed systems. This doesn't absolutely prove human minds work the same way, but it makes a compelling case that nothing beyond physical cause-and-effect is needed to explain decision-making. However, it also raises deep questions about consciousness and subjective experience, which AI currently doesn't replicate. Whether that difference is crucial for free will is part of ongoing philosophical debate. Some might cling to the hope that there is an ineffable spark in biological cognition that will forever elude mechanistic copying — and that spark might be where freedom lies. Yet, as history has shown, many capacities once thought uncopiable have been mechanized (like arithmetic, logic, even learning to some extent). The direction of progress suggests that the gap is narrowing.

Having journeyed through the inner workings of the brain, the findings of psychology, the lessons of history, and the parallels with AI, what picture emerges? It appears that at every level, from neurons to social environment to silicon chips, the evidence and analogies favour the view that decision-making follows patterns and processes that can be understood scientifically. The mystique of an uncaused will is steadily retreating under the onslaught of knowledge. Yet, we as individuals still *feel* as though we choose, deliberate, and act freely. How do we reconcile these perspectives? That is the pressing question as we move forward.

In the next chapter, we will grapple with the consequences of this deterministic understanding of the mind. If our wills are indeed part of the natural order of causes, what does that mean for our sense of self, our moral responsibility, and how we live our lives? Do we abandon the notion of personal freedom altogether, or do we redefine it in a way that harmonizes with the science? And importantly, how should we feel about ourselves and each other in a world where the mantra might be "to understand all is to forgive all," given that every action has its reasons? As we proceed, we will attempt to find a balanced view that acknowledges the realities unveiled by neuroscience and determinism while also addressing our human need for meaning and accountability. The microscope has shown us the nuts and bolts of the mind; next, we confront the human condition that emerges from that understanding.

Chapter 6

Philosophy of Freedom – The Free Will Debate

In the previous chapter, we traced how the tension between natural causation and human freedom emerged through history and science. We saw ancient philosophers clash over fate and chance, and noted how modern science's clockwork vision of nature raised new doubts about our autonomy. Now we turn directly to the age-old free will debate – a philosophical drama that asks: Are we truly free to choose our actions, or are we merely playing out a script written by prior causes? In this chapter, we will examine the major positions that thinkers have taken on this question. We begin with hard determinism, the stark view that every choice is an illusion dictated by causality. We then consider the opposite stance of libertarian free will, which insists that people have a genuine capacity to choose independently of physical determinism. After that, we explore compatibilism, an attempt to reconcile free will with a deterministic universe by redefining freedom in a more nuanced way. We'll also discuss Bertrand Russell's perspective, which brings a healthy dose of scepticism toward any absolute answers. Finally, we will look at the real-world implications of where one stands in this debate – touching on law, ethics, modern neuroscience, artificial intelligence, and our sense of meaning. Throughout, we will strive to maintain the rigorous but open-minded approach that has guided us so far, weighing each view and seeing how they connect.

By the end of this chapter, it should be clear why the free will problem remains one of the most profound and contested issues in philosophy. Yet we will also find that understanding these perspectives can illuminate practical aspects of our lives – from how we judge others' actions to how we find purpose in a world that might be fully caused. Let us now delve into the competing philosophies of freedom, starting with the uncompromising logic of hard determinism.

Hard Determinism – No Escape from Causality

Hard determinism is the position that free will is an illusion and that every event, including every human action and decision, is the inevitable result of preceding causes. According to this view, the universe is governed by unbreakable chains of cause and effect, and the human mind is no exception. If we fully knew all the conditions that led up to a person's choice – their genetics, upbringing, brain state, environment, and so on – we would see that the person *could not have done otherwise*. In other words, given those prior causes, only one outcome was ever possible. Just as a rock thrown from a cliff follows a deterministic trajectory set by gravity and its initial push, a person's "choice" follows a path set by prior events and influences. The feeling of freedom, say hard determinists, comes from our ignorance of all those causes; we *experience* decision-making without seeing the hidden gears turning under the surface.

Paul-Henri Thiry, Baron d'Holbach, an 18th-century French philosopher, was a classic champion of hard determinism. In his *System of Nature* (1770), d'Holbach argued passionately that humans are wholly part of nature's machinery. He asserted that a person's thoughts and desires are the product of their physical brain, which operates under the same natural laws as everything else. Therefore, every decision a person makes is as determined as the motion of a clock's hands. D'Holbach famously likened the idea of free will to a fly confidently carrying a carriage, unaware that the horse is actually pulling it. In another vivid analogy, he described a man in a fast-moving river who believes he's freely choosing his direction while he is in fact being carried by the current. The man *feels* free to swim wherever he likes, but the rushing water dictates his options; if the current is strong, he can't simply will himself to go upstream. Likewise, d'Holbach said, a person floating through life's stream might imagine he can choose any path, yet if we consider all the forces propelling him – his strongest desires, his fears, his ingrained habits – we find those forces inevitably push him toward one outcome. What appears to be a spontaneous choice is, in reality, the result of the strongest motive winning out, much as a weight placed on a scale will tip it according to the heavier side. For d'Holbach, free will was simply our ignorance of the real causes behind our actions. Once we understand those causes, the notion that we could have acted differently evaporates.

This hard determinist stance builds on the remarkable success of science in explaining phenomena by causes. By d'Holbach's time, Newtonian physics had demonstrated that the motions of planets and cannonballs follow precise mathematical laws. Enlightenment thinkers extended this causal determinism to living beings and the human mind. If planets obey cause and effect, why would humans be an exception? The hard determinist says they aren't – we are also part of the clockwork. In the 19th century, Pierre-Simon Laplace encapsulated this worldview with the image of an all-knowing intelligence (later dubbed "Laplace's demon") that, if it knew the position and momentum of every particle at one time, could predict the entire future of the universe with perfect accuracy. In a Laplacian universe, everything that will happen was already implicit in the state of the world moments after the Big Bang. Under such strict determinism, the notion of *choosing* differently is incoherent – the future is as fixed as the past. Even our internal deliberations would just be part of the unfolding mechanism: we deliberate because we are caused to, and we reach the decision that was predetermined by prior conditions.

Hard determinism finds support not just in classical physics but in much of modern science as well. Biology and neuroscience increasingly reveal how our behaviour is tied to physical processes. Our genes influence our temperament and tendencies. Our brains operate via electrochemical signals that follow the laws of chemistry and physics. We've learned that hormones and neural circuits can shape our moods and reactions; for example, a surge of adrenaline can make us feel fear and prompt a "fight or flight" decision, and that surge is a physiological cause, not something we wilfully conjure. Experiments in psychology show that much of our behaviour can be traced to subconscious cues or prior conditioning. Hard determinists point to classic studies like Ivan Pavlov's conditioned dogs or more broadly to our formative childhood experiences: these illustrate how responses and preferences can be programmed by earlier events. Even our creative or personal decisions might be less "free" than we think – they could stem from brain structures and past influences we never chose. For instance, a person may choose a career in medicine because they "want to help people," but a determinist will note that this desire itself grew from specific causes (perhaps a family expectation, a personal encounter with illness, certain empathic genes). If every aspect of our decision-making has some prior cause, then, as hard determinists argue, there's no room for a special freedom that escapes causality.

One might object that quantum mechanics – the 20th-century update to physics – introduces randomness and might upset the deterministic picture. It's true that at the subatomic level some events appear fundamentally unpredictable; even Laplace's demon would struggle with the exact behaviour of a single electron. However, hard determinists usually respond that *randomness is no help to free will.* If an outcome is determined, it's fixed; if it's truly random, it's out of our control – like a coin flip. Neither case grants the kind of purposeful control we associate with free will. So even if physics allows a sprinkle of randomness, that doesn't magically empower us with freedom; at best it would make some actions arbitrary. Hard determinists maintain that for all practical purposes, especially at the scale of neurons and decisions, cause and effect still reign supreme. The mind, in their view, is what the brain does, and the brain follows natural laws or probabilistic rules – either way, nothing "else" enters to override those processes.

Philosophers following in d'Holbach's footsteps (and many scientists today) have continued to argue that we never truly choose otherwise. They often highlight that our intuitive sense of having multiple possible futures is a kind of cognitive mirage. For example, when you stand at an ice cream counter and agonize between chocolate or vanilla, it *seems* you could genuinely pick either. But a determinist would say that given your taste preferences, your past experiences (maybe chocolate reminds you of childhood treats), your current brain state, and a host of subtle factors, one of those options is already favoured by the time you reach the counter. You simply don't realize all the prior causes that are tipping the scales. In hindsight, we might tell ourselves "I could have chosen the other flavour," but from the deterministic perspective, that is only a hypothetical imagining. In reality, with the universe in the exact same state up to that moment, you would make the same choice of chocolate every time. The principle of causality allows no room for deviation unless something in the prior state was different.

Contemporary defenders of hard determinism include several scientists and philosophers who emphasize the mechanistic nature of decision-making. For instance, neuroscientist Sam Harris is a vocal proponent of the view that free will is an illusion. Harris points to experiments in neuroscience that reveal brain activity corresponding to a decision *before* the person becomes conscious of deciding. In one famous type of study, participants are asked to make a spontaneous choice (say, press a button with their left or right hand) and to note when they became aware of intending to act. Remarkably, researchers find that the brain's motor regions show signs of which button will be pressed milliseconds – sometimes even seconds – before the person feels they "made" the decision. To hard determinists, such findings strongly suggest that our brain was going to do what it does, and *then* our conscious mind catches up and interprets it as a free choice. In daily life too, they argue, our choices emerge from background causes we don't control:

genetics, culture, stimuli, and so on. We are, as Harris puts it, more biochemical puppets than autonomous masters of our fate[18] (even if the strings are immensely complex and not controlled by any single puppeteer).

The hard determinist viewpoint has a certain logical and scientific starkness to it. It insists on consistency: if we accept causation and natural law everywhere else, we shouldn't make a special exception for human volition. It appeals to our demand for explanations – if someone asks "why did you do X?", we normally try to give a reason, a cause. Hard determinists say if we trace those reasons deeply enough, they will always extend beyond "just because I chose to." They will terminate in factors outside the will – perhaps in childhood conditioning or brain chemistry or universal laws. Thus, in their eyes, free will is simply a name we give to our ignorance of all the threads that pull at us.

However, this uncompromising view is deeply unsettling to many. If taken as absolute, it seems to undermine our sense of moral responsibility (after all, if one couldn't help but act as they did, can we blame them?). It also clashes with our inner experience of deliberation and choice. Most people feel that at least sometimes, they face genuine alternatives and choose one. Hard determinism tells them this feeling is false – that it was always going to be that one outcome. This has led other philosophers to push back. Some have tried to preserve a robust, "contra-causal" free will, rejecting the idea that all events are inevitable. These thinkers, the libertarians (in the metaphysical sense, not to be confused with political libertarians), hold that we do have a capacity for genuine choice that is not completely preordained by prior events.

---

[18] **Sam Harris**, Free Will (New York: Free Press, 2012), 5–7. (Harris's argument that free will is an illusion, where he likens humans to "biochemical puppets" governed by neurophysiological events beyond conscious control.)

Let us now consider their case for real freedom, and the challenges it faces.

Libertarian Free Will – The Case for Choice

Libertarian free will is the view that human beings are not entirely bound by deterministic causation – that we possess an ability to initiate actions in a way that is not just the consequence of prior physical events. In other words, when you make a choice, you could truly have done otherwise even if everything leading up to the moment had been the same. This position often involves the idea that there is something special about the human mind (or soul) that allows it to rise above mere mechanism. Libertarians about free will agree that cause-and-effect governs the physical world, but they argue that the human agent can be an original source of causation – a first cause of a new chain of events. Whereas hard determinists see us as dominoes knocked over by previous dominoes, libertarians want to say that sometimes, a person can "stand up" and topple the next domino by their own independent power, not just because another domino hit them.

Throughout history, many have found this view appealing because it secures a strong sense of responsibility, dignity, and creativity for human beings. It aligns with our intuitive feeling of freedom. When I stand before a crossroad, I genuinely feel that *I* choose the left or right path; it doesn't seem predetermined. Libertarian free will takes that feeling at face value – we do have a real ability to choose among alternatives. Our decisions are not pre-written in the stars or in our neurons; we, as conscious agents, author them in the moment.

One classical foundation for this belief comes from dualism, especially the mind-body dualism most famously articulated by René Descartes in the 17th century. Descartes argued that the mind (or soul) is an immaterial substance, fundamentally different from the material body. The body, like other physical objects, could be subject to deterministic laws (the physics of muscles, nerves, and so forth), but the mind was a thinking, unextended thing – not made of atoms – and therefore not bound by physical necessity. In Descartes' view, the mind could interact with the body (he speculated the pineal gland might be the point of contact), but it wasn't simply another cog in the material machine. This opened the door for the mind to have a will that is free. The will, Descartes believed, is by its nature free and unlimited – he even noted that in contrast to our finite knowledge, our will seems to have no bounds in what it can choose or affirm. Traditional religious viewpoints similarly hold that humans have an immaterial soul endowed with free will. For instance, in Christian, Jewish, and Islamic thought, free will is often considered a God-given capacity, necessary for moral accountability (how could God justly reward or punish us if we weren't free to choose good or evil?). These perspectives paint a picture of the human being as a composite of matter and something beyond matter, where that "beyond" part (mind or soul) can make choices independently of the deterministic push of the physical world.

However, simply positing a soul or an independent mind doesn't settle the matter. Libertarian free will faces a huge challenge: explaining how this free agency actually works without lapsing into mystery. If the will is not determined by prior events, what *does* determine it – or is it completely uncaused? Saying "the soul did it" might just restate the problem unless we understand how the soul operates. Critics often press libertarians to avoid just inserting a metaphysical black box. The question "how can an immaterial mind influence the physical brain?" is a classic mind-body problem. If the mind isn't physical, how can it push neurons around to cause my arm to lift or my mouth to speak? Descartes himself struggled with this and was mocked by some contemporaries for effectively appealing to something magical. In modern terms, allowing an immaterial mind to affect the material world seemingly violates the principle of conservation of energy (since an uncaused mental force would be adding new energy or momentum to the physical system of the brain). Libertarians have proposed various theories to address this.

One idea is known as "agent causation." Proposed by philosophers like Roderick Chisholm in the 20th century (a modern defender of free will), agent causation means that a person, as an agent, can start new causal chains that are not predetermined by prior events. Instead of events causing events, a person (agent) causes an event. In this view, you as an agent might cause your decision ex nihilo (from nothing but your own will) at that moment. For example, when confronted with a moral decision – say, whether to lie or tell the truth – nothing compels you one way or the other; you have reasons for both sides perhaps, but ultimately *you* initiate the choice to act truthfully or deceitfully. If we rewind time to the exact same circumstances, since you are an agent and not just a passive event, you truly could have initiated a different choice. It wasn't fixed until you made it. This is a strong form of freedom: you are a kind of prime mover for your actions.

Libertarians often find support in the experience of choice and the sense of moral duty. We all feel, when deliberating, that we are weighing possibilities that are genuinely open.

Take a simple daily example: this morning you might have debated whether to go for a jog or stay in bed. You weighed the value of exercise against the pleasure of extra sleep. From the inside, it seemed like you had a real ability to pick either course. Indeed, you might still think "I *could* have chosen differently." Libertarians would say this intuition shouldn't be brushed off. It's a direct insight into our free agency. We are not just spectators watching our body-mind system choose by itself; *we* are the chooser exerting our will. Moreover, our whole concept of ethics relies on the assumption that people have free will. We praise heroes because we believe they chose to act bravely when they could have cowardly shrunk away. We blame wrongdoers because we believe they could have done the right thing but wilfully did not. If none of them could have acted otherwise – if the hero was "fated" by biology to be heroic and the criminal "destined" by circumstances to commit crime – then our moral judgments seem to lose their foundation. Libertarians argue that free will is a necessary condition for moral responsibility. Without it, talking about what one "ought to do" would make little sense – ought implies *can*. If you ought to do X, it means you can do X or can refrain; if you can't (because everything is pre-decided), then moral obligation is moot.

However, for all its appeal, libertarian free will has to grapple with scientific scrutiny. Modern neuroscience, as mentioned, has found correlations between brain states and decisions, suggesting our brains follow physical processes. How can uncaused volition fit into this picture? Some libertarian-inclined thinkers have looked to quantum indeterminism as a potential opening. If at the fundamental level some events are not strictly determined, perhaps the brain could harness this indeterminism to allow the will some elbow room. The physicist Sir Arthur Eddington, for example, famously speculated that the uncertainty in atomic behaviour might enable free will – that maybe our mind could influence which way a quantum event goes, thereby influencing a neuron's firing and eventually our actions. This is a creative idea: it attempts to marry an immaterial will with a physical mechanism by positing that the will works subtly at the quantum scale. But as we've already considered, randomness by itself doesn't equate to meaningful choice. If your will "chooses" by triggering a random quantum outcome, that's not you exercising control – it's chance doing the work. And if your will can somehow reliably bias quantum events to align with your intentions, then we are back to asking how the will does that without a causal mechanism. The challenge remains: how to have a will that intervenes in the physical order without being either a deterministic part of it or a random outside influence? Libertarians are effectively asserting a special kind of causation that is neither deterministic nor random but originates with the conscious self.

To clarify libertarian free will, it might help to contrast two scenarios: Imagine a man named Alan who must decide whether to lie under pressure or tell the truth. In a deterministic view, all of Alan's background – his character shaped by genes and upbringing, the immediate situation, his brain's state – has already weighted the scales so heavily that, unbeknownst to him, the outcome is a foregone conclusion; perhaps given who Alan is at that moment, he will definitely lie (to save himself) and could not do otherwise. Alan might feel he chose freely, but the determinist says that's because he doesn't see the tight ropes of causality guiding him. Now imagine the libertarian view: Alan has those influences (character, circumstances) but they do not dictate his action;

at the crucial moment, he experiences a legitimate fork in the road. He *really can* go either way. All the influences might make lying very tempting, but Alan's will can still, by a creative act of intervention, choose the truthful path. If we rewound time, there's a genuine chance he might tell the truth in one replay and lie in another – because he, the agent, ultimately decides. In the libertarian picture, Alan is the originator of his action in a way nothing else in the universe is. This is a powerful image of human freedom: each person is a little centre of creation, capable of initiating new events that are not simply the outworking of what came before.

The problems that confront this view are acknowledged even by its advocates. First, it can conflict with our growing scientific understanding. As we map the brain and see how decisions correlate with neural processes, it becomes harder to point to a "gap" where a non-physical will could operate. The brain seems to be a closed system of neurons influencing neurons. If so, where does an immaterial choice-maker come in? Some libertarians bite the bullet and say free will might just be a fundamental exception to the usual rules – a unique feature of conscious minds that science has yet to understand. They argue that just because we can *model* or predict aspects of decision-making doesn't mean we've explained away consciousness or freedom. They might invoke the fact that consciousness itself (the experience of mind) is still not fully explained by science; if consciousness is something over and above neural firings, maybe free will is an aspect of consciousness that likewise transcends physical explanation. This is speculative, of course. It tends to rely on a dualist or non-materialist philosophy of mind: the idea that mind cannot be reduced to matter, and hence our choices might not be fully reducible to brain causality either.

Another issue is that if one claims some decisions have no cause (not even a hidden mental one), it verges on saying they happen by magic. Most libertarians don't want to say our choices are utterly random or uncaused; instead, they want *us* to be the cause. But describing that precisely is tricky. If someone asks, "Why did you choose A over B at that moment, given everything was the same?" the libertarian answer might be "Because I just chose – I am the reason." To a determinist, this sounds like evading the question; to a libertarian, it is the point: *I* am the ultimate cause of my act, not a chain of prior events. Whether this is coherent or just a leap of faith remains hotly debated.

Despite the challenges, libertarian free will has enduring appeal. Many people find it hard to imagine life without a belief in genuine choice. We often feel that "I am more than just a product of causes" – that in some important way, I define myself through my choices. Libertarians often argue that our whole sense of human dignity and creativity rests on being free in this deep way. If Shakespeare or Einstein were entirely determined by prior causes, can we really credit them for their genius? The libertarian would say yes, because they *chose* to exercise their creativity, their genius wasn't just inevitable. Furthermore, consider moral courage: someone might overcome immense internal and external pressure to do what is right. Under determinism, that outcome was already set by some prior configuration; but under a libertarian view, the person truly *rose above* their conditioning to do something new. That feels like a more meaningful victory of the will.

In summary, the case for libertarian free will hinges on the reality of our felt freedom, the requirements of morality, and often a conviction that humans have a special status in nature (be it through a soul or a non-material mind). It asserts that at least some human actions are self-determined: caused by the agent and not by prior events. This view keeps alive the idea that the future is not wholly written – that when faced with a decision, multiple futures genuinely exist until our will selects one. It's a hopeful and empowering vision of human life, granting us ultimate authorship of our choices. But it comes at the cost of explaining a mechanism that fits with everything we know about the world, which is why many philosophers find it problematic.

Having seen both the unyielding logic of hard determinism and the bold claim of libertarian free will, one might wonder if there is a middle ground. Must we either deny freedom entirely or accept a mysterious form of causation? This is where compatibilism enters the scene. Compatibilists agree with determinists that every event has a cause (no magic allowed), but they argue that this in no way eliminates free will – we simply need to understand freedom differently. Let's explore how compatibilism attempts to reinterpret free will in a deterministic framework.

Compatibilism – Reinterpreting Free Will

Compatibilism is the position that free will and determinism are not actually in conflict – that we can be fully caused in our actions and yet still be free in a meaningful sense. At first blush, this may sound paradoxical. How can my action be both determined *and* "up to me"? The compatibilist's strategy is to redefine "free will" not as an absence of causation, but as a certain kind of causation. Essentially, they say: *freedom is not about being uncaused; it's about being caused in the right way.* The key distinction they make is between internal causes and external constraints. If you do something because *you* want to do it, and nothing external is forcing or coercing you, then you acted of your own free will – even if your wanting and decision were themselves caused by prior events. What matters for freedom, in this view, is that the immediate cause of the action is your internal psychological state (your desires, intentions, character), rather than some external force overriding you or someone holding a gun to your head. As long as you are acting according to your own motivations, you are free, even though those motivations have a causal story behind them.

Compatibilism has a long pedigree. The ancient Stoics, as we noted earlier, held a form of it: they believed the universe was deterministic *and* that we are responsible for our actions, defining freedom as acting in accordance with one's nature and understanding. But a more explicit formulation came in the early modern period from philosophers like David Hume. Hume argued that the whole free will vs determinism "dilemma" was a misunderstanding – a result of using the term "free will" in a confusing way. He suggested that when we talk about a person having free will, we simply mean that the person can act according to their choices and desires *without external impediment*. For example, if I have the power to eat an apple when I decide to, and no one is tying my hands or forbidding me, then I exercise free will in eating the apple. The fact that my desire for the apple had causes (maybe I'm hungry, I like the taste, etc.) doesn't negate the freedom of the act, because I wanted to do it and I did it. Hume thought it would actually be disastrous for morality if actions were uncaused in the libertarian sense – because then they would be random, and how could we hold someone accountable for an action that popped out of nowhere? He famously said that *"Liberty"* (free will) *"by definition, consists in a power of acting or not acting, according to the determinations of the will."* And that is perfectly compatible with those determinations of the will having causes behind them.

To illustrate the compatibilist idea, consider a classic thought experiment: John is sitting in a room with an unlocked door. He decides he'd like to stay and continue reading, so he remains seated. In this case, John is staying in the room of his own free will – it's what he wants to do. Now imagine the same scenario except unbeknownst to John, someone quietly locked the door. John still *wants* to stay and reads on, never attempting to leave. Is he free? Intuitively, yes – because the fact that the door is locked never comes into play; John's action (staying) flowed from his own desire, not from the lock. He is doing exactly what he wants to do, hence he is acting freely. If John had suddenly wanted to leave and discovered the door was locked, *then* we'd say he was not free to leave. But so long as his own will aligns with what happens, the external constraint doesn't matter. This example, originally from philosopher John Locke, highlights that freedom is about acting on one's choices, not about the hypothetical ability to do otherwise if one had chosen otherwise. John could not have left the room (the door was locked), but since he didn't *want* to leave, that constraint didn't infringe on his freedom in that moment. Compatibilists generalize this: they argue that the true test of free will is *voluntariness* – are you doing what you *will* to do? – rather than some metaphysical power to have willed differently holding all else constant.

The German philosopher Arthur Schopenhauer put it succinctly: *"Man can do what he wills, but he cannot will what he wills."*[19] This pithy statement captures the compatibilist

---

[19] **Arthur Schopenhauer**, On the Freedom of the Will (1839), trans. E. F. J. Payne (Indianapolis: Bobbs-Merrill, 1960), 13. ("Man can do what he wills but

insight. You are free to act according to your will (no one is usually denying that – if you will to stand up, you normally can, unless something restrains you). But *what* you will – your desires and inclinations – is not something you simply choose out of thin air. Those are given to you by nature and nurture. In Schopenhauer's view, once your character and motives are in place, your actions flow necessarily from them. Yet we still call those actions "free" if they express *you*. So, you can do as you wish – that is your freedom – but you don't get to wish as you wish (since your wishes come from who you are, which is determined). This may sound like a limitation, but compatibilists argue it's all the freedom we need. After all, what is the alternative? If you could will what you will – if your desires had no cause – they'd come from nowhere in particular, which isn't obviously an improvement. In fact, compatibilists claim that randomness is no basis for freedom. If your choices were utterly uncaused, they would be arbitrary eruptions. How would that make you more free? If I couldn't trace my decision to any reason or propensity in me, it would feel accidental, even absurd. We normally *want* our choices to reflect our character, values, and reasoning – all of which have been shaped by causes (education, reflection, biology, etc.). Far from undermining freedom, those causes are what make our decisions *meaningful and ours*. They ensure that when I choose, say, to pursue a career in art, it's because I genuinely love art (perhaps due to childhood experiences, mentors, innate talent) – not because a random undetermined whim seized me.

Modern compatibilists like Daniel Dennett build on these points. Dennett argues that the kind of free will "worth

he cannot will what he wills." – Schopenhauer's famous statement of conditional free agency.)

wanting"[20] is not a magical ability to transcend causality, but rather the ability to act in the world in a way that is *sensitive to reasons, responsive to reflection, and representative of who we are.* In a fully deterministic but complex world, humans can develop into beings who deliberate, anticipate consequences, and adjust their behaviour – and this is what we actually value when we talk about free will. We don't actually want our decisions to be completely disconnected from our own motives and rational thought – quite opposite, we want them to *emanate* from a sound process of choosing. Compatibilism says yes, that's exactly what free will is: our capacity to make decisions in line with our motivations and reasoning, free from external coercion or compulsion.

Let's consider some everyday examples through a compatibilist lens:

- **Example 1: The Unforced Choice.** You're at a restaurant and you pick the pasta over the salad. Why? Because you felt like pasta – maybe you were in the mood for something hearty. That desire was influenced by many things (perhaps your body needs carbs, or you remember that this restaurant makes great pasta). You couldn't suddenly change what you're in the mood for by sheer will. Yet, when you order the pasta, you are exercising free will in the commonsense way: you made a choice that *you wanted* to make. No waiter or friend coerced you; you weren't suffering some compulsion that forced pasta down your throat against your true wish. The choice came from *inside you*. It was fully caused (by your

---

[20] **Daniel C. Dennett**, Elbow Room: The Varieties of Free Will Worth Wanting (Cambridge, MA: MIT Press, 1984), 15. (Dennett's discussion of what sort of freedom is actually desirable – the "free will worth having" – emphasizing practical autonomy over metaphysical indeterminism.)

hunger, taste, memory), but it was your will being carried out.

- **Example 2: The Compelled Action.** Now imagine a different scenario: Someone grabs your hand and forces you to sign a document you don't want to sign, or a neurological disorder causes your arm to move involuntarily. In those cases, you are *not* acting freely, because what happens is not aligned with your will. You didn't will to sign – you were forced; or you didn't will your arm to move – it moved on its own due to a malfunction. Here we see that freedom is not about the presence or absence of causation altogether (there were still causes in both scenarios – the assailant's force, the neuron misfire), but about the relation of the cause to the self. When the cause is *external or alien to the self*, freedom is lacking. When the cause is *your own desire or intention*, freedom is present, even though that desire has deeper causes.

Compatibilism thus shifts the question from "Are my actions caused or not?" (they are caused, says the compatibilist, because everything is) to "What kind of causes are influencing my actions?" If it's my own mind's reasons, fine – that's me acting. If it's someone else's threat or a coercive drug or a compulsion like an addiction that I utterly wish I didn't have – then my freedom is diminished. This resonates with how we assign responsibility in law and ethics: We normally hold people responsible if they acted intentionally (in line with their will). We excuse or mitigate if they acted under duress or coercion (external pressure) or due to some internal compulsion or insanity that made the act not truly reflect their will. Notice that in none of these judgments do we require that the person's mental state was

210

uncaused. We only care whether the action flowed from the person's stable intentions or from some interference. Freedom, in the practical sense, means the ability to do what you want without others stopping you or nature incapacitating you.

Another advantage compatibilists claim is that their view is scientifically respectable while preserving moral language. They accept the determinist thesis that the universe, including human behaviour, is lawful and causally connected. This aligns with the scientific enterprise of finding explanations for why people do what they do (in psychology, neuroscience, sociology, etc.). At the same time, compatibilists maintain our everyday talk of choices, responsibility, and freedom, but give those terms definitions that don't contradict causality. The notion of "could have done otherwise" is reinterpreted: it doesn't mean "could have done otherwise with exactly the same past" (as libertarians want), but rather "could have done otherwise *if I had wanted to* or if some relevant circumstance were different." That is a condition we all understand. For example: "I could have gone to law school instead of medical school" in a compatibilist sense means "If I had desired or decided to go to law school at that time, I would have done so." This statement can be true even if, in reality, my desires and decisions were such that I chose medical school. It simply says that there was no external obstacle preventing law school – it was within my capacity if my mind had leaned that way. Critics sometimes say this waters down the idea of freedom, but compatibilists respond that this is actually the only coherent way to talk about choices. It matches how we predict behaviour too: *if* someone's motives change, their action would change. That's a meaningful conditional statement, not a metaphysical one.

One might wonder: do compatibilists truly feel satisfied with this solution, or is it just a convenient redefinition? It depends. Some compatibilists, like Dennett, genuinely find this account of free will to capture all that matters about being free. They often highlight how being fully caused is actually what *gives* us power. For instance, if my decision to improve my life is caused by a firm resolve and understanding of my situation, that cause is precisely what makes the improvement happen. If my decision were uncaused, it would be erratic and unreliable. In this sense, determinism can be seen as empowering because it means effects reliably follow causes – including the effects of my *own choices*. When I decide to act, and because the world is orderly, my action will have the intended effect (assuming I predicted things correctly). If the world were not deterministic at all, outcomes would be chaotic, and my will's efficacy would actually be undermined.

However, not everyone is convinced by compatibilism. Libertarian free will advocates often accuse compatibilists of simply redefining away the problem. They say, "Sure, you can define free will as doing what you want, but that's not what we *really* mean by free will." The libertarian insists that real freedom means after everything up to the moment of choice, you still had multiple possible ways the future could go – and that compatibilism avoids that issue. Compatibilists, in turn, argue that the libertarian notion of freedom is either incoherent or unnecessary. It's a debate over intuition versus conceptual clarity: Libertarians trust the deep intuition of "I could have done otherwise," whereas compatibilists claim that intuition is misleading and can be explained away by their account (for example, you could have done otherwise if your desires were different, and you imagine they could have been).

Despite these disagreements, compatibilism remains a dominant view among philosophers because it allows one to have a consistent scientific outlook (no spooky exceptions to causality) while still preserving the language of choice and moral responsibility that guide human life. Historically, Thomas Hobbes, Baruch Spinoza, David Hume, and John Stuart Mill were all essentially compatibilists, though each had a slightly different take. In the 19th century, Schopenhauer we quoted gave a rather dark compatibilism (he believed our character is fated but as long as we act out our inner motives, we are "free" in a trivial sense). In the 20th and 21st centuries, many philosophers of mind and science – Dennett being a prime example – argue that freedom must be understood in terms of complex causation, not its absence.

To summarize compatibilism: Free will is reframed as the freedom to act according to one's determined will, without impediment. We are "free" when our actions flow from our own personality, values, and deliberations. We are "unfree" when something prevents our will from being effective (like coercion or incapacity) or when our action is forced by something that doesn't align with our genuine desires (like an addiction we wish we could shake). This notion tries to capture what is practically important about freedom: autonomy, self-governance, the ability to do what we decide. It says we don't need some mysterious contra-causal power to have morality or responsibility – we just need the capacity to reflect, to respond to reasons, and to have our actions come from who we are. All of those things can exist in a deterministic universe.

By navigating between the extremes, compatibilism might seem to offer a resolution to the free will dilemma. But not everyone finds it emotionally satisfying – some feel it still

213

doesn't give us enough agency, while others think it's perfectly sensible and that the debate is largely semantic. At this juncture, it's valuable to consider a perspective from a philosopher who was highly analytical yet remained cautious of oversimplifying such profound questions: Bertrand Russell. Russell's approach to free will and determinism exemplifies a kind of scepticism of absolutes. He recognized merits in the determinist viewpoint but also warned against dogmatic certainty on either side. Let's examine how Russell thought about this issue and why he felt people oscillate between free will and determinism based on emotion as much as logic.

Russell's Perspective – Scepticism of Absolutes

Bertrand Russell, the prominent 20th-century philosopher and logician, approached the free will problem with a characteristic blend of scientific rationality and philosophical scepticism. Russell was deeply familiar with the arguments of both sides, and he was also attuned to the psychological factors influencing people's beliefs about free will. Rather than declaring unequivocally for determinism or for free will, Russell took a nuanced stance: he was sceptical that either strict determinism or a metaphysical free will could be *proven* as an absolute truth. In practice, he leaned towards the deterministic outlook because of science's success, but he also acknowledged the limits of our knowledge and the powerful human feelings involved.

One key aspect of Russell's perspective is the distinction between science as a methodology and determinism as a universal dogma. Russell noted that science, by necessity, operates on the assumption of causality. When scientists investigate any phenomenon, they look for causes and effects

214

– they assume there are explanations governed by laws. This methodological determinism is tremendously fruitful: it has yielded technologies, medical advances, and explanatory power precisely because assuming things have causes leads us to find them. Russell had no quarrel with this; in fact, he was a great proponent of scientific thinking. However, he cautioned against turning this methodological principle into a metaphysical certainty that *"all events without exception are caused and could not be otherwise."*[21] Why the caution? Because, as he observed, such a claim goes beyond what we can empirically demonstrate. Even if every event we've examined so far has causes, we cannot conclusively prove that *every possible* event in the universe must have a cause. That is a broad extrapolation, one that might hold true, but isn't itself empirically verifiable. In Russell's view, saying "every action you take was predetermined since the beginning of time" is more a philosophical extrapolation than a scientific fact – it could be true, but we should not pretend we know it with absolute certainty. After all, in the early 20th century, physics itself introduced indeterminacy (as we discussed with quantum mechanics). Russell lived through that revolution and saw how even fundamental concepts like strict causality were being re-examined. He pointed out that the venerable "law of causation" was not a precise principle in modern physics, but rather a useful heuristic that might not apply straightforwardly at the quantum level. The lesson Russell drew was: *don't be too sure that you've figured out the metaphysical skeleton of reality.* We must be open to surprises.

---

[21] **Bertrand Russell**, "On the Notion of Cause," Proceedings of the Aristotelian Society 13 (1913): 1–26, at 12–13. (Russell observes that the "law of causation, … like much that passes for philosophy, is a relic of a bygone age," cautioning that the assumption that all events are predetermined is not empirically justified.)

At the same time, Russell was critical of the traditional notion of an uncaused will. Early in his intellectual life, he actually abandoned belief in free will when he studied the implications of physics and physiology. He quipped that the first "dogma" he discarded as a young thinker was the idea of free will, because as he understood the material world, it seemed clear that mental events must arise from physical ones, not magically diverge from them. He saw the classical free will idea as rooted in a false dichotomy: either determinism or some kind of *soulful miracle*. Russell had little patience for accepting miracles without evidence. If someone claims human decisions have no causes, that's an extraordinary claim needing proof – and in Russell's assessment, no such proof exists. On the contrary, everything we've learned about psychology, biology, and social influences indicates that our choices have explainable sources. For Russell, it would be special pleading to say "everything in nature has causes except human decisions." Such a special exception smacks of human arrogance, a remnant (as he might say) of a religious or mystical outlook that put humans above nature. Russell was a staunch naturalist: humans are part of nature, not apart from it.

Yet – and this is crucial – Russell did not simply champion hard determinism either. He was too aware of the complexities and too resistant to oversimplification. He recognized that even if one suspects determinism is true, it's difficult to *prove* it in the ultimate sense. It might turn out, for instance, that determinism is only effectively true in a macro sense, but at some level of reality (maybe in the depths of consciousness or quantum processes) there is some element of spontaneity. Russell was not endorsing that scenario, but as a good sceptic he wouldn't rule it out categorically just because we feel it *must* be one way. In fact, he sometimes

216

noted that concepts like "cause" themselves can be tricky and might not be fundamental to how the universe works (he once suggested that the notion of causality is a bit of a relic and that modern physics deals more in mathematical relations than in simple cause-effect terms). This indicates his unwillingness to nail down an absolute deterministic philosophy without reservation.

Russell also keenly observed the emotional underpinnings of the free will debate. He pointed out an interesting psychological pattern: *When considering ourselves, we strongly feel we have free will; when considering others or the world at large, we easily accept determinism.* For example, you might insist that you are free and responsible for your personal choices; but when you look at a criminal in the news, you might readily blame their upbringing or brain chemistry – essentially a deterministic explanation. Or you trust in physical causation when you operate in the world (we expect our car to start due to the mechanics, not some spontaneous whim of the engine gremlins), but we carve out our inner life as somehow special. Russell thought this was more about how we want to see things than about logical consistency. There's a kind of ego at play: it's comforting to view oneself as an unconstrained free agent, yet when dealing with others or making sense of events, we prefer the predictability and explanatory power of determinism. People often shift perspectives without noticing the inconsistency. Russell gently highlighted this hypocrisy: many who *profess* absolute free will still behave as if causes matter. They will try to educate their children morally (implying the cause-and-effect that good guidance yields good behaviour), or they will avoid certain temptations for fear of how those influences might lead them astray. In doing so, they acknowledge determinism in practice – they act as if circumstances shape outcomes – even if in theory they deny it.

Conversely, a scientific determinist in theory might still feel remorse or pride as though they had free choice; emotionally they can't escape the internal sense of freedom. Russell didn't necessarily condemn people for this toggle; he saw it as a result of how our minds work. But he believed philosophy's job was to sort out the logical from the psychological, and he strove to do so by not giving in entirely to either the comforting feeling of free will or the austere view of total determinism without reflection on its implications.

Another aspect of Russell's stance is an appreciation for uncertainty and humility in face of such questions. He would likely say: based on all available evidence, it appears that human actions have causes (in brains, environment, etc.), so the rational position is to operate under that assumption. However, if someone asserts "I am sure that *nothing* is uncaused, and free will is impossible," Russell would ask: How can you be *sure*? Have we empirically checked every corner of reality or the mind? Of course not. On the flip side, if someone asserts "I am sure that we have a special free will that defies causality," Russell would again ask: On what evidence? Isn't it more that we *feel* free and *wish* for moral responsibility to hold, rather than any proof that something non-physical overrides physical laws? In essence, Russell would advise us to be careful of convictions that outstrip the evidence.

Russell's scepticism doesn't mean he sat on the fence without any view. It might be fair to call him a determinist-leaning agnostic on free will. He clearly believed that assuming determinism is the only way science can progress –

218

for to do science we must expect order and causation. And he largely talked as though human behaviour is caused (he was influenced by thinkers like Freud and by the general milieu of science which by his time had explained so much of human behaviour in natural terms). But he refrained from saying the matter was metaphysically settled once and for all. In his writings, he often dismantled the idea of a spirit that can violate natural laws, yet he also dismantled overly confident philosophical assertions that go beyond what is observed. This balanced approach allowed him to navigate the debate without, as he saw it, sliding into unproductive metaphysics or wishful thinking.

To capture Russell's view in a relatable way: he might say free will is a useful concept for certain contexts, and determinism is a useful concept for others, but neither is an absolute "metaphysical truth" we can claim to know for certain. Practically, we treat each other as responsible agents – and that's fine, it works for ethics and society. Practically, we investigate the world including ourselves as causal systems – and that's fine, it works for knowledge and control. The problems only arise when we take the practical stances and turn them into dogmas: "I must be entirely and mysteriously free!" or "Everything must be fated with no exceptions at all!" Russell preferred a kind of pragmatic balance: use the determinist assumption to guide scientific inquiry, but remain aware that our understanding of causation is itself evolving; uphold personal freedom and responsibility in daily life, but recognize that this is, in part, a way of talking about complex causality and in part a moral construct. He often emphasized that people's passionate adherence to free will comes largely from their desire to see themselves as self-made and deserving of praise or blame, and from a fear that without free will, life would lose meaning or justice. A philosopher, Russell believed, should acknowledge these human concerns but not be governed solely by them.

In sum, Russell's perspective invites us to step back and view the free will debate itself with a bit of detachment. He encourages us to ask: Why are we so invested in one outcome or the other? Are we following the evidence or our emotions? He doesn't hand us a simple answer like "free will exists" or "determinism is true." Instead, he suggests *epistemic modesty* – an understanding that, given what we know, determinism is the framework that underlies scientific analysis (and we can't do without it), but that doesn't grant us license to claim we've solved every mystery of will and consciousness. At the same time, he dismantles the comfort of assuming we have a magical freedom, pointing out that such an assumption often crumbles in the face of how we actually explain things.

Russell's balanced scepticism provides a bridge between the theoretical debate and the practical implications we care about. And it's to those implications that we now turn. After all, this discussion is not just an abstract puzzle; what we think about free will versus determinism can profoundly affect how we view moral responsibility, justice, how we do science, even how we find meaning in our lives. Let's explore some real-world consequences of this philosophical debate and see how different stances might change our approach to law, ethics, emerging technologies like AI, and our personal sense of agency.

Real-World Implications of the Free Will Debate

The clash between "everything is determined" and "we have genuine choice" is not merely theoretical – it spills over into many areas of human life. How we resolve (or don't resolve) the free will debate can influence our legal systems, our moral practices, our interpretation of scientific findings, and even how we cope with life's ups and downs. In this section, we'll examine several key domains impacted by this age-old debate: legal responsibility, ethical accountability, the challenges posed by AI and neuroscience, and our sense of purpose and agency. As we do, it will become evident that regardless of where one stands philosophically, we often must make practical decisions and policies that assume something about human freedom. We'll see that determinism and free will, as concepts, lead to different emphases but also that a compatibilist approach can offer a pragmatic path forward in many cases.

Legal Responsibility: Crime and Punishment in a Determined World

One of the most immediate concerns people raise about determinism is what it means for legal responsibility. Our justice systems are largely predicated on the notion that individuals have free will to choose their actions, and thus can be held responsible (punished or rewarded) for them. If, however, every criminal act was the inevitable product of genetics and environment – if the thief or the violent offender literally *could not have done otherwise* given their circumstances – then the moral justification for punishment seems to waver. After all, we don't morally blame a lion for killing a gazelle or a storm for flooding a town; we see those events as blameless consequences of nature. Should we see a human who commits a crime in the same light – as a sort of biological/weather event shaped by causes, not an evil "freely choosing" agent?

Hard determinists often argue that, indeed, retributive punishment (punishing someone because they "deserve it" for freely choosing wrong) loses its justification if determinism is true. If the criminal had no true choice, punishing in the traditional sense – inflicting suffering as payback – seems as irrational as punishing a clock for ticking midnight. However, this doesn't mean a deterministic view would let criminals roam free. Instead, the focus would shift to a more utilitarian or rehabilitative approach. Even if a murderer wasn't "free" in an absolute sense, we still have to protect society and discourage future crimes. So a determinist might say: we incarcerate or rehabilitate offenders not because they metaphysically *deserve* punishment, but because these measures are causal interventions that lead to safer society or reform of the individual. In a fully deterministic understanding, a prison sentence is not "moral retribution" but rather a causal event intended to prevent further harmful effects (by deterring others, isolating the individual, or reforming their behaviour through therapy). Some thinkers call this the "quarantine" model: just as we would quarantine a person with a dangerous infectious disease (without blaming them for catching it), we might quarantine a dangerous criminal – not out of hatred or moral condemnation, but out of practical necessity and compassion for potential victims.

On the other hand, those who defend free will (or compatibilist free will) argue that our legal practices can still be perfectly justified. If we adopt the compatibilist stance that a person is free *when their action comes from their own intentions*, then criminals usually do act on their intentions –

they decided to break the law, even if reasons behind that decision can be analysed. Thus they are the authors of their acts and can be held responsible. Compatibilism, in fact, dovetails well with how the law tends to operate: it looks at issues like mens rea (state of mind) – did the person intend to do the crime? If yes (and they weren't coerced or insane), they are held accountable. If someone was coerced (say, at gunpoint) or lacked understanding (insanity or severe mental defect), the law either excuses them or lessens their culpability. Notice how this mirrors the idea that freedom is taken away by external coercion or impaired internal faculties, but not by the mere existence of causes. So, in practice, our courts don't ask "Was this act uncaused?" (they assume it wasn't uncaused); they ask "Did the defendant act on their own volition and understand what they were doing?" That is essentially a compatibilist criterion for responsibility. Therefore, many argue that even if determinism is true, it changes little in terms of how we assign legal responsibility – we can continue to hold people accountable in the compatibilist sense, ensuring that factors like coercion or mental illness are accounted for (which we already do).

However, accepting determinism deeply (especially the hard determinist view) might shift our attitudes within the legal system. For example, there might be greater emphasis on rehabilitation over pure punishment. If a person is not fundamentally an "evil chooser" but rather a product of unfortunate causes (trauma, social deprivation, perhaps a brain tumour affecting impulse control), we might feel more inclined to try to fix those causes for the future rather than simply inflict pain as punishment. Indeed, we see some movement in this direction: modern psychology and law recognize that many criminals have histories of abuse or neurological issues. In some jurisdictions, problem-solving courts (like drug courts or mental health courts) explicitly focus on treating underlying issues rather than just punishing the offense. This is in line with a deterministic understanding that by addressing the cause (addiction, illness), we can prevent the effect (crime) more humanely and effectively.

The free will debate also enters into specific legal defences. The insanity defence, for instance, is essentially saying the defendant did not have a normal capacity to choose or understand their action, so they shouldn't be held accountable as if they did. Some have wondered if, as neuroscience advances, more defences will arise like "my brain made me do it." There have been real cases: a famous example is that of a man who developed paedophilic urges due to a brain tumour; once the tumour was removed, the urges ceased. In such a case, it's hard not to see the crime as a direct result of a physical cause beyond the person's control – akin to a kind of temporary insanity. As we learn more about brain circuitry, we might identify other conditions where impulse control is severely compromised by physical factors (tumours, lesions, extreme hormonal imbalances). Determinism forces us to ask: at what point does an internal cause (like a brain state) absolve someone of responsibility? If we say "only when it's a recognized disorder," we maintain a line that upholds most responsibility. But a strict determinist could argue that even a "normal" criminal brain is just as caused as a disordered one – the difference is only quantitative, not qualitative. This suggests a potential evolution in law if society ever embraced hard determinism widely: we might pivot fully to a system aimed at *management and prevention* of harmful behaviour, rather than moralizing about it.

For now, though, our legal systems operate on a compatibilist-like rationale: People generally have the

224

capacity to understand rules and make choices, and when they wilfully break the law, they are answerable for it. Determinism hasn't stopped us from sentencing thieves and murderers, and likely it won't, because as a society we need some mechanism to regulate behaviour. But an awareness of the causes behind crime can make our justice more nuanced, focusing on correction and context. You can believe "the criminal couldn't ultimately help becoming who he is" and still believe it's necessary and right to have him off the streets and undergoing interventions – just as one might regret that a rabid dog became dangerous through no fault of its own, yet still must restrain it for safety.

Ethics and Moral Accountability: Praising, Blaming, and Understanding

Parallel to legal responsibility is the question of moral responsibility in everyday life. We constantly make ethical judgments of ourselves and others. We feel guilt when we think we've freely done wrong; we feel pride when we think we've overcome temptation by choice; we blame others when we believe they had the ability to do good but chose bad, and we admire those who choose the right path. How are these feelings and practices affected if one leans deterministic or not?

If someone sincerely adopts the hard determinist view that no one ever could do otherwise, they might cultivate a kind of radical compassion or fatalism (or both). On one hand, they might become more forgiving of others (and themselves), recognizing that "to understand all is to forgive all." If you truly see that a person's actions were the outcome of a chain of causes – maybe their upbringing, their suffering, their genes – then the attitude of harsh blame could soften.

Instead of thinking, "I would have chosen differently if I were them," you realize, "If I truly were them – same life and brain – I'd do the same." This can encourage empathy. For example, consider someone who is rude or aggressive towards you. A free-will defender might say, "They shouldn't have chosen to act like that; they're a jerk." A determinist might reflect, "I wonder what causes in their life made them this way – maybe they're under stress or were never taught kindness." This deterministic empathy doesn't excuse bad behaviour in the sense of saying it's okay, but it explains it and perhaps channels our response toward helping or avoiding future issues rather than pure anger. Some proponents of determinism even argue that it could lead to a kinder society: instead of moral outrage that seeks retribution, we adopt a problem-solving mindset that tries to heal the sources of bad behaviour.

On the other hand, a fatalistic attitude can lurk if determinism is misunderstood. Fatalism is the idea that "whatever happens is destined and inevitable, so why bother trying?" It's important to note that determinism is not the same as fatalism – in determinism, outcomes are fixed *because of preceding causes, including our efforts.* In fatalism, outcomes happen regardless of what we do. A person who conflates the two might think, "Well, if everything's predetermined, there's no point in making moral effort or trying to change myself – the chips will fall where they may." This is a misinterpretation, but it's an alluring trap. In reality, even if your efforts are determined by prior factors, it's still true that *if* you make an effort, you can achieve changes, and *if* you don't, you won't – your decisions still matter in the causal chain. So a wise determinist would say: you're determined, yes, but one of the causes in your life can be your own recognition of determinism and the deliberate changes you

226

decide to implement. For example, you might think "I'm predisposed to laziness because of my past, but knowing that, I can set up strict routines to cause myself to be productive." That "knowing and setting routines" is itself part of the causal fabric.

Moral education and improvement, from a compatibilist or determinist lens, simply become about understanding and influencing causes. If someone wants to become more virtuous, they might put themselves in environments that promote virtue (cause), avoid temptations (cause), practice habits (cause) – all deterministic interventions to shape their character. They are freely doing this in the sense that it's their own will enacting it, but they are also acknowledging that willpower alone isn't a mysterious force – it's supported by concrete strategies.

For those who hold a libertarian free will view, moral responsibility retains a more absolute flavour. They can say, "No matter what your past, at the moment of choice you could have done the right thing, so you fully deserve blame if you did wrong." This can underpin a strong sense of justice ("evil really is chosen") but can also lead to less compassion ("there's no excuse, you had free will!"). Many religious moral frameworks, for instance, hinge on the idea that each person has a God-given free will, so on Judgment Day one truly *deserves* their reward or punishment. For a strict libertarian, to suggest otherwise (that maybe severe circumstances mitigate guilt) might sound like letting people off the hook. However, even most libertarians acknowledge mitigating circumstances – they just believe that ultimately some element of freedom always remains unless one is literally not in control of oneself.

Interestingly, many philosophers and psychologists note that in practice our moral sentiments might not change drastically even if we adopt a certain theory. For example, you might intellectually endorse determinism but still *feel* anger when someone harms you, or pride when you do something good. Those feelings are deeply ingrained. Some hard determinists try to temper their reactive emotions with their beliefs – like actively reminding themselves "don't be too mad, they couldn't help it." Others may find that too much to ask; they proceed compatibilistically: "I know technically causes made them do it, but I'll treat them as responsible anyway because that's how human interactions work." There's even an argument (from philosopher P.F. Strawson) that our "reactive attitudes" – feelings like resentment, gratitude, love, moral indignation – are part of the human condition and won't be given up simply because of a theory. We are practically wired to respond to others as if they are responsible agents, and that might be okay. Compatibilists often cite this: we can acknowledge determinism in theory, but in practice continue to interact with each other with praise and blame to guide behaviour, because those interactions themselves are among the causes that shape future actions. For instance, praising a child for a good deed encourages them (a cause for them to do more good), and scolding them for a bad deed corrects them (another cause). So even if you think the bad deed was determined by their temperament and prior lack of knowledge, your response can be a determinant for better outcomes later. In that sense, moral responsibility practices (reward, punishment, praise, blame) remain meaningful because they influence people – they are part of the causal matrix that makes us who we are.

Artificial Intelligence and Neuroscience: Mechanistic Minds and the Free Will Question

Advancements in neuroscience and artificial intelligence (AI) in recent decades have added new layers to the free will debate. They prompt us to ask: if a machine can perform "decisions" or if a brain's decisions can be predicted or manipulated, what does that say about our cherished freedom?

Neuroscience, as mentioned earlier, has delivered some eye-opening findings. Beyond the Libet experiment (where unconscious brain activity precedes conscious intention), researchers have used brain scanners (like fMRI) to predict a person's choice before they themselves are aware of making it[22]. In some experiments, participants choose between two options (pressing a left or right button, for example), and scientists, by looking at their brain activity patterns, can predict with significant accuracy which they will choose a few seconds before the person consciously "decides." This suggests that what we experience as a conscious decision might actually be the culmination of subconscious neural processes that have already been set in motion. To some, this strikes a blow to the idea of a freely willing conscious self. It's as if our brain "decides" and then informs "us" of that decision, allowing us the feeling of having decided. While there's ongoing debate about how to interpret these experiments (critics note that these are often trivial choices and that people might still have a "veto" power in the last moment), they certainly support the notion that the brain is

---

[22] **Benjamin Libet, et al.**, "Unconscious Cerebral Initiative and the Role of Conscious Will in Voluntary Action," Behavioural and Brain Sciences 8, no. 4 (1985): 529–566. (Libet's experiments demonstrated measurable brain activity (Readiness Potential) occurring moments before subjects were aware of their decision to act, suggesting that the brain "decides" before the mind knows – a key empirical challenge to classical free will.)

a mechanism following physical laws, with consciousness perhaps riding on top like a passenger more than a driver.

Neuroscience also shows how manipulations of the brain can alter decisions and personality. Drugs can dramatically change behaviour and impulse control (think of someone on alcohol doing things they'd never do sober). Electrical stimulation or lesions in certain brain areas can compel or inhibit certain actions. For example, stimulating a motor cortex might make a patient move their arm, and interestingly, sometimes the patient will confabulate a reason: "Oh, I think I was trying to stretch." The brain, when action happens, often generates a narrative of why "I" did it, even if in that case the movement was externally caused. This raises the unsettling possibility that even in normal life, we might be routinely confabulating reasons for actions that were triggered by internal processes we don't see. It challenges the image of a unitary "I" in full control, and replaces it with a picture of many neural sub-systems interacting, with our conscious self taking partial credit.

Artificial intelligence brings another thought experiment to life: if we can create a machine that mimics human decision-making, does it have free will, or does it highlight our own lack of it? Today's AI systems (like advanced learning algorithms, or the AI playing strategic games, or driving cars) operate by processing inputs and producing outputs according to complex algorithms and learned patterns. They can adapt to new information, appear to "decide" (should the car turn left to avoid a pedestrian or right?), and even "learn" from mistakes. But few would argue an AI has metaphysical free will – we see it as a very sophisticated deterministic (or stochastic) system. Now, if the human brain ultimately is an organ that processes inputs (sensory data, memory) and produces outputs (actions,

230

speech) according to complex electrochemical algorithms honed by evolution and learning, one could say we are basically biological AI. This analogy can reinforce a deterministic view: we are machines, albeit organic ones of astonishing complexity. If an AI can simulate aspects of human thinking, it demystifies those aspects; it suggests that what we consider "choosing" could be, at base, algorithmic. This doesn't diminish the wonder of human consciousness (we still find AI consciousness-free, at least for now), but it does remind us that intelligence and decision processes can be fully explained in naturalistic terms.

That said, AI also pushes us to define free will carefully. If one day we develop a truly conscious AI (a being that has self-awareness and feels it is making choices), we will face the same philosophical questions from the other side: we might know exactly how we built this AI, know its code and training data (causes), yet if it insists on its own freedom, will we treat it as an agent? Compatibilism might again be our refuge: we could say if the AI's actions are the result of its own internal states (however programmed), and not directly remote-controlled by something else, maybe it has a kind of free will (and perhaps rights? That's a whole other debate). If we remain strict determinists, we'd say no, it's just following programming. But then the AI (imagine it's advanced enough to argue philosophy) might retort, "How is that different from you following your genetics and upbringing programming?" AI forces a mirror on us.

Furthermore, AI and machine learning are providing new insights into decision-making strategies – sometimes revealing that even high-level decisions can be broken down into sub-decision processes. For instance, an AI that masters chess or Go does so by evaluating countless possibilities and selecting moves that maximize some expected value (victory probability). One could argue a human chess grandmaster's brain is doing something analogous, though more intuitively. If everything we do can be in principle mimicked by algorithmic exploration (with enough computing power), it suggests our own "will" is bounded by algorithmic processes.

On the flip side, some hold out that human consciousness includes something non-algorithmic (this is speculative – like Roger Penrose's idea that consciousness might harness non-computable quantum processes). If that were true, perhaps that's where an unpredictable element could come in. But again, unpredictable isn't the same as wilful.

In summary, neuroscience tends to bolster a view of humans as biological robots (though immensely complex and capable of self-reflection), and AI shows that many tasks once thought to require a mind can be done by a machine. Together they challenge the specialness of human decision-making. Every new discovery – a gene for impulsivity, a brain network for moral reasoning, a bias in our cognitive processing – adds another link in the chain of explanation for why we choose as we do. The more complete that chain, the less room there seems to insert a free-floating "soul choice." That said, even scientists who personally believe free will is illusory often agree that society should still treat people *as if* they are responsible agents. There is even research suggesting that if people strongly disbelieve in free will, they might behave less responsibly (for example, in experiments, people who read texts undermining free will showed a higher propensity to cheat or behave aggressively shortly after). This indicates that, psychologically, the belief in free will has beneficial effects on motivation and self-control. It's almost as if evolution wired us to have the illusion of free will because it helps us function. So ironically, even if neuroscience is telling us "you're determined," neuroscience also tells us "it might be good for you to feel free." As a result, some thinkers propose a sort of dual approach: in the lab or when analysing, acknowledge determinism; in personal life, cultivate a subjective sense of freedom and responsibility because it leads to better outcomes. (This again is quite compatibilist at heart.)

Human Meaning and Purpose: Agency, Regret, and the Search for Significance

Finally, we come to the deeply personal dimension: what does the free will debate mean for how we view our lives, our choices, our sense of meaning? This philosophical question can have existential consequences. If one embraces determinism, does life become devoid of purpose, or can purpose be redefined? If one clings to free will, is it out of an emotional need – and is that a bad thing?

One common worry is that if free will is an illusion, then our sense of being agents – the authors of our lives – is false, and that might lead to a kind of nihilism or resignation. People might say, "If everything I do is preordained by circumstances, why should I strive or hope? The future will be what it will be." However, it's crucial to note that *determinism does not equate to predictability by us*. Even if your life is determined, you don't *know* your future, and neither does anyone else fully. You still have to make choices in the sense of deliberating on what to do – that deliberation is itself part of the cause-effect web that leads to outcomes. Think of life as a complex novel that's already written but you are reading it page by page, unaware of what comes next. You still experience suspense, make decisions (which are part of the story), and care about what happens. From the inside, things feel open. In fact, we cannot live our day-to-day lives except by making decisions and acting on reasons, no matter what we philosophically believe. Even the determinist, when hungry, thinks "What do I want to eat?" and goes through a choice process. It would be a mistake to throw up one's hands and say "I won't decide, determinism will make it happen." You *will* decide – or your lack of deliberation is itself a decision with consequences (maybe you'll just starve indecisively, which itself follows cause/effect but not a desirable outcome).

What determinism can change is the lens through which you interpret your life. Regret, for example, might be tempered. If you look back on a mistake, under a free-will mindset you might torture yourself: "I *should have* chosen differently, I was free and I failed." Under a deterministic mindset, you might say, "Given who I was at that time, I couldn't have done differently – but I can learn from this experience now." Some find this comforting: it can help release crippling guilt. You realize you were a product of many factors, and maybe you did the best you could at that moment, or at least the only thing you could given your state. This doesn't mean you won't apologize or make amends; you likely will want to, because now you have grown and that growth (a new cause) pushes you to rectify things. But it removes the idea of magical self-blame. Similarly, regret over missed opportunities might lessen: "It simply wasn't in the cards for me to take that path – lamenting it endlessly won't help, but what have I learned from it for the future?"

A deterministic perspective can also influence how we assign life's meaning. If one believes in a grand cosmic free will, they might think meaning comes from being the *uncaused causer* of something great – a sort of prime mover in one's own story. If one steps away from that, meaning might instead be found in understanding one's place in the bigger

234

causal tapestry. Some find awe in thinking "I am the endpoint (so far) of a long chain of events going back to the start of the universe. My actions now will ripple into the future beyond me." In this view, meaning comes from being part of something larger – the unfolding of the universe, or the human story. You might not have chosen your role initially, but you can *embrace* the role you find yourself in and play it with intention. Think of an actor who didn't write the play but can still perform it with passion and creativity. Even if a deterministic fate put you at a certain juncture, you still experience life as making choices and those choices matter for others. For many, that's enough for meaning: knowing that what I do (whatever its ultimate cause) will have effects, I want those effects to be positive.

Another source of meaning can be relationships and love. If we see others as determined creatures like ourselves, we might actually become more compassionate and connected (as mentioned in moral discussion). Rather than isolating individuals as free moral islands, determinism can highlight how interdependent we are: everyone is shaped by everyone else. In a way, this can increase a sense of unity – we're all in the causality soup together, influencing and being influenced. One could derive meaning from being a good influence in the chain: for example, maybe I was inevitably caused to become a teacher, but knowing that, I find purpose in being the best teacher I can, so that I become a positive cause in my students' lives, shaping their trajectories.

Of course, some fear determinism undermines personal achievement. If I write a great novel, but it was just determined by my genes and environment, do I get any credit? I'd answer (from a compatibilist or even a pragmatic determinist view): Yes, you do, because *you* are the unique confluence of genes and experiences that produced that novel – no one else was, and thus no one else wrote it. We can still meaningfully say "I did that," it's just that "I" is understood as the whole causal being, not a causa sui (self-caused cause). Actually, some find that determinism can be humbling in a healthy way: you recognize the role of luck and help in your achievements (genes, supportive parents, mentors, cultural heritage). That can make you more grateful and less arrogant. But you can still take *pride* in achieving something difficult – because pride can be about the effort you put in and the outcome realized through you. Even if effort is caused by internal drive, that drive is your character. Many compatibilists argue that virtues like courage or perseverance remain meaningful under determinism: a person is courageous if they reliably act bravely despite fear – it doesn't matter that their brain was determined to be courageous; in fact, that's what it *means* to be courageous (to have a character that responds in that good way).

For those who strongly endorse free will, meaning often comes from the idea that they are the captain of their soul. They might worry that without that captaincy, life is pointless. But consider: do we admire a sailor less if we learn that the wind and currents heavily influenced his voyage? Or do we still credit how he navigated those influences? Human life can be seen similarly: even if we don't control all factors, we navigate through them. And that navigation – how we respond to challenges, how we grow – can be a source of pride and purpose.

In fact, one might argue a subtle point: even under determinism, we *do* have a sort of freedom – we often can do what we *desire* to do. So much of meaning is tied to fulfilling desires and goals. If you manage to become what you wanted to become, you feel your life is meaningful. Determinism doesn't prevent that; it just explains why you had those desires to begin with and how you managed to succeed. But the satisfaction of achievement, love, creativity – those feelings are real and not diminished by knowing they have causes.

One could also find meaning in simply understanding the truth of our condition. Some philosophical individuals feel a sort of meaning or honour in *seeing clearly* how the world works. For them, accepting determinism and shedding comforting illusions is a courageous confrontation with reality, which is meaningful in itself (a kind of authenticity). Jean-Paul Sartre, an existentialist, believed in radical free will, but existentialists in general emphasize creating meaning in a world that doesn't come with pre-assigned meaning. Interestingly, if one truly abandons the idea of any cosmic guidance (which determinism might reinforce by removing any ultimate "purpose" or divine plan), one might step into an existentialist stance of self-defined meaning. Even if you're determined, you still have to define what you consider worthwhile. That act of definition and commitment to values can be empowering (even if, yes, your values have causes too).

Lastly, let's touch on agency. Agency is the feeling that I can make things happen, that I am an active participant in life. Determinism does not remove agency as an experience – you still make choices and see results. Arguably, agency is an emergent property: a chess-playing computer can have "agency" in the context of chess even though it's programmed, because it takes actions towards goals. Humans similarly have agency as an emergent story: we perceive ourselves setting goals and pursuing them. That narrative isn't negated by knowing the lower-level details. Think of a waterfall: every molecule of water follows physics, but the waterfall as a whole has a shape and flow we appreciate on a higher level. Similarly, we can appreciate human lives on the level of intentions and projects, even if underneath it's all cause and effect.

In conclusion, the free will debate does not yield easy answers to what one *should* believe. Some find comfort in free will, others find comfort in determinism, and many find some form of compatibilism as a workable middle ground that preserves moral and personal significance while acknowledging natural law. What's clear is that our stance on this issue can influence our attitudes: more blame or more understanding, more focus on retribution or on on rehabilitation, a sense of being special or a sense of being connected. There isn't a one-size-fits-all emotional resolution. But humanity has lived with these questions for millennia and still found meaning in love, art, work, discovery, and improvement.

As Bertrand Russell might remind us, we should approach these grand questions with both rational analysis and a recognition of our emotional needs. Perhaps we will never fully *solve* the free will problem to everyone's satisfaction – it may be that it's a feature of how we think about ourselves that will always invite debate. But exploring it as we have can deepen our understanding of what it means to be human: a creature of nature that contemplates itself, a link in the chain of causes that wonders if it is something more, an individual who desires freedom and a world that runs by order, both at once.

As we move to the next chapter, we will take forward this richer understanding of freedom and causation. The insights gained here will inform our continuing exploration of human nature and philosophical questions. In the chapters ahead, we might ask how to reconcile our desire for moral responsibility with a scientific worldview, or how notions of freedom play out in social and political realms. For now, we can conclude that the free will debate, far from being merely abstract, touches the core of how we view ourselves and our society. It challenges us to think deeply about choice, control, and accountability – issues that will certainly arise again as we continue our philosophical journey.

Chapter 7

Morality and Meaning in a Determined World

One of the most unsettling implications of a universe governed by strict cause and effect is what it means for our sense of right and wrong. In the previous chapter, we delved into how human behaviour might be explained by natural laws and neural processes, raising the stakes for a profound question: if every action is the inevitable result of prior causes, can anyone truly be held responsible for what they do? This question strikes at the heart of both morality and meaning. After all, much of the meaning we ascribe to our lives comes from the belief that our choices matter—that we can deserve praise for kindness or blame for cruelty. If free will is an illusion, does that erode the very foundation of ethics and our personal sense of purpose?

In this chapter, we explore how a determined world challenges and reshapes our notions of moral responsibility. We will examine arguments that in a fully deterministic

241

universe, traditional ideas of praise and blame might need to be rethought—since people, it seems, *could never have done otherwise* than what they did. We will also consider the counterarguments of compatibilists, philosophers who maintain that even if our decisions have prior causes, we can still meaningfully talk about choice, responsibility, and ethics. From these theoretical debates, we move into practical terrain: how would embracing determinism alter the way we approach justice and punishment? Should a criminal be treated as morally culpable in the old sense, or more like a malfunctioning part of society to be fixed or guided? And importantly, would letting go of belief in absolute free will make us more compassionate or dangerously lax in our moral standards?

Our journey through this chapter will weave together philosophical reasoning and everyday experience. We'll look at how our intuitive sense of freedom underpins moral judgments like "you shouldn't have done that," and ask whether these judgments can survive without the idea of metaphysical free will. Alongside the theory, we'll examine psychological research revealing how people's behaviour and attitudes change when their belief in free will is shaken—or strengthened. The aim is to paint a rigorous yet humane picture of morality and meaning in a determined world. By the end, we should see clearly whether understanding the causal forces behind human behaviour undermines our ethical frameworks, or instead gives us new insight into how to live together with responsibility and purpose in a world of causes.

Responsibility Under Determinism

The idea of determinism forces us to confront a stark possibility: if every decision we make flows inexorably from our genes, our upbringing, and our brain's biochemistry, then in what sense can we be *responsible* for those decisions? Consider a simple example: a teenager shoplifts from a store. If we trace her action backward, we might find a chain of causes—perhaps peer pressure influenced her, or she inherited a thrill-seeking temperament, or maybe her family struggles financially, creating desperation. Each of these factors in turn has its own causes (her peers have their own influences, her genes came from her parents, her family's poverty has systemic roots, and so on). If we had complete knowledge, we could, in theory, draw a continuous line of causation from the Big Bang to the moment the item slipped into her pocket. This is the hard determinist perspective: every action is the result of prior events and could not have unfolded differently given those prior conditions. The teenager, in that strict sense, *could not have done otherwise* at that moment.

If this is true, it seems to undermine the very basis on which we normally praise or blame people. After all, we typically hold someone morally responsible because we assume they had a choice—they could have chosen *not* to steal, and thus we blame them for making the wrong choice. But if, in reality, her choice was the only outcome possible (given her brain state, environment, and history at that split second), blaming her in the traditional way starts to look questionable. Hard determinists argue that our usual notions of moral responsibility are built on an illusion. In their view, to scold or punish someone as if they genuinely could have chosen differently is to misunderstand the true nature of human behaviour. They liken it to praising a robot for

243

performing a task well or punishing a computer for an error—it would be absurd if we knew the machine was just following its programming. Likewise, if a person's brain was "programmed" by biology and experience to do what they did, then the concepts of guilt and merit might need to be radically revised.

One famous philosophical argument highlights this conundrum. It goes like this: *You do what you do because of the way you are.* In other words, your actions spring from your personality, values, and desires—your overall makeup as a person. But *the way you are* is something you didn't ultimately choose; it's the product of your genes and life experiences. And since you aren't responsible for being the way you are, you can't be ultimately responsible for what you do. This line of reasoning, associated with philosopher Galen Strawson, drives home the hard determinist conclusion that *ultimate* moral responsibility is an illusion. If he's right, then no one would ever truly deserve blame or praise in the deepest sense, any more than the wind or the rain would. The thief, the hero, the murderer, the saint—all are simply playing out scripts written by the conditions that came before them.

This perspective can be deeply unsettling. It challenges our intuitions and the way society has operated for centuries. For example, our legal systems, religions, and personal relationships all lean heavily on the idea that individuals are free to choose between right and wrong. Immanuel Kant, reflecting a common intuition, once argued that if our will is determined by forces beyond us, then we're no more accountable for our actions than a billiard ball is for the way it bounces. To many, a world where nobody is truly blameworthy (or praiseworthy) sounds not only counterintuitive but perhaps even dangerous: how would we enforce morality or encourage good behaviour if we believed no one could help doing what they do?

Yet not all philosophers agree that determinism negates responsibility. Enter the compatibilists. Compatibilists hold that we *can* have a meaningful notion of free will and responsibility, even in a determined world—but we might need to refine what we mean by those terms. When we normally say someone acted "of their own free will," we don't usually mean "uncaused and completely spontaneous." We mean they acted voluntarily, in line with their desires and reasoning, without external coercion or compulsion. In this view, the teenager who stole did so because she wanted whatever she took, and she formed a decision based on her own internal motives. If no one forced or manipulated her against her will, then in a practical sense she acted freely, even if her desires and thoughts have deterministic origins.

From the compatibilist perspective, moral responsibility can survive because it is defined by factors like intent, understanding, and control in the moment, rather than some metaphysical ability to have done otherwise in an identical situation. They would say: Yes, her choice was influenced by many factors, but it was still *her* choice in that it flowed from her own mind, rather than from an outside interference or a gun to her head. So we can still hold her responsible in a meaningful way—meaning we can still justifiably respond to her with social or legal consequences aimed at correcting her behaviour—because that's how we encourage better decisions in the future.

To illustrate the compatibilist view, imagine two scenarios. In scenario A, the teenager steals the item entirely on her own initiative. In scenario B, someone was standing over her with a weapon, threatening to harm her unless she committed the theft. In both cases, a determinist could say her action was caused by preceding factors. But we clearly judge these scenarios differently. In scenario B, she was under duress—her action was coerced by an external threat, so we'd likely excuse or forgive it. In scenario A, there was no coercion; the act came from her internal decision process. Compatibilists point out that this difference is crucial and remains valid even under determinism: we distinguish acts caused by the person's own intentions from acts forced upon them. The internal causes (her character, reasons, desires) make her behaviour *her* doing, whereas external compulsion undermines that. Thus, we continue to call scenario A a situation where she is responsible, and scenario B one where she is not, even if in a broad sense both had causation behind them.

Philosopher David Hume, one of the earliest compatibilists, put it succinctly: our freedom is not about being uncaused; it's about not being constrained. In a determined world, people can still be free in the sense that their actions come from their own will (even if that will has a causal story behind it). Modern compatibilists add that holding people accountable is itself part of the causal chain that shapes future behaviour. In other words, our practices of praise and blame are tools: by praising good deeds and condemning bad ones, we create incentives and social pressures that become part of the environment influencing people's future choices. So even if a person's decision today was inevitable given the past, our response to that decision can influence what they (or others who hear of it) do tomorrow. In this way, notions of responsibility and morality remain not only meaningful but essential—they are key leverage points for changing outcomes within a deterministic system.

Bertrand Russell, a philosopher deeply sympathetic to scientific thinking, argued along these lines that accepting determinism need not upend our moral framework at all. He suggested that much of the alarm about determinism wrecking morality comes from a misunderstanding. Just because our choices have causes does not mean that deliberation, effort, and ethical distinctions cease to matter. After all, we still deliberate when faced with options, and it is *we* who ultimately make the decision—even if that "we" has been shaped by prior events. Russell even turned the tables by suggesting that it's the belief in a mysterious, undetermined free will that can be problematic, because it might encourage us to ignore the real factors that influence behaviour. If we think choices just happen spontaneously, we might overlook how education, upbringing, or social conditions lead people toward good or bad actions. Determinism, by contrast, directs our attention to those factors—precisely so we can understand and improve the causes that lead to better decisions.

In summary, the debate over responsibility under determinism presents two seemingly opposite views, but both seek to preserve what is important about morality. The hard determinist urges humility and caution in blaming others (or ourselves) harshly, noting that "there but for the circumstances go I." The compatibilist, on the other hand, maintains that we can keep our concepts of responsibility by grounding them in practical realities like intention and the ability to respond to reasons. As we continue, we'll see how this philosophical debate translates into real-world attitudes—especially when it comes to how we punish wrongdoing or reward good behaviour in society.

Ethical Frameworks: Retribution vs. Rehabilitation

If we accept—even just for the sake of argument—that human actions are fully caused by prior conditions, it has far-reaching implications for how we think about *justice*. Consider how our society typically handles wrongdoing. There are roughly two broad philosophies at play whenever we decide how to respond to a crime or harmful act. One is the philosophy of retribution: the idea that a wrongdoer should suffer or be punished because they *deserve* it. This is the "eye for an eye" intuition, the notion of moral payback. We demand justice in this sense because we believe the person freely chose to do wrong and thus merits a proportionate consequence. The other philosophy is more about prevention and correction—let's call it rehabilitation, though it also includes deterrence and protection. This view focuses on the future: how do we change the offender or the situation so that harmful acts are less likely to happen going forward?

In practice, modern justice systems are a mix of these two approaches. For example, sentencing guidelines often consider both the severity of the crime (to satisfy a sense of just desert) and the likelihood of reoffending (to protect the public or reform the individual). Society's moral attitudes also reflect this mix. We sometimes feel a visceral need to see a guilty person *punished*—that is the retributive instinct. Yet we also talk about extenuating circumstances, root causes of crime, and rehabilitation programs—recognizing that people's actions are influenced by their environment and that they can change.

A deterministic outlook tends to bolster the case for the rehabilitation side of the equation. If a criminal's action stems from factors beyond their ultimate control (brain chemistry, abusive childhood, social deprivation, etc.), then punishing them purely for retribution—simply because "they deserve it"—starts to look less reasonable. After all, in a fully causal sense, what do they *deserve* for being unlucky enough to draw a hand of bad influences? It might seem more rational (and compassionate) to focus on how we can prevent such misdeeds in the future. This could mean rehabilitating the offender through therapy, education, or positive influences, so their future choices (which will also be caused by their new experiences) are better. It could also mean structuring consequences mainly as deterrents: not to inflict moral vengeance, but to create incentives for better behaviour (since knowing you'll be caught and penalized is a cause that can dissuade someone from offending).

In fact, even without explicitly invoking determinism, our society already often treats behaviour as the result of causes. Why do we invest so much in schooling children, in mentoring youth, or in anti-poverty programs? Partly because we *know* that these factors hugely influence what kind of adults they become and what choices they'll likely make. Why do we have laws at all, or punishments like fines and prison? It's not just to avenge wrongdoing, but to *shape* behaviour by altering the future environment of decision-making. We raise the cost of bad actions (like fines for littering or jail for theft) in order to discourage them—implicitly acknowledging that people respond to incentives and consequences (cause and effect again). Why do courts consider an offender's background or mental state? Because it changes how we interpret their actions: if someone committed a crime under severe duress or due to a mental illness, we instinctively shift from pure blame to understanding that there were causal circumstances significantly influencing them. In all these ways, aspects of a deterministic understanding are already woven into our moral and legal practices. We know people are not just independent atoms freely choosing in a vacuum; they are creatures shaped by their upbringing, society, and biology.

So what would it mean to fully embrace a deterministic perspective in our ethical frameworks? It might mean doubling down on those practices that treat wrongdoing as a human problem to be solved rather than an evil to be stigmatized and avenged. For instance, prisons might look less like dungeons for the wicked and more like hospitals or schools—places where offenders are held, yes (society needs protection from harmful behaviours), but also places where the aim is to heal whatever can be healed, to educate and reform. The emphasis would be on returning someone to society better equipped to make pro-social choices, rather than simply making them suffer for what they did. We might expand mental health services, recognizing how often crime is linked to untreated disorders or trauma that could be addressed. We might also put more effort into *preventative* measures: if we understand the causes of crime, we can work to mitigate those causes before they result in harm (improving education, economic opportunities, family services in troubled communities, etc.).

Even our interpersonal attitudes could shift. Picture a scenario in a family: a teenager is caught vandalizing a neighbour's property. A retributive response might be the parents expressing outrage and imposing a harsh punishment to "teach a lesson" in a purely punitive sense. A more causally informed response would be to ask: why did he do this? Is he acting out because of emotional stress, peer pressure, or some unmet need? Addressing those causes—getting him counselling, talking through his issues, finding a constructive outlet for his energy—would likely be more effective in the long run than simply grounding him in anger. The "lesson" in a deterministic framework comes from understanding consequences (he has to clean up the mess, apologize, and repair trust) and learning better ways to handle whatever drove him to do it, rather than from instilling fear or retribution alone.

However, critics of a purely deterministic approach to justice raise an important concern: could emphasizing causal factors end up *undermining* personal responsibility in a way that makes things worse? There's a worry that if people start believing "It's not really my fault, my genes or my childhood made me do it," they might feel freer to misbehave or less motivated to make moral choices. This is sometimes phrased as the "excuse" problem: determinism, if misused, could become a universal excuse for bad behaviour. "Don't blame me, blame my circumstances," one might say. If society were to accept that at face value for everyone, would that erode the deterrent effect of moral disapproval and punishment?

This is a legitimate point to grapple with. A world where everyone shrugs off their misdeeds as inevitable is not a morally healthy world. But proponents of the deterministic outlook would reply that understanding causes is not the same as letting people off the hook in practice. In fact, holding someone accountable can still happen in a deterministic framework—it just means we do so with a different attitude. We would hold them accountable not to exact cosmic justice for a freely willed sin, but to correct behaviour and protect others. For example, even if a person's criminal tendencies can be traced to an abusive upbringing, we don't simply say, "Oh well, he couldn't help it, let's ignore it." We might feel sympathetic to their background, but we still need to intervene—maybe through mandated therapy and supervised rehabilitation rather than just retributive punishment, but *some* intervention is necessary. The difference is that we carry it out without hatred or the notion of moral stain; instead, we act as a society to fix a problem.

Think of it this way: if a boulder rolls down a hill and threatens to crush a village, the villagers will try to divert or stop it. They don't blame the boulder as "evil," but they still must deal with the danger it poses. Similarly, if a person is on a path that harms others, we intervene not because we think they are a freely evil villain who "deserves" suffering, but because we need to protect the community and hopefully redirect that person's life for the better. Unlike a boulder, of course, a person can respond to reasoning and rehabilitation—so our response to human wrongdoing is much more nuanced. We use restraint (prison or other measures) as needed to prevent immediate harm, and simultaneously we try to address the reasons behind the wrongdoing, knowing that those reasons can be altered.

It's also worth noting that even in a deterministic worldview, consequences still matter. If someone believes "my circumstances made me do it," that belief itself becomes part of their causal chain and future circumstances. If society responds to wrongdoing with clear consequences (like legal penalties or social disapproval), those consequences become new causes that shape future behaviour. In other words, saying "I couldn't help it" doesn't stop the fact that you will face results from your action which will influence you and others. A person might claim their anger is just in their nature (a product of genes and upbringing), but if that anger leads them to punch a wall and break their hand, they'll still feel pain and learn a lesson from it. Similarly, society can maintain strong disincentives against harmful acts, so even if one intellectually thinks "Well, technically it's not my fault," they still have plenty of practical reasons to control themselves (knowing they'll go to jail, lose friends, etc., if they don't).

The key, then, is how we frame responsibility. A deterministic ethic might say: "No, you didn't create yourself, but you *are* the current steward of your behaviour. Society will treat you as responsible in the sense that our reactions aim to influence you going forward." Thus, we still praise generosity to encourage more of it, and we still punish theft to discourage it—but we do so with an eye on changing outcomes, not on moral vengeance. This approach can foster a more compassionate society, as we recognize that *anyone* might have ended up in the same place as the wrongdoer had they lived the same life. This recognition could reduce hatred and increase efforts to help those who go astray. At the same time, it keeps in place the necessary structure of incentives and consequences that guide behaviour.

In sum, adopting a deterministic perspective doesn't mean we abandon the ideas of right and wrong or consequence. Instead, it shifts our emphasis. We move from a model of retribution—punishing because a person supposedly chose evil out of sheer free will—to a model of rehabilitation and prevention—addressing wrongdoing by understanding its causes and working to alter those causes. We would still hold people accountable, but our goal would be to improve them and protect others, rather than to satisfy a metaphysical notion of "just deserts." The challenge is ensuring that in doing so, we don't accidentally send the message that people have no agency at all. It's a delicate balance: seeing humans as part of nature's causal web while also empowering them (through education, social support, and fair consequences) to be the best versions of themselves within that web.

This reimagining of justice is not just abstract philosophy; it dovetails with ongoing debates in criminal justice reform and psychology. And it leads naturally to the next question: How do these ideas play out in the everyday moral choices and intuitions we all experience, outside of courts and formal systems?

Free Will, Moral Intuition, and Everyday Life

Up to now, we've discussed high-level notions of responsibility and justice. But how does determinism—or the lack of absolute free will—affect the moral dimension of our day-to-day lives and personal relationships? Most of us aren't judges or philosophers in our daily interactions. We're friends, parents, coworkers, neighbours. We constantly make moral judgments on a small scale: we feel pride when we resist temptation or do the right thing, we feel guilty when we hurt someone, we tell others they *ought* to do this or *ought not* to do that. These intuitions and reactions form the fabric of our moral life. So, do they all collapse if we accept that every action has a cause?

Our sense of free will is deeply ingrained. When you decide whether to have a second slice of cake or to tell a difficult truth to a friend, it *feels* like you are freely weighing the options and could genuinely choose either way. Philosophers might call this an impression of "could have done otherwise." It's no wonder that our moral intuitions are built on this impression—holding someone accountable assumes they could have chosen differently. Yet, even if determinism suggests that in the precise moment of decision only one outcome was actually possible, it doesn't render our deliberations or moral intuitions irrelevant. We still go

254

through the process of thinking, imagining consequences, and making choices, and those processes matter enormously.

Let's consider a simple moral judgment we often make: telling someone, "You shouldn't have done that." Imagine a close friend betrays your trust by sharing a secret of yours. You confront them and say, "What you did was wrong. You shouldn't have told others about something I confided in you." Now, if we pause and put on our determinist hat, we might ask: was it really *possible* for the friend to have done otherwise? If we rewound the universe to the moment of temptation, with every molecule and thought the same, determinism says they would do the same thing and spill the secret again. Does that make your moral criticism pointless? Not necessarily. Criticism and advice are themselves part of the causal chain. When you tell your friend "You shouldn't have done that," you're adding a new cause into the mix— your words, conveying disapproval and hurt. This becomes a part of your friend's future mental landscape. They might feel remorse, reflect on their action, and resolve not to do it again. In a sense, your moral judgment *helps make it true* that next time they could do otherwise, because next time the situation won't be identical: it will include the memory of your confrontation and its emotional impact.

This illustrates a key compatibilist insight: our everyday practice of holding each other accountable isn't predicated on a magical ability to violate causality; it's predicated on the idea that people can respond to moral reasons. Your friend had the capacity to respond to reasons too—perhaps they just failed to consider them in the moment. By reproaching them, you sharpen their sensitivity to those reasons going forward. So when we say, "You *should not* have done X," we usually mean "You did X, but that was not aligned with the values or expectations we share, and you *could* have acted differently if you had focused on those values. Please do so in the future." Determinism doesn't negate that statement because it's forward-looking as much as (or more than) backward-looking.

We see a similar dynamic with praise and encouragement. If your coworker goes out of their way to help you finish a project, you'll likely thank them and tell them they did the right thing. You're acknowledging their effort. Now, if everything including their helpful impulse was determined by prior causes (maybe they were raised to be generous, maybe they happened to be in a good mood that day), does your praise matter? Absolutely—because praise reinforces the behaviour. It makes your coworker feel valued and likely encourages them (and even others who hear about it) to help again in the future. In other words, praise is another causal factor that feeds into the chain. It's a reward that shapes future dispositions.

What about our internal moral life—feelings of guilt, regret, pride, and a sense of moral "desert" (as in deserving blame or praise)? These feelings don't vanish in a deterministic worldview, but we might reinterpret them. Take guilt and regret: if you do something that hurts someone, you'll probably feel bad about it later, especially if you empathize with the person you hurt. Determinism might tell you, "Given who you were at that moment, you couldn't have done otherwise." But that's not the end of the story. The *you* of now, who is reflecting on the action, is a slightly different you—one who has seen the outcome and perhaps learned something from it. That new perspective means next time you truly *will* do otherwise, because now the causes acting on you include the memory of this guilt. In essence, regret is the mind's way of flagging an action as undesirable so that it influences your future self. Whether or not you could have avoided the mistake the first time, feeling remorse is crucial for doing better moving forward.

However, determinism could help us refine these feelings and avoid destructive extremes. If someone becomes consumed by guilt for a mistake, believing they are irredeemably evil or that they freely chose to be bad, that can be paralyzing. A deterministic perspective, oddly enough, might introduce some self-compassion: "I am not fundamentally evil; I made a mistake because of certain factors, and now I can work on changing those factors." It shifts guilt toward a healthier form of responsibility: acknowledging harm and taking steps to repair it, rather than wallowing in self-loathing. Similarly, pride in accomplishments can remain intact, though perhaps tempered with a bit more humility. If you work hard and succeed at a goal, you'll feel pride. Knowing that your work ethic was instilled by various influences doesn't have to dampen the satisfaction. You still identify with the goal and the effort you put in. A determinist might simply add, "I'm grateful to everyone and everything that made me the kind of person who could achieve this." This could actually enhance a sense of connectedness and gratitude, making pride less about ego and more about appreciation of the fortunate circumstances and personal perseverance that led to success.

Now, let's address the idea of moral desert—the notion that people truly deserve praise or blame (or reward and punishment) in some ultimate moral sense. Without libertarian free will (the kind that implies a person could have absolutely acted differently in a given moment), many philosophers argue that strict moral desert is an illusion. It might not be cosmically true that someone "deserves" to suffer for what they've done, or that someone else "deserves" all the accolades for being virtuous, since none of us ultimately authored our own existence. This is a challenging idea because a lot of our moral language, especially in religion and law, leans on desert. "He got what he deserved" is a common refrain when a bad person faces consequences. If we take determinism seriously, we might have to drop the idea that anyone inherently deserves anything—instead, we justify consequences on other grounds (like protection, rehabilitation, deterrence, or simply rewarding good behaviour to encourage more of it).

Does losing the idea of pure desert undercut our moral motivation? Not necessarily. Many compatibilists say that what we *really* care about, deep down, isn't that people deserve punishment for its own sake, but that good is rewarded and harm is mitigated in society. We can fulfil those pragmatic and ethical goals without invoking metaphysical desert. When you refrain from stealing not just because you fear punishment but because you feel it's wrong, you're guided by empathy and principles, not the abstract idea of deserving punishment. Those moral sentiments remain unchanged by determinism—they may even be strengthened by understanding causes. For instance, empathy might increase when you realize the person you're about to judge harshly didn't come from the same supportive background you did.

In everyday life, we constantly balance understanding and accountability. Think about how we treat children versus adults. If a six-year-old breaks a vase, parents typically don't punish them the same way they would a malicious act by an older teen or adult. We say, "They're just a child; they don't know any better," and we try to teach them rather than punish severely. Why? Because we implicitly recognize the child's decision-making capabilities are not fully developed—they are more a product of impulses and lack of knowledge (causes they can't yet control well). This is a partially determinist stance; it acknowledges the limits of the child's freedom in a practical sense. As the child grows, we increase the expectations and hold them more accountable because we see their ability to understand consequences and control actions has grown. What's notable is that at no point do we require the child to have some magic free will; we just require them to have the cognitive and emotional tools to respond to moral reasons.

This is much like the compatibilist view of all persons: we hold each other accountable to the extent that we are capable of understanding and responding to moral reasons. If someone cannot (for instance, due to a severe mental illness or extreme coercion), we temper our judgments. Determinism simply universalizes this perspective: everyone is influenced by factors, but most adults have the capacity to reflect on their actions and adjust them in light of criticism or praise. That capacity is what we appeal to when we engage in moral discourse.

So our everyday moral intuitions—blaming, praising, feeling guilty or proud, saying "should" and "shouldn't"— can remain quite intact under determinism once we interpret them in this light. We may become a bit more understanding of others' missteps, knowing there are reasons behind them, and perhaps more modest about our own virtues, recognizing our luck. But we still genuinely care about right and wrong. We still get angry when someone harms us deliberately (though maybe we'll direct that anger more constructively). We still admire acts of kindness and courage. We continue to use our reactions—anger, gratitude, encouragement, condemnation—as feedback in the grand causal network to promote the behaviours we value.

Ultimately, human beings will likely continue to feel as though they have free will in the moment of choice; that subjective experience isn't going away. What determinism asks is that we reinterpret what's happening: behind the scenes of our conscious feeling of freedom, there is a chain of events leading us to choose as we do. But that doesn't make the choice any less *our choice*, nor does it make its consequences any less real. Our moral intuitions evolved to help us live together harmoniously, and they can still serve that purpose. By infusing those intuitions with a better understanding of why people act as they do, we might become wiser in applying praise and blame—using them to heal and guide rather than simply to vent outrage or bestow uncritical adulation. In a determined world, our moral life becomes, if anything, an even more conscious dance of influence: we hold others (and ourselves) accountable in order to continually shape each other for the better, recognizing all along that this process is part of the natural unfolding of causes and effects.

Belief in Determinism: Effects on Behaviour and Society

So far, we've been exploring how one *could* view morality under determinism in principle. But there's another layer to consider: how do people behave when they *believe* (or disbelieve) in free will? Does simply holding a determinist worldview change the way we act? Interestingly, psychologists have conducted experiments to test this, and the results tell a cautionary tale about the power of belief itself.

Imagine you're participating in a psychological study. You're given an essay to read that argues free will is an

260

illusion—that scientists have discovered human decisions are entirely the result of neurons firing in the brain, obeying the laws of physics. After reading this, you move on to what you think is an unrelated task: solving some puzzles or taking a test, where you have opportunities to cheat without anyone noticing. It turns out you're part of a group reading the anti-free-will essay. Another group of participants reads a neutral essay that doesn't mention free will at all. What researchers have found is that the group exposed to the "free will is an illusion" message tends to cheat more often than the control group. In other words, when people are momentarily convinced that their choices aren't really "up to them," some take that as a license to break the rules if they think they won't get caught.

This kind of study has been run multiple times with variations: some measure willingness to help others, or propensity to be aggressive versus kind, after manipulating beliefs about free will. The pattern that emerged is a bit disconcerting: when people's belief in their own free will is weakened, they may exhibit less ethical behaviour, at least in the short term. Why might this be? One interpretation is that if you tell someone "You are a sophisticated biological machine with no free will," they might feel less accountable for their actions—after all, if it's not *really* "me" making the choice (just my neurons or my genetics), then perhaps I'm not really blameworthy if I slack off or indulge my selfish impulses. It's a bit like a psychological trick: remove the sense of personal agency, and some people lower their guard against temptation or selfishness.

However, this is not the whole story. There's an important nuance: these studies often capture an immediate reaction to a new idea. If someone hasn't deeply reflected on what determinism means and just hears "no free will," they might jump to a simplistic conclusion: "Nothing I do matters, so why not cheat?" But someone who has a more nuanced understanding of determinism might think differently. And indeed, there are positive behavioural effects associated with a determinist or at least a causally minded outlook— especially regarding how we treat *others*.

Consider how we react when someone wrongs us. The natural impulse can be anger, even hatred, and a desire to see them punished. But if we adopt a perspective that they are a product of their circumstances, it can soften that anger. We might still hold them accountable, but with more empathy. A classic example is how we view people with clear mental illnesses. If a person with severe schizophrenia does something harmful during a psychotic episode, we don't react with the same anger we would if a sane person did the same thing for malicious reasons. We recognize the illness drove their action; we might feel sadness or concern more than fury, and we focus on getting them help (and protecting others in the meantime). Now extend that thinking to more common scenarios: say, a friend lashes out at you verbally. If you know they've been under enormous stress or were sleep-deprived (factors causing their irritability), you're more likely to be forgiving, or at least understanding, rather than immediately lash back in anger. In daily life, when we remind ourselves "There's probably a reason behind so-and-so's behaviour," we are practicing a kind of determinist compassion—we're acknowledging causality in human behaviour, and that dampens our instinct for pure retribution.

There is some evidence that people who see behaviour in terms of causes and conditions tend to support more constructive approaches to justice. For instance, if you present people with a story about a criminal and include details about how his brain physiology or upbringing contributed to his crime, people generally recommend less harsh punishment and more rehabilitation. Knowing the causes invites compassion. In a societal sense, widespread acceptance of determinism could potentially lead to more support for social programs that address the root causes of problems (like crime, poverty, addiction) rather than just punishing symptoms. If we truly believe that genes and environment underlie much of behaviour, we might invest more in early education, mental health care, and reducing social inequalities as moral imperatives. We might also be more patient and willing to help those who have faltered, seeing them not as simply "bad" but as individuals who need guidance or support to do better.

That said, the worry remains: how to reap the compassion of determinism without the apathy or excuse-making. It's a bit of a balancing act. Some philosophers, noting the experimental findings, have even suggested what might sound ironic: that society might function best if people in general *don't* dwell too much on determinism when it comes to their own actions, because a strong personal feeling of agency can encourage ethical behaviour. In other words, it might be useful for each of us to *feel* as though we have free will in order to stay motivated and conscientious, but at the same time for us to recognize others as influenced by circumstance, to treat them kindly. This one-way street ("free will for me, but not for thee") is hard to justify intellectually, but it captures the intuition that believing in your own agency is motivating, while attributing others' misdeeds to circumstance is humane.

However, a more integrated approach—and one compatibilists would favour—is to refine what we mean by personal agency so that we can accept determinism without losing our moral drive. This means educating ourselves and others that determinism is not fatalism. Determinism doesn't mean your effort doesn't matter; it means your effort is a crucial part of the chain of cause and effect that leads to outcomes. If anything, determinism should motivate us to put effort into the *right causes*. For example, if a student thinks, "Whether I study or not, whatever grade I get is already determined," that's a misunderstanding. If she doesn't study, the poor grade is determined by that choice; if she does study, a better grade is determined by that effort. The outcome is determined by the input, which includes her studying. So her sense of agency—her knowledge that her actions have consequences—should remain intact. This is something important to emphasize: your choices *do* matter greatly, because they are the mechanism through which change happens, even if those choices have antecedents.

Education about determinism could actually bolster moral responsibility by shifting it from a metaphysical idea ("you could have done absolutely otherwise") to a practical one ("your actions have effects, and you are part of society's causal network for promoting good"). People can be taught that yes, we understand you are shaped by your circumstances, but *now that you are aware* of that, you have the ability to seek out better influences, to reflect on your impulses, and to make decisions that, in turn, reshape who you are. Over time, you can become a different person by deliberately exposing yourself to good causes—like learning, practice, and supportive environments. In this view, self-improvement and moral effort are not only still meaningful; they are reimagined as a cause-and-effect project. You are, in a sense, a gardener tending the garden of your mind and character, knowing full well that growth follows the laws of nature which you can learn and harness.

264

Social cohesion in a deterministic world might actually improve if these ideas are embraced wisely. Imagine a community where, instead of jumping to blame and division when problems occur, people ask, "What caused this, and how can we work to fix those causes?" It could foster more collaboration and less stigma. For example, addiction might be addressed fully as an illness to be treated rather than as a moral failing to be shunned. Criminals who serve their time might be welcomed back with support to integrate them, rather than being permanently branded and ostracized (which itself often leads to more crime). People might be more open about their struggles ("I'm dealing with anger issues, which probably stem from some trauma; I need help addressing it") if they know others won't immediately judge them as simply a "bad person," but will see a person with a problem that has origins and potential solutions.

Of course, one cannot ignore potential pitfalls. A society that too casually absolves individuals of responsibility might find some taking advantage of that leniency. If consequences are seen as only rehabilitation and not punishment at all, would that diminish the deterrent effect? It's a delicate policy question: how do we integrate compassion with effective prevention? One suggestion is to borrow a public health approach to issues like crime, treating harmful behaviour somewhat like a disease outbreak—compassionately but firmly. For example, such an approach might involve:

- Quarantining those who are immediately dangerous to others (incapacitating offenders to protect the public).

- Treating the underlying issues driving their behaviour (providing rehabilitation through therapy, education, or medical care).

265

- Vaccinating against future cases by improving the social conditions that breed such behaviour (preventive measures like better education, mental health support, and economic opportunities).

This can be done without anger or the notion of moral hatred. But it must be done with a resolve that society will not allow harmful behaviour to go unchecked.

Ultimately, the practical impact of embracing determinism comes down to how well people understand it. If it's misunderstood as "nothing matters, I can't change anything," it could erode personal responsibility and effort. If it's understood as "things have causes, and we can be deliberate about being good causes," it could inspire a more thoughtful, compassionate, and proactive approach to ethics. Our stance on free will versus determinism, then, isn't just a dry philosophical position—it has real stakes for how we raise our children, how we punish or forgive, how we motivate ourselves and others, and how we construct our social institutions.

The message of this chapter has been that a determined world need not be a world without morality or meaning. Instead, it can be a world where we trade in a punitive, blame-heavy moral mindset for one that is deeply responsible in a different way: responsible for understanding the web of causes and for navigating it toward better outcomes. We've seen that our beliefs about free will can shift behaviour—toward either callousness or compassion—and it's up to us to choose the path that leads to a more humane society.

With these insights, we find ourselves at a crossroads of understanding. We can no longer see human actions as isolated, freely willed events; they are part of a vast tapestry of causality. How we respond to that knowledge will define the ethical meaning we create. As we move forward, let's consider how this more nuanced view of human behaviour influences not just our judgments of right and wrong, but also our personal quest for purpose. After all, morality is one avenue through which we seek significance in a law-governed universe. In the next chapter, we will delve deeper into how we find meaning and construct values in a world that, on its face, is indifferent and determined—an exploration that will tie together the threads of understanding we've developed so far.

Chapter 8

Society, Technology, and the Future of Determinism

After journeying through the philosophical and scientific underpinnings of determinism—from the clockwork laws of physics to the intricate wiring of the human brain and the thorny questions of moral responsibility—we now turn to the broader world we all inhabit. In the pages ahead, our focus widens to society at large and the technological forces shaping our future. How does the age-old debate over determinism and free will play out in an era of intelligent machines and big data? What happens when algorithms can anticipate our wants and actions, seemingly confirming that we are creatures of habit and cause? And in our social systems, from economics to education, to what extent are our choices a product of circumstances beyond our control?

This chapter tackles these questions head-on. We will explore artificial intelligence as a case of "mechanistic minds," examining whether a machine following code can ever be said to act freely—and what that implies about our own mental machinery. We then delve into the realm of big data and predictive algorithms, where modern technology edges eerily close to Laplace's dream of a predictive engine, forecasting human behaviour with uncanny accuracy. From there, we'll consider social determinism through the lenses of economics, sociology, and psychology, asking how much individuals are moulded by societal forces and what that means for personal agency and public policy. Finally, we confront the danger of fatalism, clarifying why accepting causality does not doom us to passivity or despair. If anything, understanding how cause and effect shape outcomes can empower us to make better choices—since we, too, are part of the causal chain that can shape the future.

By the end of this chapter, we aim to have a clear view of determinism not just as an abstract principle but as a living reality in our high-tech, interconnected world. The discussion will range from philosophical thought experiments to real-world examples—from the logic circuits of a computer chip to the social currents that guide a generation. Throughout, we maintain the same spirit of careful reasoning and curiosity that has guided us thus far. Society, Technology, and the Future of Determinism invites us to see the unfolding of cause and effect in new domains, and challenges us to think about what freedom and responsibility mean in the face of predictive machines and powerful social forces. Let us begin by examining the minds we have built in silicon, and what they teach us about the nature of choice.

Artificial Intelligence – Mechanistic Minds

Consider a modern chess-playing computer that makes a move so clever it astonishes grandmasters. The machine seems to have "decided" on a brilliant strategy. But did it really choose in any meaningful sense? Under the hood, every action of an artificial intelligence (AI) is the result of computations following set rules. AI systems operate by taking inputs (like the state of a chessboard or data from a camera), running them through algorithms, and producing outputs (the chosen move or an identification of what's in an image). In traditional software, this process is explicitly programmed: a given input will always yield the same output because the code is deterministic. Even in more advanced AI like neural networks, which learn from experience, the end result is still a network of mathematical weights and operations. Once the learning phase is complete, the AI's responses to any particular input are fixed by those learned parameters. In short, a machine intelligence is fundamentally a mechanistic entity: if we could reset it to the same state and give it the same input again, it would behave identically (barring any random number generator influencing it – and even that "randomness" is typically a predictable pseudorandom process).

This inherent determinism in AI leads to a provocative thought experiment: imagine an intelligent robot asserting, "I made this choice freely." We would likely smile at the notion. We know that its every decision traces back to lines of code or the statistical patterns in its training data. If an autonomous car swerves left instead of right, it's not because the car "willed" it in the way a human might feel they do; it's because its programming calculated that left was the better option given the situation (perhaps to avoid an obstacle). We do not attribute moral responsibility or true agency to the car; rather, we credit the engineers who programmed it or the data that shaped its driving model. In our eyes, the AI is an instrument executing instructions—even if those instructions are very complex and allow for adaptive behaviour. The AI may *appear* to reason or choose, but we interpret everything it does as ultimately stemming from its design and inputs, not from its own spontaneous volition.

Some philosophers and scientists argue that this captures the essence of what an AI is: an extension of human determinism. We built the algorithms; we curated the training data; therefore, whatever the AI does can be seen as a product of those initial human causes. By this view, an AI's "choices" are really just indirect outcomes of human choices, plus some statistical rules. The machine is a marionette whose strings are invisible mathematical parameters rather than visible ropes, but we believe firmly that there are strings. No matter how sophisticated the program, the AI cannot transcend the instructions and examples it was given. Even machine-learning systems that modify themselves (tweaking their own parameters as they learn) do so only within the confines of their programming. They are following a script that says, in effect, "adjust your approach to minimize error according to the data." There is no ghost in the machine, no mysterious inner will that breaks it free of cause and effect.

Yet others wonder if something new might emerge once a machine's complexity reaches a certain threshold. They point out that AI has surprised us on many occasions, performing actions its programmers did not explicitly anticipate. For example, when DeepMind's AlphaGo program made an unconventional Go move that confounded expert human players, it seemed almost creative. Such moments make people ask: could an AI develop a kind of spontaneity or emergent agency not directly traceable to a specific human directive? After all, we often can't pinpoint the exact chain of cause within a neural network that led to a given decision—it's a black box of layered calculations. Could genuine autonomy arise from such complexity? This is a speculative leap. Most researchers would answer that "surprise" is not the same as free will. The AI's move, however inventive it appeared, was still the result of the program's internal logic responding to the situation – a logic put in place by its creators and training. The system didn't decide to be creative; it simply followed its algorithms, which sometimes yield outcomes that surprise even the programmers because of the system's complexity. Complexity can breed unpredictability, especially to observers, but unpredictability is different from true freedom. We encountered a similar idea when discussing chaos theory earlier: a purely deterministic system can behave in ways so intricate that its outcomes feel random or novel. Likewise, an AI might be perfectly deterministic and yet non-obvious in its behaviour. That doesn't grant it an independent will; it only means its determinism can mimic the appearance of choice to those of us who don't see every calculation.

The debate over AI "free will" often circles back to an analogy with human cognition. If we hesitate to ascribe free will to a machine that processes inputs and outputs based on causal rules, on what grounds do we attribute it to ourselves? Human beings, after all, are often described as biological machines. Our brains take in inputs (sensory information, memories), process them through networks of neurons according to electrochemical laws, and produce outputs (actions, decisions, speech). Neuroscience has shown that our decision-making involves electrical signals and neurotransmitters following physical principles. In earlier chapters, we noted experiments where scientists could predict a person's simple choices by watching brain activity, even before the person felt they had decided. This suggests that, at least for those decisions, the brain was working through its "algorithm" prior to our conscious awareness. If an AI is a soulless input-output device, is a person so different? We certainly *feel* different; we experience our deliberations as if something more than chemistry is at play. But feeling isn't proof of a special exemption from causality. It's entirely possible that our sense of freely willing our actions is a byproduct of complex neural processes, an emergent property of a very sophisticated machine made of flesh. In other words, we might be sophisticated robots who don't realize we're robots—much like an AI might "feel" independent if it were complex enough to have feelings at all.

Pushing this analogy further, imagine a future where engineers do create an AI so advanced that it exhibits human-like self-awareness. Suppose this AI writes an essay about its own will, insisting that it has desires and can choose its path. From our perspective, knowing we assembled its circuits and code, we might be sceptical: "It's just saying what it was programmed to say (or what it learned from data)." We could maintain that stance even if the AI begins to surprise us, because we remember that however autonomous it seems, every facet was once a result of some cause we (or the environment) set in motion for it. But now reflect on ourselves: if an outside observer knew every detail of our brain's construction—our genes, our upbringing, the experiences that "programmed" us—might they not say the same of us? "Of course Jane feels like she made a choice, but given her neural wiring and history, she could not have chosen otherwise." In essence, advanced AI forces us to hold up a mirror to human nature. It provokes us with a challenging question: Is there any evidence that we humans have an agency fundamentally different in kind from that of a very complex computer?

So far, no one has identified a clear factor that grants humans absolute free will while machines remain mere automatons. Some have speculated that consciousness might be the secret ingredient—that subjective experience, which as far as we know humans possess and current AIs do not, could be tied to a special kind of freedom. Others have gone further to suggest exotic physics at work in the brain, as if quantum uncertainty or some non-computable process might inject a little indeterminism into our thoughts. But these ideas remain unproven and highly contentious. And even if true, randomness or quantum indeterminacy wouldn't equate to the kind of intentional free will people imagine; it would just add unpredictability, not control. As it stands, the simpler explanation is appealing: that both man and machine are governed by cause and effect. A human mind may be astronomically more complex than any AI we've built so far, but complexity alone doesn't break the bonds of determinism—it only obscures them.

The point is not to reduce humans to "mere machines" in a trivializing way; rather, it is to recognize that if we attribute our own actions to a causal network (genes, neurons, environment), then we should be consistent when thinking about AI, and vice versa. We hesitate to grant a robot true freedom because we see its mechanisms plainly. We don't see all the mechanisms inside ourselves, so we're inclined to feel special. Yet as our understanding of brains and computers grows, that gap in perception narrows. Realizing this can be humbling. It doesn't necessarily strip life of meaning—after all, a being can be determined and still be intelligent, loving, creative, and self-reflective (a point we've made about human life). But it does challenge us to find a non-arbitrary basis if we want to maintain that humans have free will while AIs do not. Perhaps one day we'll have to decide whether a very advanced AI deserves to be treated as having a will of its own. Our answer will inevitably reflect what we believe about our own nature.

For now, artificial intelligences remain firmly under the umbrella of determinism as we understand it. They are mechanistic minds, marvels of engineering that follow the instructions encoded in silicon pathways. And interestingly, their very success in domains like chess, driving, or medical diagnosis highlights determinism in action: they show that even tasks requiring judgment can be broken down into computations. In doing so, AIs do not diminish the human mind, but rather illuminate it. They suggest that what we call "choosing" or "thinking" need not rely on any mysterious free will—it can emerge from a sufficiently complex deterministic process. This insight leads us to consider another development of our time that reinforces the power of prediction and pattern: the rise of big data. If AI demonstrates determinism through machines, big data does so through vast information about ourselves. How far have we gone toward predicting human behaviour? As we shall see, the new engines of data and algorithms are making the world more predictable than ever—and raising their own host of questions about autonomy and control.

Big Data and Predictive Algorithms

In 1814, the mathematician Pierre-Simon Laplace imagined an intellect so vast that, could it know all the positions and motions of every particle at one time, it could foresee the future with perfect certainty. This vision of total predictability remained a thought experiment for centuries. But in our modern world, we are beginning to see glimmers of Laplace's dream in action, not through divine omniscience, but via something more humble: data. Every day, human activities generate billions of data points – our clicks and likes on social media, our GPS locations, our online searches and shopping choices, even our heart rates from smartwatches. With the rise of big data and powerful computing, these countless particulars can be analysed to reveal patterns and probabilities. The result is a suite of predictive algorithms that eerily anticipates what individuals will do, want, or need. We live under a kind of statistical foresight: not perfect like Laplace's demon would have, but impressive enough to feel almost like a form of everyday mind-reading.

Anyone who uses the internet has experienced this. Perhaps you've noticed that as soon as you think about buying a new appliance, ads for that very item pop up on your screen. Or you finish a series on a streaming service and find that the next show recommended is uncannily aligned with your tastes. It's not magic – it's prediction. Companies like Netflix, Amazon, and YouTube deploy sophisticated recommendation systems that compare your past behaviour with millions of others. Given what you've watched or purchased, they can predict with high probability what you might enjoy next. Often, they're correct. Similarly, social media feeds are curated by algorithms that learn your preferences: they seem to know which posts will keep you scrolling. While it can feel creepy to have a machine know you so well, it's essentially an application of determinism. You are being treated as a being whose future choices can be inferred from past ones. In a sense, the algorithm is saying: "Given the causes we've observed (your prior clicks and linger times), we can foresee the effect (you'll like this content)." The same input tends to produce the same output — just as determinism would predict.

The predictive power of big data extends beyond entertainment and shopping. In law enforcement, some cities have experimented with "predictive policing" software that analyses crime data to forecast where crimes are likely to occur, or even who might be at higher risk of committing them. The idea is to allocate police or social resources proactively to those areas or individuals, potentially preventing crime before it happens. Likewise, in public health, researchers analyse search engine queries and social media mentions to predict disease outbreaks (for example, a spike in people searching for "flu symptoms" in a region can warn of a brewing flu outbreak). Doctors are beginning to use algorithms that crunch patient data to predict who is at risk of conditions like heart disease or depression, allowing earlier intervention. Even our cars and appliances are getting predictive: modern thermostats learn your schedule and start adjusting the temperature before you even walk through the door, and navigation apps suggest when to leave for an appointment based on predicted traffic.

In many ways, these technologies fulfil aspects of the old deterministic ideal: they demonstrate that much of human behaviour is not random at all but follows discernible patterns. If a company can predict that a certain teenager is likely pregnant based on changes in her shopping habits (a real-life case that made headlines when targeted ads revealed a girl's pregnancy to her family), it underscores that our personal choices often flow from regular causes that data can pick up. If a credit card fraud detection system flags a transaction as suspicious because it doesn't fit your usual spending pattern, it's leveraging the fact that you have a

278

"usual pattern" to begin with. All these systems assume that given similar conditions, you will act in similar ways—that there is continuity in your behaviour which can be modelled and anticipated.

Does the success of these predictions confirm that determinism is true? It certainly bolsters the deterministic perspective, at least in practice. The more we can predict, the more it appears that our actions are governed by knowable factors. If humans had complete free whim unbound by any prior tendencies, our behaviour would likely be too erratic to forecast. The fact that algorithms can, with reasonable accuracy, anticipate what you'll do suggests that you operate to a significant degree by patterns—patterns shaped by your past choices, your demographic, even the time of day. Of course, predictive algorithms are not infallible or all-knowing. They deal in probabilities, not certainties. A recommendation might be wrong; an unexpected event can throw off a forecast. Sometimes people act "out of character" or genuinely surprise those who know them (and thus also surprise the algorithms that shadow them). So we haven't turned into perfectly predictable clockwork dolls—each individual still has some capacity to deviate from the model. However, it's telling that our deviations too often have explanations: perhaps the algorithm didn't have data on a new interest you developed, or you deliberately acted differently because you didn't want to be predictable (ironically, a tendency that could itself be predicted if known—some people by personality will go left if everyone else goes right). In the grand scheme, what big data reveals is that, especially in aggregate, human behaviour has regularities. On a large scale, these regularities can be astonishingly robust: one year to the next, the number of car accidents, or marriages, or even suicides in a large population

279

tends to be stable relative to the population size. We'll discuss the social implications of that soon. The point here is that as the scale and detail of data grow, the space left for completely capricious, unforeseeable action shrinks correspondingly.

The rise of predictive algorithms brings great promise alongside great peril. On the positive side, if we can anticipate problems, we can potentially solve them before they grow. Imagine a city using data to identify intersections where accidents are likely and redesigning them pre-emptively, or a health app that alerts you of a potential illness before you feel any symptoms. There is a clear benefit in using our knowledge of cause and effect to improve lives—this is determinism applied for good. If certain behaviours reliably lead to certain outcomes, then understanding those links can help us intervene for the better. For instance, predictive policing, in its ideal form, isn't about arresting someone for a crime they haven't committed (that would be dystopian), but rather about community outreach: if data shows a particular neighbourhood is at risk for gang violence, authorities might increase youth programs or job opportunities there to change the causal chain before crime occurs. In education, if analytics suggest a student is likely to fall behind, teachers can provide extra support early on. Personalized medicine might monitor your biomarkers continuously and catch an oncoming disease at its earliest, most treatable stage. All these examples hinge on the idea that by treating certain indicators as causes-in-motion, we can redirect outcomes. This is determinism as a tool: it says "A tends to lead to B, so if we don't want B, we had better intervene in A."

However, the very same capabilities raise thorny ethical and philosophical issues. The darker side of a predictive world is the potential loss of individuality and autonomy. If algorithms pigeonhole us based on data, we might start to live in self-fulfilling prophecies. Being constantly predicted can feel like being constantly monitored and subtly guided. Consider personalized advertising: you might think you chose to buy a gadget because you wanted it, but what if the desire was stoked by a precisely targeted ad that appeared at just the right moment, exploiting your known preferences and mood? When does persuasion become a form of control? Another concern is the fairness and bias of these systems. Predictive policing has faced criticism because if the data used reflects past biases (for example, heavier policing of certain minority neighbourhoods in the past leads to more recorded incidents there), the algorithm might simply perpetuate those biases, directing more surveillance to those areas and creating a cycle that looks like destiny but is really a product of feedback loops. In other words, a false aura of determinism can arise: the prediction comes true because the system is nudging it to. We must ask: are we discovering determinism or imposing it?

The notion of "pre-crime" — punishing or restraining someone for what they *might* do — is especially problematic. It runs counter to basic principles of justice and our intuitive sense of free will. After all, if we treat a person as guilty based on a prediction, we are essentially saying their future is fixed and that no choice they make could avert it. That crosses into the realm of fatalism (the idea that outcomes will happen no matter what), which even a strict determinist should avoid. Determinism says "if you continue on this trajectory, then X will likely happen," but it doesn't say the trajectory cannot be altered. The proper use of prediction, many ethicists argue, is to empower individuals and authorities to make better choices, not to eliminate choice. For example, informing someone "Our data suggests people with your profile often develop diabetes in five years" could be used to encourage them to change their diet and exercise (thus using causal knowledge to help them avoid that fate). In contrast, using that data to, say, deny them health insurance outright would be punitive and could remove their incentive to improve (if they're doomed to be judged anyway). Similarly, a police department might use forecasts to offer community support and address causes of crime rather than simply pre-emptively jailing someone.

Another risk is that people might internalize predictions in a way that diminishes their sense of agency. If every app and platform around you seems to "know" what you'll do, you might start to feel like you're on rails, that your life is just following a script. For instance, when your navigation app tells you exactly when to leave and which route to take, you might stop making any decisions about your commute at all. When your streaming service auto-plays the next show it knows you'll enjoy, you might stop browsing for new or challenging content outside your usual tastes. Bit by bit, one could surrender a certain freedom of spontaneity, not because some law of physics compels it, but because an overly helpful algorithm smooths the path so much that you passively go along. It's a subtle psychological effect: determinism in society can become a self-fulfilling prophecy as we conform to the patterns expected of us. Maintaining awareness and deliberation becomes key to preserving a sense of autonomy: we can use the recommendations and predictions as tools, but we also can choose to go against them at times, just to remind ourselves that we can.

In summary, the era of big data has moved determinism from philosophical thought experiment to everyday experience. We are both witnessing and participating in a grand natural experiment: to what extent can human behaviour be predicted if enough information is available? So far, the answer seems to be: to a remarkable extent, though not perfectly. This doesn't conclusively prove that free will is an illusion, but it certainly nudges us toward viewing our choices as part of larger causal patterns. It's a bit disconcerting to realize that an algorithm might understand parts of your behaviour better than you do (for example, predicting you are falling in love with a genre of music before you consciously realize it, simply by noting your listening habits). However, rather than see this as a threat, we might frame it as feedback—an opportunity to understand ourselves through the patterns we produce, and thereby perhaps change those patterns if we wish. Ultimately, big data's lesson is similar to Laplace's original insight: given enough knowledge, much of what we consider personal and spontaneous can be anticipated. This leads us naturally to a broader consideration beyond individual data points: the social and economic forces that shape our lives. Long before "algorithms" and "big data" became buzzwords, thinkers in economics, sociology, and psychology were uncovering systematic causes behind human actions. It is to those social determinants that we now turn.

Social Determinism – Economics, Sociology, and Beyond

For as long as people have reflected on human nature, there's been a tension between seeing individuals as self-made agents or as products of their environment. Modern social sciences largely tilt toward the latter view: that who we become and what we do are profoundly shaped by external forces—our economic conditions, our cultural upbringing, our family dynamics, education, peer influence, and so on. This perspective is sometimes called social determinism, the idea that the individual is, in important respects, a reflection of their society. Unlike the hard physical determinism of, say, physics, social determinism doesn't claim mathematical precision or inevitability; rather, it posits that our choices are heavily conditioned (and in extreme views, almost dictated) by social causes. It's an extension of the deterministic principle into the realm of human behaviour and institutions.

Consider how economists analyse decisions. Classical economic theory often pictures people as rational actors responding to incentives: if the price of something goes up, you buy less of it; if taxes are cut, you work or invest more, and so forth. Though we now know humans aren't always perfectly rational, much of our economic behaviour does follow predictable patterns. We react to scarcity, we seek rewards, we avoid losses in systematic ways. This is why entire industries rely on forecasting market behaviour. An investor assumes that under certain conditions (like low interest rates), most people will invest in stocks rather than save in banks. These predictions hold true enough to be the basis of economic policy. In effect, our aggregate financial choices can often be treated as determined by factors like income, prices, and policy. Even deviations (like bursts of irrational exuberance or panic) happen in patterns—bubbles and crashes that, in retrospect, have logical triggers. Economists of a more radical bent, such as Karl Marx, took determinism further: Marx argued that the material economic conditions of a society ("the mode of production") essentially determine its politics, laws, and even its prevailing ideas. To him, individual beliefs and choices were largely a reflection of one's class interests and socioeconomic position. In a famous line, Marx stated that "men make their own history, but not under circumstances of their own choosing." He acknowledged that people act and thus shape history, but those actions are moulded and constrained by the historical and social context they inherit. A peasant in feudal Europe could not simply decide to become a capitalist factory owner; society's structure made certain paths available and others nearly impossible. In Marx's theory of history, each stage (feudalism, capitalism, etc.) follows necessarily from the prior conditions, almost as if social evolution is pre-scripted—though driven by human conflicts and choices, those choices are themselves products of deeper economic forces.

Sociology, as a discipline, was founded on the insight that many personal outcomes have social causes. Émile Durkheim, one of its pioneers, demonstrated this vividly in his study of suicide. We think of suicide as the most personal, individual decision imaginable. Yet Durkheim found statistical patterns: for example, suicide rates were consistently higher among Protestants than Catholics, and higher among unmarried people than married people. He argued that differences in social integration and social regulation explained these patterns. Catholics (in 19th-century Europe) tended to have tighter-knit communities and more binding shared beliefs, which he believed offered protection against suicidal impulses, whereas Protestants had more individualistic, less communal lifestyles on average, correlating with higher suicide rates. Likewise, being married often meant more social ties and obligations than being single, potentially anchoring individuals against despair. The specifics of Durkheim's explanations can be debated, but the overarching point remains powerful: even our most intimate acts can reflect the influence of social conditions like religious tradition or marital status. Later sociologists

285

continued in this vein, showing how phenomena like crime, educational achievement, or health are not merely a matter of individual choice or ability, but are strongly affected by one's environment: poverty levels, family structure, quality of schooling, peer groups, and cultural norms. When we see a statistic like "children from low-income neighbourhoods are significantly less likely to attend college," we are confronting a form of social determinism—it tells us that an individual's life path is statistically constrained by socio-economic factors beyond their choosing.

Psychology, too, has grappled with determinism. In the early 20th century, behaviourists like John Watson and B.F. Skinner argued that much, if not all, of human (and animal) behaviour could be explained by conditioning and responses to stimuli. Watson famously claimed, with some exaggeration, "Give me a dozen healthy infants and my own specified world to bring them up in, and I'll guarantee to take any one at random and train him to become any type of specialist I might select—doctor, lawyer, artist, merchant-chief, and yes, even beggar-man and thief, regardless of his talents, penchants, tendencies…" His point was that upbringing and environment, not innate free will or even innate talents, largely determine outcomes. While we now recognize genetic influences too, the essential insight remains: our behaviours are shaped by what we learn and experience. Skinner went so far as to suggest that our sense of autonomy is an illusion and that, if we want a better society, we should stop fixating on an imagined free will and instead use behavioural science to engineer better environments. In his book *Beyond Freedom and Dignity*, Skinner proposed that by understanding the environmental causes of behaviour, society could deliberately shape people's actions towards positive ends—much like training animals, but applied to humans (with their consent, one hopes). Although Skinner's views were and are controversial, they encapsulate the extreme of social determinism: seeing individuals as malleable products of external reinforcement, to be moulded for collective well-being.

Even outside these schools of thought, everyday reasoning often acknowledges social determinism. We say "He didn't have a chance in life, growing up like that," or "She is who she is because of how she was raised," implicitly recognizing that circumstances channel behaviour. The debate lies in how *much* they determine it. Hard social determinists might say that, given a person's genes and environment, they could not have turned out much differently than they did. More moderate views allow that individuals find wiggle room to resist or reinterpret their influences. Indeed, history gives examples of people who defied their circumstances—a child from adversity who grows into a successful, kind adult despite the odds, or an individual who rejects their community's values to follow a personal calling. These cases show that social influences are powerful but not absolute destiny; however, they are often notable precisely because they stand out from the trend. For one person who breaks the mould, there are many who fit it, which is why social statistics and predictions work more often than not.

If we embrace the idea that many undesired behaviours (crime, addiction, violence) have social causes, it has profound policy implications. It suggests that to reduce crime, for example, we should fight poverty, improve education, and build healthier communities, rather than simply intensify punishments after crimes occur. This perspective has gained traction in various ways. The public health approach to violence treats crime like an epidemic: identify the risk factors (unemployment, exposure to

287

violence, lack of positive role models) and intervene to reduce those risks, much as you might target the breeding grounds of a virus. Some countries, when dealing with drug abuse, focus less on jailing users and more on addressing the socioeconomic and psychological factors that lead to addiction. If a young man joins a gang, a social determinist lens asks: what influences in his life led to that decision? Maybe his school was underfunded and his family situation unstable, and the gang offered belonging and income. Those are causes we can change—provide better schools, mentor programs, job opportunities—and thereby prevent others from following the same path. This doesn't excuse harmful actions, but it reframes them: the individual still carried out the act, but we look at them more like the end-point of a chain of events. To truly stop the act from happening, one must intervene earlier in the chain.

Such approaches are often contrasted with a pure "individual responsibility" stance, which might emphasize punishment and personal accountability without much concern for background conditions. The truth is, society needs a balance of both views. Leaning too far into social determinism, one could end up absolving individuals of all blame ("society made me do it" becomes a universal excuse) and potentially eroding any incentive for personal effort or moral reflection. Leaning too far the other way, ignoring social causes, can lead to harsh systems that treat every failing as solely the fault of the individual, which is not only uncompassionate but often ineffective (since it doesn't remove the root causes, leading to repeat problems in each generation). As with the personal free will debate, a compatibilist stance might be healthiest: yes, people make choices and should be encouraged to make good ones, but those choices are made within contexts, and improving the context will lead to better choices on average.

We can illustrate this balance with the example of criminal justice. If someone commits a crime, society rightfully holds them accountable; there are consequences like arrest or imprisonment to protect others and signal that the behaviour is not acceptable. That addresses the immediate fact that a harmful action occurred. But then a determinist-minded approach asks: what can we do to ensure that once this person has served their consequence, they won't simply fall back into the same pattern? That leads to rehabilitation efforts—education in prison, psychological counselling, job training—treating the causes that might have contributed to the criminal behaviour. It also leads to efforts outside the justice system: preventing crime through social programs. Notably, countries that have adopted more determinism-informed justice policies (emphasizing rehabilitation and social support) often have lower crime rates and lower recidivism (repeat offense) rates than those that focus purely on retribution. For example, many Scandinavian countries offer extensive rehabilitation for prisoners and support systems upon re-entry to society; their recidivism rates are much lower than in countries that mainly punish. This isn't solely due to one factor (societies differ in many ways), but it aligns with the idea that addressing the determinants of behaviour yields better results than expecting willpower alone to solve everything.

Social determinism also influences how we assign praise, not just blame. If someone achieves great success, a purely individualistic view might laud them as inherently more talented or hardworking than others. A social perspective points out that their success likely drew on many advantages: perhaps supportive parents, good schools, a safe neighbourhood, the cultural capital to navigate institutions, maybe even a bit of luck in opportunities. Recognizing this doesn't belittle their hard work; it just contextualizes it. It can make successful individuals more humble and willing to "give back," realizing their achievement wasn't in a vacuum. And it can spur efforts to extend those advantages to more people, so that success isn't so contingent on birthplace or social status. The goal of acknowledging determinism in society is not to rob anyone of credit or blame, but to foster empathy and intelligent problem-solving. It invites us to see each person as part of a larger story—a story we collectively write through our social policies and culture.

The power of social influences on behaviour has been dramatically demonstrated in psychological experiments as well. In the 1960s, Stanley Milgram's obedience experiments showed that ordinary people, when instructed by an authority figure in a white lab coat, were willing to deliver what they believed were painful electric shocks to a stranger. Despite their personal misgivings, a large percentage complied with the authority's commands to an alarming extent. This suggests that situational factors (the presence of an authority and the structure of the setting) can drive behaviour even when it conflicts with an individual's personal morals. Similarly, Philip Zimbardo's Stanford prison experiment had to be cut short when college students randomly assigned to play "guards" in a simulated prison rapidly began abusing students playing "prisoners." The experiment horrified observers by revealing how quickly people internalized roles and how social context (the power dynamics of a prison setting) elicited cruel behaviour from otherwise normal individuals. While ethically controversial, these studies underscore a key point: context can strongly govern conduct. Good people can do bad things in bad environments, which again implies that if we want to promote good behaviour, we must pay attention to shaping environments, not just lecturing individuals.

Understanding the sway of societal factors helps cultivate compassion. When we learn that a friend's erratic behaviour stems from trauma or that a stranger's rudeness is fuelled by stresses we can't see, we often shift from anger to empathy. At a societal level, this understanding can lead to more patient and constructive approaches to social problems. It echoes that old saying, "To understand all is to forgive all." We might not go so far as to forgive all, but to understand the causes behind actions certainly tempers the harshness of our judgments. It's harder to simply write someone off as "bad" when you see the complex web that led them there. That compassion, however, should not slide into a fatalistic passivity (a topic we address next). Knowing the causes of behaviour is empowering: just as a doctor finds empowerment, not despair, in diagnosing the cause of an illness (because a cause suggests a cure or treatment), so too can society find empowerment in diagnosing the causes of its ills.

Social determinism, then, invites us to take a proactive stance: if we want better outcomes, we have to alter the conditions that breed those outcomes. It's an optimistic message in a way. Rather than throwing up our hands and saying "people will always do X, you can't change human nature," it says human nature in practice is quite changeable if you change what humans are dealing with. History provides evidence of this: when societies alter their structures—expanding education, improving equality, fostering community engagement—people's behaviour often changes accordingly (crime drops, innovation rises, etc.). We are adaptable creatures, for better or worse shaped by our context. The challenge is that we are also the ones creating that context, which means we have a responsibility to get it right.

By seeing individuals as part of a causal network of society, we also extend responsibility outward. It's not only the criminal who must make better choices; it's all of us who must make choices that reduce crime (for instance, voting for policies that reduce poverty or improve justice). It's not only the struggling student who must "work harder"; it's teachers, parents, and policymakers who must strive to provide the conditions where that student can thrive. In a deterministic framework, responsibility is not eliminated; it's distributed. Everyone plays a role in the chain of causes. You can no longer complacently say, "That's not my problem," because if you are in the same society, you are part of the matrix of causes that produce good or bad outcomes.

Before we conclude that determinism erases the individual, it's important to acknowledge that individuals are not just passive receivers of influence. People can often become aware of the forces acting on them and, in that awareness, find some degree of freedom to manoeuvre. For example, someone realizing "I tend to react angrily because I grew up in a hostile environment" might, through reflection or therapy, begin to respond differently and break a cycle that was passed down. Human beings uniquely can reflect on their own conditioning and sometimes transcend it. This means that while social determinism is real, it's not an absolute doom. It just means that achieving that transcendence usually requires specific conditions itself (like support, knowledge, or a transformative experience). In general, the safe bet in predicting human behaviour is still that we will follow our conditioning. But the possibility of change is always there, keeping the door open for personal growth and social reform.

All told, acknowledging social determinism deeply influences how we approach everything from justice to education to personal relationships. It encourages preventative and restorative actions over purely punitive or dismissive ones. It asks us to look at the broader picture whenever we're confronted with a human outcome. As we've woven through these examples—from economic behaviour and crime to psychological experiments—we see the recurring lesson: factors outside the individual strongly channel what the individual does. This insight pairs naturally with the content of the previous section on big data, which highlighted patterns in personal choices, and it sets the stage for our final discussion. Because if we come to see so much of life as governed by causes, an uneasy question arises: should we resign ourselves to these causal laws and just go with the flow? Are we at risk of falling into a kind of fatalism, believing that everything is preordained no matter what we do? In our final section, we address precisely this concern and clarify why recognizing causation in society and in ourselves should empower, not paralyze, us.

The Danger of Fatalism (and how to avoid it)

By this point, one might worry: if everything truly follows from prior causes, does that mean our future is already sealed, and our efforts don't matter? This concern arises from conflating *determinism* with *fatalism*. Though they sound similar, the two ideas are importantly different. Determinism, as we have used the term, is the doctrine that every event has a cause and unfolds from prior conditions in accordance with laws (whether physical, psychological, or social laws).

293

Fatalism, on the other hand, is the belief that outcomes will happen no matter what we do—that certain events are fixed to occur regardless of our choices or actions. In a fatalistic story, a person's attempts to avoid their fate are futile; in a deterministic story, a person's attempts are themselves part of the causal process that leads to the outcome (or leads to a different outcome if those attempts succeed).

An ancient Greek tragedy illustrates fatalism well: the myth of Oedipus. Told that he is destined to kill his father and marry his mother, Oedipus desperately tries to escape this fate by leaving his home—only to unwittingly fulfil the prophecy through the very actions meant to avoid it. This creates the sense that the outcome was "written in stone" and nothing Oedipus did could have changed it. That is fatalism: the idea that "what will be, will be," regardless of human intervention. Now contrast that with a deterministic scenario: imagine a pool table where a cue ball strikes another ball, sending it toward a pocket. If nothing interferes, the second ball will go in—deterministically following the laws of physics from the initial push. But if I place a block on the table, the ball will strike the block and stop, thus changing the outcome. The ball was not "fated" to go in the pocket no matter what; its journey just followed cause and effect. My intervention (placing the block) became a new cause that altered the course. In life, determinism tells us that certain outcomes will happen *if* things continue on their present course. Fatalism would claim the outcome will happen *regardless* of what course we take.

Understanding this distinction is crucial. Determinism does not mean that our choices don't matter; it means our choices do matter, because they are part of the fabric of causality. If you make a choice, that choice will have consequences—specific effects that follow from it. If you refrain from making a choice, that too has consequences. Fatalism incorrectly treats outcomes as independent of the choices, whereas determinism ties outcomes firmly to choices (and other factors). In a deterministic world, to get a particular result, you had better take the actions that lead to it; in a fatalistic world, it doesn't matter what you do, the result will happen (or won't happen) regardless.

Let's make this concrete. Suppose a student has an exam coming up. A fatalistic attitude would be: "Whatever grade I'm going to get is already set. If I'm meant to pass, I'll pass even if I don't study; if I'm meant to fail, studying won't change it. So why bother studying?" A deterministic (but not fatalistic) perspective would say: "Whether I pass or fail will be determined by a host of factors—how much I prepare, how I'm feeling that day, the difficulty of the test, etc. Studying is a cause that will very likely improve my knowledge and therefore my grade. If I choose not to study, that decision will play into the cause-and-effect chain leading to a poor grade." In the deterministic view, the student's efforts are absolutely relevant: they are among the causes that will determine the outcome. The fatalistic mindset, by denying this, can become a self-fulfilling prophecy for failure.

Why do people slip into fatalistic thinking? Often, it's because the idea of determinism is misunderstood or feels emotionally overwhelming. If one hears "everything is determined by prior causes," it might sound as if our fate is out of our hands. But determinism doesn't say outcomes happen without causes; it says outcomes happen because of causes. And who or what provides those causes? In many cases, we do. We are agents—that is, entities that cause things to happen. True, we cause things because of prior causes in us (our genetics, experiences, desires), but that doesn't make our involvement any less significant. A simple analogy: consider a row of standing dominos. If the first domino falls, it will knock over the second, which knocks the third, and so on—deterministically. Now imagine one of those dominos has the ability to move itself or position another domino in a different spot. That domino's movement is itself caused (say, it's on a motor and a timer), but by moving, it can break the chain or redirect it. We are like moving dominos in the chain of events. We may be set in motion by prior conditions, but we are also movers that affect subsequent outcomes.

The philosopher Bertrand Russell pointed out that recognizing causation is empowering, not enfeebling. In a world where events follow from causes, we can intentionally arrange causes to bring about desired effects. This is, in fact, what humans have been doing for millennia as we learned about our world. A farmer doesn't assume "If fate wills a harvest, there will be a harvest." Instead, the farmer tills, plants, waters, and weeds—knowing that these actions (causes) will lead to a good harvest (effect) if all goes well. The farmer operates under an implicit determinism: crops grow because of soil, water, and sunlight, not by sheer chance or fate. If the farmer believed in fatalism ("no matter what I do, the harvest will be the same"), he might not bother farming at all—and surely, the harvest would fail. We can generalize this lesson: nearly every practical endeavour of our lives, from engineering to education, assumes that input affects outcome. We study hard to get a degree, we train in sports to improve performance, we design bridges with calculations to ensure they stand. These are acts of faith in causality: a faith that doing certain things will reliably produce certain results. Imagine if we truly thought outcomes were divorced from our actions—civilization would grind to a halt, as no one would see any point in exerting effort.

Thus, there is a kind of irony: believing in a lawful, cause-and-effect universe motivates us to take action (because we expect our actions to have effects), whereas believing "whatever will be, will be" can lead to passivity. One might say determinism is actually the antidote to fatalism. If you believe things happen for reasons, you will be inclined to figure out those reasons and harness them. If you believe things just happen inevitably, you have no incentive to do anything. A deterministic outlook and a sense of agency are compatible: you view yourself as an instrument through which causes can be channelled to produce outcomes you care about. You might not have *ultimate* free will in the metaphysical sense, but you still have wants, goals, and knowledge, and those translate into actions that make a difference in the world.

It's worth noting that even in a fully determined world, from the inside, we experience life as choosing and doing. You wake up and make decisions—what to eat, where to go, how to respond to emails. Those decisions have real consequences. Understanding that your decisions have causes behind them doesn't change the fact that they are *your* decisions and they will shape your day. If anything, understanding those causes can help you make better decisions. For example, if you realize you tend to make impulsive choices when you're tired (a causal insight), you might decide not to do online shopping late at night, thereby avoiding some poor purchases. In doing so, you've used determinism (knowledge of what causes your impulses) to improve your exercise of agency.

This relates to what we discussed about knowledge being power. If you know the causal factors at play in your life, you are better positioned to steer outcomes. Recognizing determinism is essentially recognizing how the world (and we ourselves) work. It should equip us to work with the grain of causality to shape the future, much as a sailor uses knowledge of wind and currents to navigate the sea. A fatalist would simply drift, saying "the winds will take me wherever." The determinist sailor trims the sails and charts a course, knowing full well that the winds and currents are natural forces, not random whim. The sailor's actions are determined too (perhaps by a desire to reach land and knowledge of sailing), but that doesn't negate the fact that those determined actions are necessary for the ship to reach its destination.

There is also a subtle but important emotional shift that happens when moving from a fatalistic attitude to a deterministic-yet-engaged attitude. Fatalism often comes with resignation or despair—"nothing I do matters" can be a depressing thought. It can lead to apathy or a sense of helplessness. When people first grapple with the idea that free will might be an illusion, some do react in this way: "If I'm just a cog in a machine, why should I care about anything?" But this reaction overlooks that even as a 'cog', you have a role and function that affects the whole machine. The proper response is arguably the opposite of despair: it's responsibility. If anything, determinism should make us feel *more* responsible for outcomes, not less. Because if outcomes flow from conditions, and we are among those conditions for many outcomes, then what we choose to do carries weight. We cannot just throw up our hands and wait for fate, because fate is not something separate from the chain of cause and effect—it works through that chain, and we are links in it.

298

Let's revisit the scenario of someone saying "It's all determined, so I can't change anything." If taken literally, that statement is paradoxical, because if it's truly determined that you will do nothing, then indeed nothing will change—but not because determinism per se prohibits change, rather because you've decided not to be an agent of change. However, if it were determined (by prior causes such as your character and understanding) that you *will* take action, then change will happen through you. In other words, determinism doesn't tell us what is predetermined; it only says *something* is (namely, things follow from what came before). It's up to the actual causes in play to decide what happens—and your attitude can be one of those causes. Adopting a defeatist attitude tends to lead to worse outcomes; adopting a proactive attitude tends to lead to better ones. Both attitudes might be caused by something (say, your upbringing or your philosophical beliefs), but understanding that, you can also intentionally feed yourself a different perspective. This book's aim, in part, is to provide that perspective: a way to see determinism not as a sentence to nihilism, but as insight that can enhance how effectively and compassionately we navigate life.

We should also recall our discussion in earlier chapters about moral responsibility in a deterministic framework. We concluded that dropping belief in absolute contra-causal free will doesn't mean giving up on ethics or improvement; instead, it refocuses our approach. Similarly, dropping a belief in metaphysical freedom doesn't mean dropping your will to shape your life. It just means you now understand your will as operating within a causal network. You still set goals and pursue them—you simply do so with a clearer recognition of the influences on you and the influences you can have. In fact, believing in cause and effect can make you more effective at achieving goals. For example, if you accept that your health is largely a result of diet, exercise, and stress (rather than pure chance or destiny), you'll be more inclined to eat well, stay active, and manage stress—concrete actions that deterministically lead to better health. A fatalistic approach ("I'll live as long as I'm fated to, it doesn't matter what I do") might lead one to neglect those factors, with poor health as a result.

Philosopher Bertrand Russell, along with many scientists, championed the idea that understanding the world's causality is key to progress. When we see a problem—be it a disease, a social ill, or a personal struggle—our first question should be: what causes underlie this, and how can we change them? That question itself is an embrace of determinism. It rejects the fatalistic shrug of "nothing to be done," and instead asserts that by altering inputs we can alter outputs. Russell also believed that acknowledging our place in nature (as determined beings) can instil a kind of calm and acceptance of things beyond our control, while simultaneously motivating us to control what we can. His view aligns with an even older wisdom: the Stoic idea of distinguishing between what we can change and what we cannot. The Stoics believed in a fated order to the universe (they were determinists in their own way), yet they emphasized acting virtuously and dealing with what is up to us—our own judgments and actions. They counselled to not waste energy lamenting what must be, but also to never shy away from doing what one can. In essence, they were saying: accept determinism without falling into lazy fatalism.

Finally, it's worth reflecting on an empowering thought: if the future is determined, it is not determined in spite of us, but through us. We are part of the unfolding of the universe. The chain of causation that will be tomorrow's reality runs through our choices today. This gives our lives significance, even if one believes those choices are themselves determined by prior causes. We become the conduits by which certain possibilities become actual. For instance, it might be true that given the state of the world now, someone is determined to invent a new technology next year—but that invention will occur through the hard work and creativity of that person. It doesn't happen automatically. The deterministic view doesn't mean we sit back; it means we recognize that everything we do now will have reverberations. It puts a kind of responsibility on our present actions: since they will echo into the future, we ought to choose them carefully (to the extent that we can choose).

In short, understanding determinism should lead not to fatalistic inaction, but to a thoughtful engagement with life. It replaces the notion of an arbitrary fate with the reality of cause and effect—a reality in which our efforts are integral. By clarifying the distinction between "inevitable no matter what" and "inevitable only if nothing changes," we reclaim the importance of making changes. We started this chapter asking whether knowing more about causes (in technology, in society, in ourselves) undermines our freedom. We end it by seeing that, on the contrary, such knowledge hands us the reins to the extent they can be held. Embracing determinism means accepting that the world has structure and order—but within that order, it matters greatly what we do. Far from resigning us to passivity, this realization can energize us to be active participants in the grand causal drama, aiming to steer it toward outcomes we value.

With the discussion above, we have navigated the complex interplay of determinism with modern society and technology. We've seen that the algorithmic engines of AI and big data reflect deterministic principles in action, and that social systems powerfully shape individual destinies through cause and effect. Yet we've also affirmed that understanding these forces does not condemn us to fatalism; rather, it equips us to act more effectively and compassionately. In recognizing the chains of cause around us, we learn how to tug those chains in better directions. This brings us to a final consideration that looms over the entire free will versus determinism debate: how do we find meaning and construct values if the world is, at its base, governed by impersonal laws? In the next chapter, we will confront that question directly, tying together all the threads—from physics and biology to ethics and society—that we have unravelled so far, to see what kind of personal purpose and moral vision can guide us in a universe of causes.

Chapter 9

Conclusion – Freedom, Knowledge, and the Unbroken Chain

Revisiting the Chain

Our journey through the realms of history, science, and philosophy has brought us face to face with the profound idea of determinism. From the earliest myths and metaphysical musings to the latest scientific theories, we have traced the evolving concept of an unbroken chain of cause and effect running through reality. Now, at the end of this journey, it is fitting to step back and consider how these pieces come together. What have we learned about the notion that every event is linked by causality? How has our understanding of this "chain" changed from ancient times to the present day? In revisiting the key milestones, we uncover a theme that is both remarkably persistent and subtly transformed over the ages.

Ancient roots. The idea that events do not happen in isolation has deep roots in antiquity. Long before modern science, thinkers and storytellers grappled with whether the

303

cosmos was orderly or capricious. Many ancient cultures personified fate as a powerful force weaving the destinies of gods and humans alike. In Greek mythology, for instance, the Fates spun the threads of each life—a vivid image of an ordained sequence of events. Philosophy soon took up these questions in a more analytical way. By the 5th century BCE, the earliest philosophers were offering naturalistic explanations for why things happen. On one side, the atomists like *Leucippus* and *Democritus* argued that nothing occurs at random; everything unfolds from prior conditions by necessity. According to Democritus's bold vision, reality consists of atoms moving in the void, and all phenomena— including human thoughts and choices—result from the lawful interactions of those atoms. If one could know the precise arrangement of atoms at any moment, one could in principle foresee the next outcome. This was one of the first explicit formulations of determinism: the belief that every event has a cause and, given that cause, could not happen otherwise.

Not all agreed. Other Greek thinkers emphasized spontaneity, chance, or genuine choice. *Aristotle*, for example, acknowledged causation but believed that not every outcome is fated from the beginning; he allowed for accidents and contingencies that could have been otherwise. In a famous illustration of this tension, Aristotle considered the statement "There will be a sea-battle tomorrow." He realized that if such a statement were already true or false in advance, then the future would be fixed—either the battle inevitably happens or it cannot happen at all. To preserve the possibility that human decisions (to go to battle or not) still matter, Aristotle concluded that propositions about future events don't have a definite truth value in the present. In essence, he was resisting a strictly deterministic logic by arguing that the future remains open until it becomes present. Likewise, the philosopher *Epicurus* took a bold step to safeguard free will: he proposed that atoms occasionally "swerve" unpredictably, introducing a tiny element of randomness into the otherwise lawful atomic motions. Epicurus's idea was meant to break the bonds of determinism just enough to allow human volition a foothold. Though modern physics has long since moved beyond Epicurean atoms, the core philosophical worry he addressed is timeless—how to reconcile a lawful universe with our sense of freedom.

Between these poles, the Stoic philosophers crafted a worldview that tightly embraced cosmic determinism while trying to maintain moral responsibility. The Stoics believed that a divine rational principle (the Logos) pervaded nature, ensuring that everything unfolds according to fate. To them, even the most unexpected twist of fortune was *in principle* woven into the universe's rational plan. A Stoic might counsel that if you stubbed your toe, it was ultimately because the cosmos willed it so at the highest level of reason. Yet the Stoics also taught that humans must live virtuously and play our part—essentially advocating a form of compatibilism long before the term existed. In Stoic ethics, you are free and responsible as long as your will aligns with the inevitable progression of events. Ancient debates thus already featured many of the key themes that would echo through later ages: some thinkers saw an unbreakable causal order, others carved out space for chance or choice, and many struggled to balance these views.

Medieval and religious perspectives.

As history moved forward, the discussion took on theological dimensions. In late antiquity and the Middle

Ages, the determinism question became entwined with religious doctrines of divine foreknowledge and providence. If an omniscient God already knows or decrees everything that will happen, does that not imply that the chain of events is fixed from eternity? This problem preoccupied thinkers in the Judeo-Christian-Islamic traditions. *Saint Augustine*, wrestling with heretical ideas of cosmic fatalism, argued passionately that humans still possess a will and are responsible for sin, even though God is all-knowing. He distinguished between God's knowledge and human causation, suggesting that God's foreknowledge doesn't *force* us to choose what we do—a subtle argument that many after him would refine. In medieval scholasticism, philosophers like *Thomas Aquinas* attempted to reconcile human free will with an omnipotent, omniscient deity by proposing that divine knowledge exists on a different plane than time-bound human choice. Similarly, the Jewish philosopher *Maimonides* contended that we shouldn't think of God's knowledge as a literal pre-recording of events, because God's way of knowing is not like ours. These theologians, in effect, did intellectual somersaults to affirm both: that an unbroken chain of divine causality sustains the world *and* that humans can be held accountable for their actions. The tension was never fully resolved, but throughout the medieval period the idea of an orderly, law-governed universe—whether by nature or by God—remained strong. Even when miracles or mysteries were allowed, most thinkers assumed that events were not arbitrary. The universe was seen as a grand design rather than a chaos of accidents, and that assumption of underlying order set the stage for the scientific revolution.

Clockwork universe: the rise of scientific determinism.

With the dawn of modern science in the 17th century, the concept of an unbroken causal chain gained dramatic new support. *Isaac Newton* and his contemporaries discovered mathematical laws that could predict the motion of planets and projectiles with astounding accuracy. Suddenly, the age-old notion that nature follows dependable rules was not just a philosophical speculation but an empirical reality demonstrated by physics. The success of Newtonian mechanics painted a picture of nature as a vast machine—intricate but fundamentally predictable if you knew the mechanisms. Thinkers began to suggest that, just as planets orbit the sun by lawful necessity, perhaps every physical event has a precise cause. The image of the universe as a perfectly regulated clockwork emerged: God (or nature) as a master clockmaker who set the cosmos in motion according to perfect laws. In this view, every tick of the clock and every future tick were determined at the moment of creation.

By the 18th century, deterministic thinking had extended beyond physics. Enlightenment philosophers applied the idea of natural laws to human behaviour, society, and even the workings of the mind. The French philosophe *Baron d'Holbach*, for example, argued that humans are wholly part of nature and therefore subject to the same causal laws—our notions of free choice, he claimed, are illusions born of ignorance of the causes that compel us. Others in the Enlightenment were more moderate, but a general optimism prevailed that science would eventually explain *everything*, from the fall of an apple to the decisions of a person, through universal laws. This sentiment was epitomized by *Pierre-Simon Laplace*, a French mathematician and astronomer who in 1814 articulated what has become the classic thought experiment of strict determinism. Laplace asked us to imagine an intelligence (later often called "Laplace's Demon") that knows the exact state of every particle in the universe at one time. If such a being also knew all the laws of nature, Laplace declared, then "nothing would be uncertain" for it—the future and the past would be as clear as the present. In other words, if the positions and velocities of all atoms were known, this super-intelligence could compute every future event and retrodict every past event with perfect accuracy. Laplace confidently asserted that any appearance of chance in our world is only due to human ignorance; underlying it all is a firm chain of causes.

This vision of a perfectly deterministic universe captured the imaginations of the 18th and 19th centuries. It was more than just a physics principle—it was a sweeping worldview. Nature was a vast, unerring calculus of cause and effect. Many intellectuals of Laplace's era believed that Newton's laws (perhaps extended by undiscovered principles for chemistry, biology, and society) would eventually explain everything. For instance, early biologists searched for strict laws of heredity and physiology that would make life processes as predictable as planetary orbits. Social thinkers like *Karl Marx* later spoke of "historical laws" driving the destiny of societies, implying a kind of determinism in economics and class struggle. Determinism, in short, became entwined with the notion of scientific progress and rationality. The world was viewed as a gigantic puzzle that, in principle, could be solved if we had enough information and computing power. By the late 1800s, many scientists and philosophers felt that the chain of causation was indeed unbroken—and that human knowledge was approaching the point of tracing those links with confidence in domain after domain.

Cracks in the armour: chaos and quantum uncertainty.

Just when determinism seemed almost unassailable, new discoveries began to complicate the picture. The late 19th and early 20th centuries brought phenomena that didn't fit neatly into the clockwork scheme. One challenge came from within classical physics itself: the problem of *chaotic dynamics*. In 1890, the mathematician *Henri Poincaré* discovered that the gravitational interaction of even just three bodies (say, the Sun, Earth, and Moon) can be inherently unpredictable in the long term. Tiny differences in initial positions or speeds can lead to vastly different outcomes over time—a finding that later blossomed into chaos theory. This was unsettling: it suggested that even systems governed by deterministic laws could defy precise prediction, not because the laws were wrong but because the systems were exquisitely sensitive to initial conditions. Much later, in the 1960s, meteorologist *Edward Lorenz* famously described this phenomenon as the "butterfly effect"—the idea that a butterfly flapping its wings might ultimately influence the formation of a tornado weeks later. The essence of chaos is that for certain complex systems (weather, ecosystems, perhaps economies), one would need impossibly perfect knowledge of the present to predict the future accurately. Any slight uncertainty about the present multiplies over time into complete unpredictability. Importantly, chaos does not break the causal chain—each event still has its causes. It only hides the pattern from our view by making it exceedingly complicated. For scientists raised on Laplace's dream, however, it was a humbling reminder that determinism in theory is not the same as determinism in practice. The chain might be unbroken, but it could be so entangled that we effectively experience it as unpredictable or random.

An even more dramatic challenge to classical determinism arrived with the new physics of the quantum realm. In the early 20th century, experiments with atoms and subatomic particles revealed phenomena that no classical law could explain. To account for these, physicists developed quantum mechanics—a revolutionary theoretical framework that succeeded beyond expectation in predicting the *probabilities* of microscopic events. But it came with an unsettling implication: at a fundamental level, nature might be governed by chance. According to the standard interpretation of quantum mechanics, you cannot predict the exact outcome of a single radioactive decay or the precise path of a single electron; you can only calculate the probabilities of different outcomes. For example, if we have one unstable atom, physics can tell us its half-life (the time by which there's a 50% chance it will have decayed), but it cannot tell us *exactly when* any given atom will decay. There seems to be no hidden clock or mechanism that triggers the decay at a set time—it just happens. Einstein, who had grown up intellectually during the heyday of strict determinism, found this deeply unsatisfactory. His famous protest was, "God does not play dice with the universe," expressing his belief that there must be some deeper law beneath quantum randomness. Yet repeated experiments have consistently validated the quantum predictions of genuine randomness (at least in the sense of unpredictability). In fact, by the 1980s, physicists such as Alain Aspect and his colleagues had performed tests that strongly suggested no local hidden variables can explain away quantum indeterminacy—nature really behaves as if certain events have no specific cause but are instead irreducibly probabilistic.

The philosophical implications of quantum mechanics are still debated. Some interpretations of quantum theory (such as the *Many-Worlds Interpretation*) actually keep determinism intact by positing that all possible outcomes occur in branching parallel universes, so there is no randomness in the broader multiverse—though in any single branch (the one we experience), events appear random. Other interpretations hold onto determinism by imagining unknown variables or a deeper level of reality (as Einstein hoped) that we simply haven't discovered yet. However, the mainstream view among working physicists is more pragmatic: quantum mechanics works extremely well as a predictive tool, so whether each event is truly uncaused or just caused by something hidden is seen as an almost metaphysical question. For practical purposes, scientists accept that at least on the scale of particles, outcomes can only be predicted in terms of probabilities. The upshot is a shift in how we conceive the causal chain: it's no longer seen as ironclad in the Laplacean sense. Modern science instead describes a chain that is statistical or probabilistic in certain respects. The causal links are still there, but they are not always one-to-one links; sometimes one cause can lead to multiple possible effects, with known probabilities but no way to foretell which effect will happen in a given instance.

An evolving understanding.

As we reach the present day, the concept of determinism has been refined and tempered. We saw it grow from a philosophical principle to a triumphant scientific paradigm, and then become a subject of subtle nuance in the face of new evidence. Does the universe follow an unbroken chain of cause and effect? In a general sense, much of our exploration suggests yes—the success of science in every field depends on finding dependable connections between past events and future outcomes. We have not discovered any domain in which pure chaos (in the sense of utterly uncaused happenings) reigns. Even quantum randomness occurs within a framework of well-defined probabilities and constraints, and at larger scales those quantum uncertainties often average out to the stable, reliable patterns we observe. For all practical purposes, cause and effect remain enormously robust. When you flip a light switch, the lamp will reliably turn on (barring a burned-out bulb or a power outage). When an apple detaches from a tree, gravity ensures it will fall to the ground. When people take a medication, we expect consistent physiological responses according to chemistry and biology. Our entire technology and industry are built on the expectation that causes lead to effects in predictable ways. In that sense, the chain of causality is alive and well.

Yet, our journey also revealed that our knowledge of this chain is incomplete and always will be. We cannot trace every link, and some links seem to have a looseness to them. We learned that even in a deterministic system, if it is complex enough (like the climate or the human brain), we may be unable to predict its exact state far into the future—our calculations become overwhelmed by complexity. And we learned that on the smallest scales, the universe may possess a fundamental element of indeterminacy, meaning even with perfect information some events would remain unpredictable except in probabilistic terms. In short, the "unbroken chain" of cause and effect remains a guiding ideal, but we approach it now with greater humility. Modern determinism is not the rigid, absolute certainty that Laplace's generation envisioned; it is a recognition of the patterns and regularities that underlie phenomena, coupled with an understanding that there is still mystery at the edges. We find ourselves, then, in a world where causality is immensely powerful but not all-powerful—at least not in any way humans can fully grasp. The chain of events that shapes our lives is exceedingly strong, but it is also intricate, sometimes hidden, and perhaps threaded with a touch of genuine unpredictability.

That brings us to a crucial insight as we conclude this review of determinism's evolution: believing in the principle of cause and effect doesn't mean claiming we know every cause or can control every effect. Determinism as a concept has matured from a dogma about certainty into a nuanced framework that guides inquiry. This sets the stage for our next consideration. If the world is largely governed by causal laws but our understanding of those laws is probabilistic and incomplete, how should we regard extreme claims on either side of the free will debate? To answer that, we turn now to the value of maintaining a balanced perspective—one that is pragmatic in seeking explanations but humble about what we truly know.

Pragmatism and Humility

If our exploration has taught us anything, it is caution against absolutism. Grand questions like "Is everything fated or do we have free will?" tend to lure people toward extreme answers. One person might claim that *absolutely everything* is predetermined down to the last detail; another might insist that humans possess a mystical freedom wholly outside the chain of cause and effect. But the lessons of history and science urge a more nuanced view. Extreme positions—dogmatic determinism on one hand or a dogmatic belief in unrestricted free will on the other—are philosophically hazardous when taken as articles of faith. They each run

313

ahead of what we can firmly know, and they can distort our interpretation of new evidence.

Consider first the allure of absolute determinism. After Laplace, it was tempting to believe the universe is like a perfect equation: solve for the initial conditions and you solve for all time. Some thinkers did speak as if this were a settled truth—that every action, every thought, every breeze and every starquake was fixed since the dawn of creation. The trouble with holding this view too tightly is that it can become a kind of blindfold. Someone convinced that "everything is 100% predetermined" might be inclined to dismiss or downplay phenomena that don't neatly fit a clockwork picture. We saw, for example, how the early 20th-century discovery of quantum randomness shocked those with Laplacean expectations. A rigid determinist could respond to such surprises in two unhelpful ways: either by denying the new findings ("there *must* be a hidden cause; I don't care what the experiments say"), or by misinterpreting determinism in a fatalistic manner ("if it's all predetermined, then our efforts don't matter"). Both reactions miss the mark. The history of science shows that even our best theories can be incomplete, and reality can defy our certainties. Clinging to absolute determinism as a dogma can close our minds to the possibility that nature has more nuances in store.

On the other side, the allure of absolute free will has its own risks. It often stems from a deeply felt intuition that we are not mere puppets—that we can genuinely choose and could have chosen otherwise. Many religious and humanistic traditions uphold that people have a soul or self that is outside the brute mechanics of nature, capable of initiating actions independently. Taken to an extreme, this view posits that some events (notably human decisions) have no cause

314

whatsoever except the mysterious power of the will. The hazard here is a different kind of blindfold: a person convinced of total free will might reject well-founded evidence that our choices are influenced by genes, brain chemistry, upbringing, and other factors. For instance, psychology and neuroscience have catalogued countless ways in which decisions can be predicted or manipulated by altering their antecedents (whether through advertising, brain stimulation, or social conditioning). If someone insists that free will is absolute, they may ignore these causal factors and thus miss important truths about human behaviour. In the realm of ethics, an exaggerated belief in unconstrained free will can breed harsh attitudes—imagine blaming someone for not "just choosing" to be mentally healthy or morally perfect, as if their background or biology meant nothing. Just as the hard determinist can become too cynical about personal effort ("why try, if the future is already written?"), the hard libertarian (champion of pure free will) can become too judgmental or naive about the forces that drive people's actions ("everyone has total control, so any failing is purely their fault"). Both extremes, in different ways, lead to unwise conclusions.

The remedy for these extremes is a healthy dose of pragmatism and humility. Pragmatism here means grounding our beliefs in what is actually known and what actually works, rather than in sweeping absolutes. And humility means recognizing the limits of our knowledge. A wonderful example of this balanced mindset comes from the philosopher *Bertrand Russell*. Russell engaged the free will vs. determinism debate in light of modern science, and his stance was neither black nor white. He noted that on the one hand, the method of science presumes determinism: scientists constantly seek causes for observed effects and

315

have been extraordinarily successful in finding them. This working assumption—"there must be an explanation"—is pragmatic because it leads to discovery. It would be foolish to abandon the search for causes just because some questions are hard; indeed, the scientific approach has time and again turned mysteries into understanding by doggedly looking for lawful regularities. Russell had no quarrel with this aspect: determinism as a methodological principle is the engine of scientific progress. We assume there's order, and we thereby uncover order.

However, Russell also cautioned against leaping from the success of this method to the metaphysical claim that determinism holds without exception in every corner of reality. Science's track record supports believing that events have causes, but it does not prove that *all* events are rigidly predestined or that our theories will never meet anomalies. In the early 20th century, Russell saw quantum physics forcing thinkers to re-examine whether the "law of causality" was absolute. He counselled that we should of course keep investigating causes everywhere, but we should not claim we already know as a fact that literally everything is fixed in advance. In plain terms, don't become so sure of determinism that you treat it as infallible dogma. Reality has surprised us before and could do so again. Maintaining this humility ensures that if truly acausal phenomena exist, we won't be blind to them out of stubborn philosophy.

At the same time, Russell was equally critical of the opposite dogma—the claim that human will is somehow exempt from causality. He pointed out that declaring an event uncaused (especially something as complex as a human decision) is an extraordinary claim that demands extraordinary evidence. To simply assume our choices "float" free of any prior influences would be, in his view, a relic of mystical thinking left over from an earlier age. Everything we've learned in fields like biology, psychology, and neuroscience indicates that our mental life is intertwined with the physical processes of our brains and shaped by our environments. Thus, to carve out one special part of nature (human volition) and say "here, the laws of cause and effect break down" is a kind of special pleading. It elevates human beings to a miraculous status without proof. Russell, ever the naturalist, suggested that humans are part of nature, not apart from it. We are likely subject to causation just as much as other creatures, even if we do not yet understand all the subtle mechanisms at work.

In essence, this balanced perspective tells us: keep an open mind, but also keep a critical eye. We shouldn't be too quick to shout "miracle!" and abandon the search for causes whenever we encounter something we don't yet understand. History shows that many mysteries eventually get natural explanations. But we also shouldn't presume that our current scientific understanding is the final word on reality. The wise course is to remain curious and cautious. Perhaps determinism is nearly universally true but has a few fundamental exceptions; or perhaps what looks like an exception today will be explained tomorrow. Until we have incontrovertible evidence one way or the other, the prudent stance is neither to dogmatically affirm nor to dogmatically deny absolute determinism.

This attitude is not a lukewarm compromise for its own sake; it is an acknowledgment of the complexity of the issue. It allows us to navigate between the extremes, taking the best of both. We affirm the pragmatic value of seeking causes— after all, assuming there is a causal explanation has been an immensely fruitful strategy in science and daily life. At the same time, we practice intellectual humility—recognizing that our understanding of those causes is always provisional and subject to revision. In practical terms, this means treating determinism as a working hypothesis and guide, not as an untouchable dogma, and treating free will (in the radical, "uncaused" sense) as unproven, while still respecting our lived experience of making choices.

Science, importantly, remains open-ended. A good scientist (or philosopher) must be ready to say "I don't know for sure" and adjust their model of the world as new data come in. So far, no experiment has reliably demonstrated a breach of causality—no one has shown an event that clearly had no cause at all. Conversely, it's impossible to prove beyond doubt that *every* event is predetermined, because we cannot test every corner of the universe across all time. In light of that, our stance should be one of cautious exploration. The burden of proof is high for anyone asserting the absolute: whether it's "some events have no cause" or "everything was fixed since the beginning of time." These claims, if true, would reshape how we see ourselves, but they remain hypotheses to be examined against evidence.

Adopting pragmatism and humility doesn't mean we throw up our hands and refuse to take any position. It simply means we proceed carefully. We lean on evidence and reason, and we avoid the temptation of all-or-nothing thinking. This mindset allows us to appreciate the richness of the determinism debate: it's not a simple binary where one side must be entirely right and the other entirely wrong. The truth may lie in a subtle middle ground—or in some synthesis we have yet to fully imagine. With this balanced perspective in mind, we can now turn to the human level. Given that the universe seems law-governed but not transparently predictable, and given that we neither hail ourselves as sorcerers outside of nature nor reduce ourselves to passively ticking clocks, how do we find meaning in our lives? Does a largely deterministic framework diminish our humanity, or can it coexist with the values and sense of purpose that drive us? These questions of human meaning and values will occupy us next.

Human Meaning and Values

One might worry that a largely deterministic universe leaves little room for human meaning. If our choices and actions are all products of prior causes, is everything we do somehow less genuine or important? This concern has haunted the determinism debate from the start: what becomes of love, creativity, moral responsibility, or personal achievement if we are, in a sense, "programmed" by circumstances and biology? It is a serious question, but the conclusion of our journey offers an encouraging answer. Causation does not rob life of significance. In fact, understanding how and why things happen can *enhance* our sense of meaning and guide us to live more purposefully. We still fall in love, invent new things, compose songs, raise children, and dream about the future—and all these actions matter, perhaps even more so, when seen as part of the grand chain of events. Far from being nullified by determinism, our human experiences and values find a solid place within a causally connected world.

First, let's dispel the notion that if something has a cause it is automatically devoid of value. We sometimes hear the lament: "If my feelings and choices have physical or psychological causes, then maybe they're not *really* mine." But consider the opposite: would your love for your best friend be more meaningful if it appeared entirely out of nowhere, with no basis in your past experiences or their qualities? Or is it meaningful precisely because it *grows out of* a shared history, mutual understanding, and kindness exchanged (all causes and conditions)? Most of us would agree it's the latter. Love isn't less special because we can trace its development; if anything, knowing the story of how two people came to care for each other deepens its significance. Similarly, an artist's creative genius often has discernible sources—perhaps years of practice, influences from earlier artists, or even a neurological quirk. Those origins don't make the artwork any less magnificent; they merely tell us *how* it came to be. Value and meaning thrive in a context of causation. A life story is meaningful because of the connections between events, not in spite of them.

In a deterministic framework, our actions have *consequences*, and that is exactly why they matter. If anything, a world of dependable cause and effect gives our choices a certain weight: what you do now will ripple out into the future. Recall the idea we encountered earlier: if the future is determined, it is determined through our present actions, not around them. When you work hard to learn a difficult skill, that effort is a cause that will have real effects—perhaps a new career opportunity down the line, or the creation of something that outlasts you. If you decide to show kindness to a stranger, that act might set off a chain of positivity in that person's life (or it might not, depending on other factors—but it clearly *has the potential* because cause and effect allow it). If everything were pure chance or whim with no causal continuity, then your efforts and intentions would have no guarantee of making any difference. It is precisely because the world has reliable pathways that planting a seed, literally or metaphorically, can lead to a tree later on. We find meaning in life by recognizing that our choices shape outcomes. Determinism, understood properly, underscores that fact rather than undermining it.

What about moral values and responsibility? On the surface, determinism might seem to dissolve personal responsibility—after all, if someone's actions were the inevitable results of prior causes, how can we hold them accountable? This is a profound ethical puzzle, but throughout our exploration we've seen that acknowledging causation can actually *strengthen* our moral framework by making it more compassionate and more effective. Understanding the causes behind behaviour tends to foster empathy. For example, if we learn that a person who committed a crime was raised in dire circumstances, with abuse and lack of education, we gain insight into the chain of events that led to that outcome. We are less likely to write the person off as simply "evil" (a label that explains nothing) and more likely to consider how to help them or how to prevent such situations in the future. This doesn't mean we deny the person's agency or excuse the harm done; rather, we shift our focus toward addressing root causes. A justice system informed by determinism would emphasize rehabilitation (changing the offender's future causes for action) and prevention (changing social conditions that breed crime) over pure retribution. In fact, many Enlightenment reformers and modern thinkers have argued just that: once we see that people's actions flow from prior causes, we can tailor our social responses to *change* those causes going forward, reducing harm for everyone. Punishment becomes not an angry act of vengeance, but one element in a causal feedback loop aimed at improving behaviour and protecting the community.

Far from making morality meaningless, a causal perspective grounds it in reality. It tells us that if we want better outcomes—less crime, more kindness, greater well-being—we must understand what causes lead to those results and then work to implement or encourage those causes. "To understand all is to forgive all," says an old proverb. While it exaggerates (complete understanding doesn't automatically equal total forgiveness), the saying captures a truth: deep understanding of someone's story usually increases our compassion for them. Determinism invites us to adopt this understanding stance. When we realize how much a person's upbringing, genes, and life experiences have shaped their character, it softens the sharp, reflexive judgment that "they could simply have chosen to do better." We see instead that their very ability to choose wisely was influenced by factors beyond their control up to that point. This perspective can make us more forgiving of others and also more committed to helping them overcome their circumstances. It encourages what you might call an "ethic of care" rather than an "ethic of blame." We shift from merely assigning guilt to asking: *How did this happen, and how can we prevent it from happening again?*

Importantly, recognizing causal influences does not mean denying the reality of our deliberation and decision-making. Whether or not ultimate free will exists in some metaphysical sense, humans *experience* themselves as making choices, weighing reasons, and controlling their actions to a significant degree. That experience is not an illusion to be discarded; it is a crucial part of how the chain of causality operates in our lives. Our ability to reflect, consider different possibilities, and restrain or enact impulses is itself a product of evolution and development—a set of capacities with causes behind them, yes, but also one that gives us a powerful form of agency. Think of it this way: your deliberative mind is the *mechanism* by which many causes (your knowledge, desires, fears, memories, and so on) come together to yield an action. It's a high-level causal process that integrates lots of inputs. If you decide after careful thought to change careers, that decision might be influenced by a dozen factors—financial concerns, passion for the new field, advice from friends, personal values—but *you are the one doing the integrating and deciding*. The decision is "yours" because it happens through your conscious reasoning and reflects your personality and priorities, even if those, in turn, have antecedents. In a deterministic (or mostly deterministic) universe, our capacity for reason and foresight doesn't vanish—on the contrary, it becomes the linchpin of how change occurs.

Seen in this light, we can define a kind of freedom that is compatible with causality. This compatibilist notion of freedom does not require magical independence from cause and effect. It simply requires that our actions flow from our *internal* desires, intentions, and rational deliberations, rather than from external coercion or constraints that force us to act against our will. If my choices are caused by *me* (that is, by my brain and mind, shaped by my genetics, experiences, and character) and not by some external force or random accident, then in a meaningful sense they are my choices. I can own them, take responsibility for them, and work to change them if needed, because they reflect who I am. This view preserves moral responsibility: we hold people responsible not because we assume they had some supernatural ability to do otherwise in exactly the same situation, but because their actions flow from their character and reasons, and responding to those actions (through praise, blame, sanctions, or support) is part of how we influence their future behaviour and the behaviour of others. Responsibility, in this understanding, is forward-looking—

it's about guiding future causes—rather than a mere backward-looking blame for past inevitabilities.

Moreover, if we embrace this understanding, we gain the ability to cultivate freedom and meaning by shaping the causes that shape us. We become, as it were, gardeners of our own lives and societies. For instance, if you know that your environment heavily influences your habits, you can design your environment to encourage the habits you *want*. Want to read more books and watch less mindless television? A deterministic insight might lead you to set up a causal structure: keep books by your bedside and put the TV remote in an inconvenient spot. You haven't made yourself magically "free" of the temptation of TV, but you have effectively used cause and effect to give your preferred behaviour the upper hand. By creating the right causes (easy access to books, minor obstacles to TV watching), you increase the likelihood that the effect will be you reading at night. On a community scale, if we want the next generation to lead meaningful, productive lives, we can invest in education, mentorship, and a nurturing social environment—causes that we know tend to empower individuals later on. In doing so, we are leveraging determinism to our advantage: because certain inputs reliably yield better outcomes, we intentionally provide those inputs.

In this way, understanding causation becomes a roadmap to greater human freedom (in the practical sense) and flourishing. It teaches us that freedom is not a static, all-or-nothing property that we either have or don't; it's something we can have *more or less of*, depending on the conditions. A person with more knowledge, who has cultivated self-discipline and critical thinking, and who lives in a society that provides opportunities and doesn't oppress—such a person has more effective freedom than someone who is ignorant, impulsive, or living under tyranny. None of those conditions violate determinism; they are all about setting up the right causes for freedom. Thus, determinism and human freedom are not adversaries, once we clarify what we mean by freedom. Rather, determinism can be the mechanism by which we achieve the kind of freedom that matters: the freedom to act according to our own motivations and values, with an understanding of their sources.

Life's meaning, similarly, is something we construct through causes and effects. We derive meaning from relationships, achievements, learning, and contributing to something larger than ourselves. Every one of those sources of meaning is realized by actions within the web of causality. If I find meaning in helping others, it's precisely because my actions can alleviate someone's suffering (cause leading to effect). If I find meaning in artistic creation, it's because I can actually produce a painting or poem that moves people (again, a causal chain from my efforts to their emotional response). Determinism does not stand in the way of these meanings—it is the stage on which they play out. It is the canvas on which we paint our lives. A blank canvas on which colours appeared with no rhyme or reason, purely by chance, would hardly make for a meaningful artwork. Likewise, a life where events had no rhyme or reason would not magically be meaningful—it would be disorienting and impossible to navigate. We are fortunate that the world has enough regularity and continuity that we *can* make sense of our actions and build a meaningful story. In fact, the dependable connections between cause and effect are what allow our choices and projects to have lasting significance.

Finally, recognizing the connectivity of all things can itself be a source of awe and purpose. Many spiritual and philosophical traditions emphasize the interdependence of life. In a thoroughly causal universe, that interdependence is literal: every person is who they are because of a vast network of influences—family, culture, biology, chance encounters— and each of us in turn influences others. In a way, we are *all in this together*, bound by the chains of cause and effect that weave through society and nature. One could draw a kind of existential meaning from this: we are participants in a larger whole, contributors to the tapestry of reality. The way we live will echo into others' lives (and into future generations, and even into the natural environment). Knowing this can inspire a sense of responsibility and also a sense of belonging. Even if ultimately our choices were determined by prior states of the universe, those choices *are* the means by which the future unfolds—so the story of the world includes our input. We are characters in the grand narrative of the cosmos, and that narrative moves through our decisions. There is poetry in that, a marriage of fate and freedom: we are at once authored by the past and authors of the future.

In summary, living under a largely deterministic framework does not deprive life of meaning or value. On the contrary, it situates our lives within a vast causal web that gives context to our struggles and our joys. It tells us that causes matter—so our efforts matter. It reminds us that understanding why things happen can empower us to shape what will happen next. We find that love, creativity, and moral striving are all compatible with a universe of laws; indeed, they depend on such a universe to have lasting effects. Whether or not we possess an ultimate "contra-causal" free will, we experience purpose, make choices aligned with our goals, and care about outcomes—and those experiences are not illusions, but integral parts of how the world's causal fabric operates through us. By embracing this view, we don't become resigned automatons; rather, we become enlightened agents who know the stakes of each action. We can let go of the notion that meaning requires magical free will, and instead find meaning in the very real impact we have as links in the unbroken chain. Armed with that understanding, we can pursue lives of significance, compassion, and wisdom, working within the network of causes to bring about the ends we cherish.

Looking Forward

Our exploration of determinism has, until now, looked backward through history and examined the state of current knowledge. But what about the future? The quest to comprehend causality and freedom is far from over. In fact, we live in an age when new insights are constantly emerging, and the coming decades promise to shed more light on these age-old questions. It is both exciting and humbling to realize that determinism is not a simple yes/no issue to be settled once and for all, but rather a rich and evolving field of inquiry. As we look forward, we can anticipate advances in physics, neuroscience, and artificial intelligence that may deepen—and perhaps revise—our understanding of how fate and choice intertwine.

The frontiers of physics.

One area to watch is fundamental physics, where the nature of causation at the deepest level of reality remains an open question. Physicists today are searching for a unified theory that can reconcile quantum mechanics (with its apparent indeterminacy) and general relativity (Einstein's deterministic theory of gravity) into a single framework. Such a theory might reveal new principles governing the universe.

It could be that when quantum theory and gravity are finally merged, the result will show that what we now call randomness is an emergent phenomenon, arising from causes that operate at some deeper level or on unimaginably small scales. In other words, it's conceivable that determinism will make a comeback at the fundamental level, with currently unknown variables accounting for quantum uncertainty. On the other hand, the opposite could happen: we might find that indeterminism is even more deeply woven into the fabric of reality than we thought, and that even space and time themselves have an inherent probabilistic quality. Either outcome—or something in between—would have profound implications for philosophy. The important point is that physics has not settled the determinism question yet.

With experiments probing ever deeper, we may get clues that tip the balance. New tests of quantum mechanics continue to be devised to challenge the presence of any hidden causal factors. For example, some recent experiments use distant starlight to choose detector settings in quantum tests, ensuring that any "hidden cause" would have to have been set in motion billions of years ago—an ingenious way to close loopholes. Meanwhile, theoretical efforts like superstring theory and loop quantum gravity are reshaping how we think about space and time; some proposals even suggest that cause and effect might not be fundamental ingredients at the Planck scale (the very smallest scales of nature), but rather emergent properties of a deeper reality. It may turn out that our classical intuitions about causality need revision when we finally understand what space, time, and matter are really made of.

Cosmology, too, feeds into this picture. We can ask about the ultimate origin of the cosmic causal chain: the Big Bang. Was it itself determined by a prior state, or was it a spontaneous, uncaused "first event"? Some speculative theories imagine a multiverse where Big Bangs happen as part of a larger cosmic landscape, implying that our universe's birth had a cause of sorts (perhaps the collision of branes in string theory, or a fluctuation in a primordial field). Other approaches hold that "before" the Big Bang isn't even a meaningful concept, which would mean asking for a cause of it is futile. As scientists refine our understanding of the very early universe and the beginning of time (if time had a beginning), they are essentially grappling with whether causality has an absolute starting point or extends infinitely. Though these cosmological musings can feel distant from daily human concerns, they influence how we view determinism as a whole. If someday we learn that our universe is one of many, spawned according to some higher-level laws, then even the existence of our world has a causal explanation within a larger framework. And if we find hints that time loops or other exotic causal structures are possible (as some solutions to Einstein's equations hint), philosophers and scientists will face new puzzles about free will—imagine a scenario where effects could precede causes in a time loop, challenging the very meaning of an "unbroken" chain.

In short, as physics marches on, it will almost certainly revisit the core questions of law, chance, and predictability. Each new discovery—be it a particle, a force, or a novel principle—has the potential to either reinforce the idea that events follow dependable rules or to reveal new layers of unpredictability. We should remain prepared for surprises. The confident determinism of the late 19th century was shaken by the revolutions of the 20th; the 21st (and 22nd…) century could hold its own upheavals. Whatever comes, the approach we've cultivated will serve us well: we will examine new evidence with an open yet critical mind, neither clinging dogmatically to old certainties nor leaping to unwarranted conclusions. The chain of cause and effect is a topic that science will continue to explore, and each insight will refine our philosophical understanding of determinism.

Deeper into the mind.

Equally promising and complex is the field of neuroscience and the study of consciousness. We have made great strides in understanding the brain, yet the nature of conscious decision-making remains partly mysterious. In recent years, neuroscientists have used brain scanners to peek at neural activity in real time. Famously, some experiments have shown that the brain may exhibit signs of a decision (say, a characteristic "readiness potential" in the motor cortex indicating you're about to press a button) a fraction of a second before you become aware of deciding. At first glance, such results can be interpreted in a deterministic light: they suggest our brain might initiate decisions non-consciously, with our conscious mind only later catching up. Some have taken this as evidence that free will (at least for simple actions in laboratory settings) is an illusion, that the deterministic brain has already set things in motion before "we" (as conscious agents) even know it.

However, these experiments are limited to very simple choices and very short time scales. As technology improves, scientists are designing more nuanced studies: for example, trying to predict more complex decisions or examining how conscious deliberation can veto or modify an initial impulse. It's plausible that within a few decades, brain monitoring will become so advanced that we can predict certain decisions well in advance—perhaps seconds or even minutes before they manifest. If those predictions become reliable for complex decisions, it will be harder to argue that there is any mysterious, uncaused element in our choices. We might come to see the mind as a highly complex but ultimately lawful system, where given enough data and computing power, one could foresee a person's behaviour the way we forecast the weather (not with certainty, but within statistical ranges of probability).

Yet neuroscience might also reveal new layers of complexity that complicate a straightforward deterministic story. The brain is not a static set of circuits; it is plastic, constantly rewiring itself based on experience and learning. It is also potentially chaotic in the scientific sense—tiny fluctuations in brain chemistry or electrical activity could be amplified into significant differences in thought or behaviour. If that is the case, then even if the brain is in principle deterministic, in practice it might never be perfectly predictable (much like we discussed with weather systems). Moreover, some researchers speculate that quantum effects in neurons (however minute) might influence mental processes; if that turned out to be true, it could inject a bit of fundamental unpredictability into our thought patterns. (It's worth noting that mainstream neuroscience does not consider this a major factor at present, but the idea is out there.) The question of consciousness itself—the subjective "inner life" we all experience—remains a wild card. We don't yet know if consciousness is purely an emergent property of complex brain activity (which would fit neatly with determinism) or if it involves some fundamentally new principle that we haven't grasped. If, by some twist, consciousness possessed causal powers that aren't reducible to neural mechanisms, that would be a game-changer for the free will debate. More likely, however, consciousness will be explained in terms of brain networks interacting in rich ways, and as those explanations firm up, they will demystify our mental life further. The more we learn, the more the needle seems to move toward seeing our mental states as part of the causal continuum of nature, not apart from it.

As neuroscience progresses, society will have to grapple with the implications. We might develop ways to intervene in the brain to change behaviour—imagine a hypothetical "impulse control" device or drug that could increase someone's self-discipline. Would using such a tool enhance free will (by giving a person more control over their actions) or undermine it (by showing how mechanistically we can be manipulated)? Similarly, brain-computer interfaces are already allowing paralyzed patients to move robotic limbs via thought; in the future, such interfaces might blur the line between our decisions and machine operations, raising questions about what counts as *us* acting. These trends all point to an ever-tightening connection between the mental and the physical. As that connection becomes more explicit, the evidence for a causally closed explanation of human thought will grow. Yet, as we've argued, that need not diminish our sense of self or freedom—it could instead give us unprecedented power to understand and shape ourselves.

Artificial agents and decision-making.

The rise of artificial intelligence is another frontier that will inform the determinism question. In Chapter 8, we explored how advanced AI and algorithms demonstrate deterministic principles in action: machines following rules (or learned patterns) to produce intelligent behaviour. Looking ahead, AI may evolve from specialized systems (like chess-playing programs or recommendation algorithms) into more general intelligences that rival or surpass human cognitive abilities. If and when that happens, we will face a remarkable mirror: a created intelligence that can potentially reflect our own decision-making processes back to us. Suppose we build a highly advanced AI that can learn, adapt, and converse in a way indistinguishable from a human. We know this AI is a product of code, mathematics, and hardware—there is no mysterious soul inside, and any randomness in its operation is either deliberately programmed or drawn from physical randomizers. If such an AI begins to behave as if it has intentions, makes plans, and even claims to have conscious experiences, it will press us to answer, "What is the difference between its 'will' and ours?" It might become very hard to say that every action of ours is *truly free* while the AI's actions are "just computation"—especially if the AI itself insists that it experiences making choices. In all likelihood, we would conclude that the AI's choices are meaningful *to it* (assuming it truly has understanding and feelings) despite arising from deterministic processes. And that conclusion would reinforce the view that our own meaningful choices can also arise from deterministic processes. In other words, creating AI could bolster compatibilism: showing that what matters for things like moral agency or meaningful decision-making is not the metaphysical origin of the choice, but the complexity of reasoning and the responsiveness to information.

Even before we reach science-fiction levels of AI, the algorithms already in use are teaching us about predictability and control. Machine-learning systems can analyse troves of data to predict human preferences and behaviours with uncanny accuracy. As this technology advances, we might see predictive models that can anticipate individual actions. For instance, an AI might forecast a person's likelihood of developing a certain habit or making a significant life decision, based purely on subtle patterns in their digital footprint. Imagine an AI that looks at your online behaviour and biometric data and says, "Within two years, you'll probably change careers," or "Next month, you're likely to start a new hobby"—and imagine it's often correct. That sort of predictive power encroaches on territory once reserved for personal introspection or chance. It could make people feel that they are not as unpredictable or unique as they thought—essentially, it's like a mini Laplace's Demon peering into our lives. Society will have to decide how to use such power. Do we want to be told what we're likely to do? Would that knowledge help us (by alerting us to opportunities or risks) or would it become a self-fulfilling prophecy that further locks in our path? These are practical ethical questions, but they tie back to determinism. The more we succeed at forecasting and influencing human behaviour with AI, the more it will seem that we are, in practice, mechanistic creatures responding to inputs—though always with the caveat that these forecasts deal in probabilities, not certainties, and human beings can still surprise us.

Conversely, the advancement of AI might highlight the limits of prediction. Highly complex AI systems can develop behaviours that even their creators cannot foresee. We already encounter this in machine learning: an algorithm trained on vast data might make a decision and we struggle to explain exactly why, even though we know it followed the rules of its training. So, even though each step of an AI's operation is deterministic, the overall outcome can be unexpected and not transparently traceable. This mirrors our own condition: even if our brains follow natural laws, the emergent results—our personalities, our creative ideas, our one-time decisions—can astonish us (and others). In complexity, determinism and unpredictability coexist. AI will no doubt provide vivid case studies of this fact, perhaps reminding us yet again that "deterministic" does not mean "easily predictable" when systems are intricate.

An ongoing journey.

The takeaway as we gaze ahead is that determinism vs. free will should not be seen as a stark yes/no verdict to be delivered. It is more like a landscape that we are mapping with increasing detail. As we push into new territories of knowledge, we add detail to the map. Some regions that once seemed flat and clear (like the realm of Newtonian physics) turned out to have intricate mountain ranges (quantum phenomena) that forced us to redraw boundaries. Other areas that seemed dark and unfathomable (like the workings of the brain) are gradually being illuminated, revealing underlying structures and pathways. We may never achieve a godlike view where everything is known and settled—likely we will not, given the limitations of any finite mind—but our perspective can continually broaden and become more refined.

This means the philosophical conversation will remain rich and evolving. We should be prepared to refine our definitions of "free will" and "causation" as we learn more. For instance, if one day consciousness is fully explained in neural and computational terms, philosophers might pivot to defining free will in terms of certain cognitive architectures or degrees of self-awareness rather than some mysterious contra-causal power. If, alternatively, some fundamental indeterminism is conclusively demonstrated in nature, we will need to ask what that means for human freedom—does a bit of quantum randomness in our neurons actually enhance our freedom, or would we still ground freedom and responsibility in the *process* of reasoning and wanting, rather than in uncaused blips? The debate may shift from "Is everything determined, yes or no?" to "*In what ways* and at *what levels* is the universe deterministic, and how do those levels interact with the phenomena of human life?" In many ways, we've already shifted toward that more nuanced approach, and ongoing discoveries will continue to push us in that direction.

Empowering wisdom.

As we conclude, it's worth emphasizing why all of this exploration matters. It's not just an abstract intellectual puzzle for philosophers to ponder. How we view determinism and freedom influences how we do science, how we structure society, and how we understand ourselves. Believing in an unbroken chain of cause and effect has driven scientists to search for cures and solutions—because they assume nothing happens without a reason. In our personal lives, believing that effects have causes can motivate us to make thoughtful choices (knowing those choices will have consequences). Recognizing the limitations of our knowledge, on the other hand, keeps us humble and cautious, preventing the kind of dogmatism that can lead to folly. And perhaps most importantly, seeing the world as connected by causality cultivates a sense of responsibility and agency. We realize that we cannot simply wish outcomes into being—we must identify and enact the causes that lead to those outcomes. If we desire a kinder world, we must sow the seeds of kindness through education, policy, and personal example. If we hope for a meaningful life, we must engage with the causes of meaning: building relationships, pursuing worthy goals, and reflecting on our experiences to grow.

The chain of cause and effect that links the cosmos together is truly awe-inspiring. From the fusion reactions in distant stars that forged the atoms in our bodies, to the chain of biological heredity that connects us to our ancestors, to the neural impulses that give rise to our thoughts—when one contemplates these countless linkages, one cannot help but feel a sense of wonder. We are embedded in this grand tapestry of causation. Understanding it, even partially, is a source of empowerment. No, we cannot step outside of the cosmic chain and pull its strings from above—there is no escaping the network of causes, no magical vantage point outside the system. But we *are* part of the system, and that means we can *influence* parts of it from within. In every domain—science, ethics, personal growth—knowledge of causal relationships gives us tools to make a difference. We have seen how clarifying the distinction between determinism and fatalism keeps us from falling into passivity. Accepting causality doesn't mean we must give up on changing the world; on the contrary, it means our efforts are integral to how the world changes.

As we move forward, we carry with us the insight that to understand the chain is to navigate it wisely. The future will undoubtedly bring new challenges and choices that test our beliefs about freedom and fate. By staying curious and open-minded, by valuing evidence over dogma, we can adapt our understanding as needed. And by remembering that our place in the unbroken chain is as agents of cause and effect, we maintain our sense of purpose.

In the end, the chain of cause and effect that connects everything in the universe is not a prison but a pathway. It is the very thing that allows our actions to matter. Every link in the chain is an opportunity—an opportunity to add the weight of our intentions and actions to tip the scales of events. By understanding this, we empower ourselves not to escape the chain, but to engage with it meaningfully. The unbroken chain of causality can be our guide: by working *with* it—by aligning our efforts with an understanding of causes— we become more effective architects of change, aiming to steer outcomes toward those we value.

If this book has demonstrated anything, it is that determinism is not a sentence to passivity, nor is it an argument against meaning. Rather, it is an invitation to understand the deep structure of reality—to recognize that everything we do is part of the grand causal web, and that within this web, our actions still matter immensely.

We began with the question of whether we are truly free, and we have seen that freedom and causation are not necessarily in conflict. Understanding determinism does not mean surrendering to fate but learning how to navigate the world with greater clarity and purpose. Just as a sailor does not curse the wind but learns to work with it, we do not need to lament cause and effect—we can use our knowledge of it to shape better futures.

The knowledge that our actions are shaped by causes should not make us passive but rather encourage us to cultivate the causes that lead to better outcomes—in our own lives, in society, and in the world at large. We shape our lives by understanding the forces that shape us.

In the end, determinism is not a prison—it is the structure within which all meaning is made. The question is not whether we are bound by cause and effect, but rather:

knowing this, how will we shape the causes that define our future?

References

Augustine, St. *On the Predestination of the Saints* and *On Grace and Free Will*. In *Nicene and Post-Nicene Fathers*, Series 1, Vol. 5, edited by Philip Schaff. Reprint, Peabody, MA: Hendrickson, 1994. (Augustine's late-4th/early-5th-century works discussing free will and divine grace.)

Bobzien, Susanne. "Did Epicurus Discover the Free Will Problem?" *Oxford Studies in Ancient Philosophy* 19 (2000): 287–337.

Cicero, Marcus Tullius. *De Fato* (On Fate). In *Cicero: De Natura Deorum; Academica*, translated by H. Rackham. Cambridge, MA: Harvard University Press, 1933.

Dennett, Daniel C. *Elbow Room: The Varieties of Free Will Worth Wanting*. Cambridge, MA: MIT Press, 1984.

Doyle, Bob. "Democritus." *Information Philosopher*. (Analysis of Democritus' deterministic philosophy and its implications.)

Harris, Sam. *Free Will*. New York: Free Press, 2012.

Hobbes, Thomas. *Leviathan* (1651). Edited by Edwin Curley. Indianapolis: Hackett, 1994.

Hume, David. *An Enquiry Concerning Human Understanding* (1748). Edited by Tom L. Beauchamp. Oxford: Oxford University Press, 1999.

Kant, Immanuel. *Critique of Practical Reason* (1788). Translated by Lewis White Beck. New York: Macmillan, 1956.

Kant, Immanuel. *Critique of Pure Reason* (1781). Translated by Norman Kemp Smith. London: Macmillan, 1929.

Laplace, Pierre-Simon. *A Philosophical Essay on Probabilities.* Translated by F. W. Truscott and F. L. Emory. New York: Dover Publications, 1951.

Libet, Benjamin, et al. "Unconscious Cerebral Initiative and the Role of Conscious Will in Voluntary Action." *Behavioral and Brain Sciences* 8, no. 4 (1985): 529–566.

Leucippus. In *The Presocratic Philosophers*, 2nd ed., edited by G. S. Kirk, J. E. Raven, and M. Schofield, 410. Cambridge: Cambridge University Press, 1983.

Lucretius, Titus Carus. *De Rerum Natura* (On the Nature of Things). Translated by W. H. D. Rouse, revised by Martin F. Smith. Cambridge, MA: Harvard University Press, 1992.

Milton, John. *Paradise Lost* (1667). Edited by John Leonard. London: Penguin Classics, 2000.

Routledge Encyclopedia of Philosophy. "Epicureanism (Free Will)." Edited by Edward Craig. London: Routledge, 1998. (Entry discussing Epicurus's contribution to the free will question.)

Russell, Bertrand. "On the Notion of Cause." *Proceedings of the Aristotelian Society* 13 (1913): 1–26.

Schopenhauer, Arthur. *On the Freedom of the Will* (1839). Edited by Günter Zöller. Cambridge: Cambridge University Press, 1999. (Schopenhauer's prize essay, which includes the quote "Man can do what he wills, but he cannot will what he wills.")

Spinoza, Baruch. *The Collected Works of Spinoza*, Vol. 2. Edited and translated by Edwin Curley. Princeton: Princeton University Press, 2016. (Includes Spinoza's letters; Letter 58 contains the "thinking stone" thought experiment regarding free will.)

Stoic Philosophers (Chrysippus et al.). *Stoicorum Veterum Fragmenta*, Vol. 2, edited by Hans von Arnim. Leipzig: Teubner, 1903. (Refer to fragment reporting Chrysippus's criticism of Epicurus's atomic swerve as an unwarranted hypothesis introduced to avoid determinism.)

Further Reading

Contemporary Analyses and Overviews

- Dennett, Daniel C. (2003). *Freedom Evolves*. Viking Press.

- Fischer, John Martin; Kane, Robert; Pereboom, Derk; and Vargas, Manuel (2007). *Four Views on Free Will*. Wiley-Blackwell.

- Kane, Robert (1998). *The Significance of Free Will*. Oxford University Press.

- Kane, Robert (ed.) (2002). *The Oxford Handbook of Free Will*. Oxford University Press.

- Kane, Robert (2005). *A Contemporary Introduction to Free Will*. Oxford University Press.

- Pink, Thomas (2004). *Free Will: A Very Short Introduction*. Oxford University Press.

- Smilansky, Saul (2000). *Free Will and Illusion*. Oxford University Press.

- Strawson, Galen (1986). *Freedom and Belief.* Oxford University Press. (Revised ed. 2010).

Classical and Modern Philosophical Sources

- Aristotle (4th century☐BCE). *On Interpretation.* (Chapter 9 presents the famous sea-battle argument on future contingents.)

- Augustine of Hippo (c. 395☐CE). *On Free Choice of the Will (De libero arbitrio).*

- Boethius, Anicius Manlius Severinus (524☐CE). *The Consolation of Philosophy.* (Discusses God's foreknowledge and its relation to free will.)

- Descartes, René (1641). *Meditations on First Philosophy.* (See especially Meditation IV, which deals with truth, error, and free will.)

- Spinoza, Baruch (1677). *Ethics.* (Argues for strict causal determinism under the guise of "God or Nature.")

- Ayer, A. J. (1946). "Freedom and Necessity." (Classic compatibilist essay, published in *Philosophical Essays.*)

- Strawson, P. F. (1962). "Freedom and Resentment." *Proceedings of the British Academy*, 48: 187–211.

- Chisholm, Roderick (1967). "He Could Have Done Otherwise." *Journal of Philosophy*, 64(15): 409–417.

- Frankfurt, Harry (1969). "Alternate Possibilities and Moral Responsibility." *Journal of Philosophy*, 66(23): 829–839.

- Frankfurt, Harry (1971). "Freedom of the Will and the Concept of a Person." *Journal of Philosophy*, 68(1): 5–20.

- Lewis, David (1981). "Are We Free to Break the Laws?" *Theoria*, 47(3): 113–121.

- Strawson, Galen (1994). "The Impossibility of Moral Responsibility." *Philosophical Studies*, 75(1–2): 5–24.

Scientific and Interdisciplinary Works

- Heisenberg, Werner (1958). *Physics and Philosophy: The Revolution in Modern Science*. (Discusses the uncertainty principle and the limits of determinism in quantum physics.)

- Hawking, Stephen (1988). *A Brief History of Time*. Bantam Books. (See Chapter 4 on quantum uncertainty and the breakdown of strict determinism.)

- Wegner, Daniel M. (2002). *The Illusion of Conscious Will*. MIT Press. (Explores psychological evidence that our sense of willing an action may be an illusion.)

- Libet, Benjamin (2004). *Mind Time: The Temporal Factor in Consciousness*. MIT Press. (Presents Libet's pioneering neuroscience experiments on the timing of conscious will.)

- Gazzaniga, Michael S. (2011). *Who's in Charge? Free Will and the Science of the Brain*. HarperCollins. (A neuroscientist's perspective on responsibility and the brain's decision-making processes.)

About the Author

Thomas W. Smith is a writer and decommissioning engineer based in Scotland. Specializing in waste regulations, compliance, and environmental management, he works in North Sea offshore decommissioning, ensuring the safe and responsible dismantling of offshore assets. His professional background has given him a deep appreciation for the complex systems that govern both industry and the natural world—a perspective that influences his philosophical inquiries.

Outside of work, Thomas enjoys reading, writing, and exploring the big questions of existence. *The Unbroken Chain* is a reflection of his fascination with determinism, free will, and the forces that shape human decision-making. When he's not immersed in philosophy and science, he cherishes time with his family and the quiet moments of everyday life.

Thank You for Reading

I appreciate you taking the time to read *The Unbroken Chain: Determinism, Free Will, and the Nature of Choice.* I hope it has given you new perspectives on determinism, free will, and the forces that shape our lives.

If this book has sparked new thoughts or questions, I would love to know what you took away from it. Reflections, discussions, and shared ideas help keep these topics alive.

Thank you for being part of this journey.

Printed in Great Britain
by Amazon